TABLE OF CONTENTS

SUMMER 2023
VOLUME 3, NUMBER 4

EDITOR
LEON WIESELTIER

MANAGING EDITOR
CELESTE MARCUS

PUBLISHER
BILL REICHBLUM

JOURNAL DESIGN
WILLIAM VAN RODEN

WEB DESIGN
BRICK FACTORY

EDITORIAL ASSISTANT
DARIUS RUBIN

Liberties is a publication of the Liberties Journal Foundation, a nonpartisan 501(c)(3) organization based in Washington, D.C. devoted to educating the general public about the history, current trends, and possibilities of culture and politics. The Foundation seeks to inform today's cultural and political leaders, deepen the understanding of citizens, and inspire the next generation to participate in the democratic process and public service.

Engage
To learn more please go to libertiesjournal.com

Subscribe
To subscribe or with any questions about your subscription, please go to libertiesjournal.com

ISBN 979-8-9854302-1-9
ISSN 2692-3904

EDITORIAL OFFICES
1101 30th Street NW, Suite 310
Washington, DC 20007

DIGITAL
@READLIBERTIES
LIBERTIESJOURNAL.COM

Liberties

KATHERINE C. EPSTEIN

Scholarship and the Future of Society

Historians like to say that correlation is not the same as causation. But evidence of correlation is often the starting point for inquiry into causation. Here is one such inquiry: How might the loss of humanistic thinking generally, and historical thinking specifically, be connected to the current dysfunction of American politics and to the erosion of America's position in the world?

In asking this question, I do not mean to suggest that the loss of humanistic and historical thinking is the only cause, or even most important one; clearly there are many causes. Some very important ones relate to form or structure, such as closed primaries and gerrymandering. But a quasi-mechanistic diagnosis of what ails the United States is inadequate. Something even more fundamental has gone wrong — a sickness of the soul, not just a sickness of the body. A sickness of the body calls for the sciences. A sickness of the soul calls for the humanities. The difficulty is that the humanities, as currently constituted, are in no position to provide a remedy, having themselves contributed to the illness in the first place.

Properly understood, the scholarly humanities have both substantive and procedural commitments, which feed each other. The substantive commitment is that human beings are worth trying to understand in all their diversity and complexity. The procedural commitment is that there are certain rules, particularly concerning the use of evidence, that one must follow in attempting to understand human beings. These two commitments secure each other: we have rules to ensure that we are trying to understand people on their own terms, because it is so tempting to narcissistically impose our own humanity on others; and we see people in all their complexity because our rules encourage us to do so. The importance of rules is why the scholarly fields are called the scholarly disciplines, and not the scholarly do-whatever-you-wants.

All the humanities enlarge our understanding of what it means to be human, but only the study of history does so by tethering that understanding to the largest store of facts (however they are interpreted) about real human behavior that we have, which is the past. This axiomatic realism is what distinguishes history from literature. While the other humanistic disciplines cultivate similar qualities of empathy and imagination, only the study of history subjects those qualities to the procedural requirements governing the interpretation of historical evidence. Unlike writers and poets and painters, historians must answer to those requirements: they are obliged to refrain from cherry-picking or inventing evidence, to consider alternative explanations, to test their hypotheses, and so forth, not only for the sake of intellectual rigor but also because we study real people, with no more or less human dignity than we ourselves possess.

The complex interplay between the study of human beings who lived in the past and the rules governing that study are essential to the formation of a humane sense of self — one bounded by, and bounding, a sense of other selves. The historian and philosopher R. G. Collingwood called this interplay "re-enactment" and saw it as fundamental to self-knowledge and the knowledge of others. From his perspective, re-enactment involves a delicate balancing act between self-surrender and self-assertion, passivity and activity, altruism and narcissism. On the one hand, it requires trying to set one's own ego aside in order to see the world through someone else's eyes. On the other hand, the only way to translate, or make sense of, someone else's life experience is in the context of one's own. This attempt at sense-making is active, not passive: the historian re-enacting another's knowledge "criticizes it, forms his own judgement of its value, corrects whatever errors he can discern in it." Hence, Collingwood reasoned, "it may thus be said that historical inquiry reveals to the historian the powers of his own mind." Since people can gain these forms of self-knowledge and knowledge of others only through the historical method, it is as vital in the present as it is for the past: "If it is by historical thinking that we re-think and so rediscover the thought of Hammurabi or Solon, it is in the same way that we discover the thought of a friend who writes us a letter, or a stranger who crosses the street." People who cannot think historically, in other words, are cut off from their own humanity and that of others, cut off from Milton's "human face divine."

Much as historical thinking nurtures inter-subjective humility, so it nurtures inter-generational humility. If "re-enactment" of another's experiences is how we establish our sense of self in space, then it is also how we establish our sense of self in time. The historian William Appleman Williams beautifully connected the methods of the historical discipline to its inter-generational substance:

> The method of history is neither to by-pass and dismiss nor to pick and choose according to preconceived notions; rather it is a study of the past so that we can come back into our own time of troubles having shared with the men of the past their dilemmas, having learned from the experiences, having been buoyed up by their courage and creativeness and sobered by their shortsightedness and failures. We shall then be better equipped to redefine our own dilemmas and problems as opportunities and possibilities and to proceed with positive rather than negative programs and policies. This enrichment and improvement through research and reflection is the essence of being human, and it is the heart of the historical method.

Practicing the historical method cultivates, or ought to cultivate, a humble sense of our own temporal finitude, and along with it a sense of inter-generational stewardship. In effect, it extends the golden rule through time: do unto past generations as you would like future generations to do unto you. By treating past generations as subjects to be understood, rather than as objects to be manipulated for contemporary advantage, the present generation stakes its moral claim to be treated with the same respect by future generations.

Indeed, one way to convey the social, cultural, and political stakes of the scholarly humanities is to say that they secularize the moral and epistemological dilemma at the heart of the Christian doctrine of original sin. The dilemma consists of being unable to have knowledge — of self and of goodness — without disunion from God and each other, and of being unable to be self-knowing and good without union with God and each other. This is the great theme of Genesis and of its finest exegesis, Milton's *Paradise Lost.* Until Adam and Eve eat from the tree of knowledge of good and evil, they live in perfect union with God and with each other, and their bliss is ignorance. God himself creates the possibility of disunity by giving them free will, because He understands that unity without freedom lacks faith and goodness ("Not free, what proof could they have giv'n sincere / of true allegiance, constant faith or love, / Where only what they needs must do, appeared, / Not what they would?"). Total unity is, in a sense, totalitarian. Adam's and Eve's decision to eat from the tree constitutes the first act of human freedom and the origins of knowledge — of good as different from evil, of humanity as different from God, of human beings as different from each other. In *Paradise Lost*, it also constitutes the beginning of history, which will end at the time of the Second Coming, when Milton's God (as in 1 Corinthians 15:28) will once again be "All in All" — a state of perfect unity.

During this period of history, humankind exists in a state

of epistemological and moral dilemma. We cannot know ourselves without having a sense of otherness, but a sense of otherness easily transmutes into a sense of self-inadequacy (self-abnegation) or justifies a sense of self-superiority (narcissism). As Reinhold Niebuhr put it,

> Self-consciousness means the recognition of finiteness within infinity. The mind recognizes the *ego* as an insignificant point amidst the immensities of the world. In all vital self-consciousness there is a note of protest against this finiteness. It may express itself in religion by the desire to be absorbed in infinitude. On the secular level it expresses itself in man's effort to universalize himself and give his life a significance beyond himself. The root of imperialism is therefore in all self-consciousness.

Here is expressed the basic dilemma of historical re-enactment identified by Collingwood. Historians can enlarge their self-knowledge only by acquiring knowledge of others. But that attempt to understand others easily transmutes into a loss of sense of self, whereby one becomes subsumed into the infinitude of evidence (and never publishes), or into a tyrannical sense of self, whereby one imposes one's own selfhood on others (by cherry-picking evidence in support of one's preferred thesis). The same dilemma exists across time as well as space. Historians can become so absorbed in the past that they cannot translate it to the present (antiquarianism), or they can become so dominated by the present that they refuse to try to understand the past on its own terms (presentism). Historical re-enactment is thus a constant toggling between what Martin Buber called "I-thou" relationships and "I-it" relationships, between empathizing with others as subjects through unity with their consciousness and studying them as objects through disunity with their consciousness.

By accustoming people to live with this dilemma, the scholarly humanities tend to inoculate against humanity's worst scourges: the perennial false promise of ideological absolutism, and the distinctively modern false promise of technocratic optimization. Both of these are forms of anti-politics, to borrow David Bell's term in these pages, pretending to offer an escape from the world of dilemma, which is to say from the world of liberal-democratic politics — the world of compromise, of messiness, of choosing between bad and worse options rather than between good and bad options. Like Christian humanism, secular humanism teaches that the acceptance of dilemma is humane, while attempts to escape it lead to gross inhumanity. The similarities go farther still. Both Christian and secular humanism seek goodness rather than perfection, because both understand that perfection belongs to an inhuman realm, and thus that any human quest for perfection is hubristic. Both are anti-utopian. Both have a sense of limits, especially of self-limitation, as an ethical imperative, so as to honor the humanity of others and acknowledge the imperfections of one's own. Both accept the impossibility of fully straightening out humankind's crooked timber; both see that attempts to do so must lead to great evil. Both have a conservative streak, which does not prevent them from pursuing progress but does make them sensitive to its imperfections and downsides.

Both also involve living with doubt about how well or badly one is doing as measured against a sense of the absolute, which is how Niebuhr defined religion. In Christianity, the absolute is God; in the scholarly humanities, the absolute is what Donne called "that library where every book shall lie open to one another." For Donne, God, and only God, was the perfect scholar, whose hand was capable of translating the chapters of human life into a better language and re-binding the leaves that scattered with original sin. But Donne encouraged the pursuit of scholarship by heeding the message of the tolling bell, which calls us to read as many chapters of humanity as we can in our fallen state. Partial failure is guaranteed. Thus scholars who hear the tolling bell feels both a sense of the absolute and a sense of doubt about their proximity to it.

Humanistic proceduralism, the imperative of method, which has the moral force of the biblical commandments, exists to calibrate scholars' doubt. On the one hand, following procedure gives scholars confidence in the integrity of their work. On the other hand, following procedure prevents this confidence from transmuting into arrogance, a false belief in the definitiveness of their work. Procedure forces humanists to slow down, to be attentive to the complexity of evidence that narcissists, imperialists, and tyrants try to over-simplify. Scholars submit to the discipline of procedure, even — especially — when they would rather rush into print, in order to ensure that they treat their subjects as real people to be understood and explained, not as abstract projections of their own egos to be praised or blamed.

This scholarly practice is also a political one. Understanding its politics is critical to defending liberalism against its opponents.

The most common scholarly analogy for liberalism is science, and understandably, given that its historical instantiations have tended to believe in the scientistic trinity of rationalism, technology, and progress. In its scientific mode, liberalism is apt to be experienced as cold, lonely, and alienating. It lacks a sense of connection to other human beings as thinking, feeling creatures. But liberalism also has a humanistic mode, which cultivates empathy where scientific liberalism does not. Empathy need not lead to feelings of warmth — it can lead to revulsion, as indeed it sometimes should — but it is a precondition for friendship and love. How can any human union — marital, national, or otherwise — survive without friendship and love, without re-enacting at human scale what the religious mind understands as the communion between God and man?

The strongest humanistic scholarship supplies the strongest possible basis for mutual understanding, and therefore for the strongest secular unions. Those bonds are humanistic bonds. In a wonderful essay in these pages, Michael Ignatieff correctly observed that rigorous scholarship, whether humanistic or scientific, has an "intransigently solitary" quality that places it "in radical contradiction" with "the ethos that liberal democracy encourages — civility, deliberation, compromise." But as he himself notes, rigorous scholarship also "demands a difficult kind of honesty, a willingness to concede defeat when the evidence is against you, and enough resilience to resume the search for the answer that still eludes you." Given that "the evidence" in the humanities consists of other human beings, scholarship has a profoundly social as well as solitary (or anti-social) quality. The willingness to concede when the human evidence gathered by the scholarly process fails to provide the outcome one wants — this is the essence of liberal democracy. If following the rules doesn't get you the result you want, you don't get to change the rules.

Like liberal democracy, humanism, whether religious or scholarly, balances rights and obligations, self-assertion and self-restraint. The "post-liberals" on the right today err by reducing liberalism to the former and ignoring the latter. Liberalism evolved its balance of rights and restraints in reaction against the violence caused by political and religious absolutism. Liberalism diagnosed this violence as stemming, in a sense, from narcissism — from the monarchical or religious ego run imperialistically amok, as concerned with its own rights as it was unconcerned with anyone else's. Liberalism did not oppose religion *per se* — if it did, it would not protect religious liberty alongside other liberties — but rather a particular kind of religiosity, one whose anti-humanism and inhumaneness made its earthly as well as heavenly ambitions totalitarian. Liberalism's conceptualization of the rights-bearing individual as the proper locus of political order was indeed a major innovation, but so, too, was its insight that nothing, not even religion or kingship, licensed the abrogation of individual rights. All people, religious or otherwise, however convinced of their own righteousness, were obliged to limit the pursuit of their own perceived rights within the bounds of non-conflict with others' rights.

Liberalism thus evolved as an antidote to authoritarian libertinism, not as a license to it, contra the post-liberals. Its innovation of the rights-bearing individual was necessarily accompanied by the innovation of the obligations-bearing individual. The bearer is individual, but the obligations are communal. This dual innovation so closely mimics the logic of Christian humanism as to call into question whether it was any more an Enlightenment innovation, which is how some of its defenders as well as its opponents understand it, than a religious bequest. In effect, liberal democracy, like scholarly humanism, has the functional equivalent of the doctrine of original sin.

This functionally religious logic helps to explain why liberal democracy attracts opposition not only from religious absolutists but also from neo-Nietzscheans, with whom the religionists sometimes make strange bedfellows. If liberal democracy had no restraints, if it were truly a system of libertinism and licentiousness, neo-Nietzscheans would have nothing to complain about. They could pursue meaning and authenticity however they wished; they could be supermen, and beyond good and evil. But liberal democracy does not permit them to do so. It demands that they, like everyone else, balance their self-assertion with their self-restraint.

Historically, liberal conceptions of self-restraint have extended from the political to the sexual realm, and this extension helps to explain why the counter-reaction to liberalism so often focuses on gender and sexuality. A defining characteristic of the premier liberals of the nineteenth century, the Victorians, was their ethic of sexual self-restraint (which disappears in post-liberals' account of liberalism as libertine). This ethic had a strong norm, however honored in the breach, against men having sex outside of marriage; it sought to domesticate testosterone, so to speak, and thus can be seen as feminizing. Unsurprisingly, some particularly trenchant critics of liberalism have been men — such as Nietzsche, Foucault, and Costin Alamariu (a.k.a. "Bronze Age Pervert," a prominent thinker on the "new right") — whose sexuality has not conformed to Victorian norms.

These men, whose politics do not fall neatly on a left-right spectrum, take liberalism's bourgeois sexual repressiveness as a metaphor for liberalism as a whole. For them, liberalism is simply a mask for power, one that in some profound sense alienates humanity from itself. The queer theory of Foucault's disciples, the gay aestheticism of Diaghilev, and fascism's "aestheticization of politics" (to borrow Modris Eksteins' borrowing of Walter Benjamin) all owe an intellectual debt to this neo-Nietzschean tradition. Wokeness is the political project associated with the intellectual tradition of queer theory, a branch of critical theory; fascism is the political project associated with that of Nietzscheanism. Although the historical instantiation that dominates our image of fascism — Nazism — was deeply homophobic, fascism need not be; indeed the homo-sociality of the trench spirit that the Nazis sought to create, as well as the homo-eroticism of Nazi art, reflect the neo-Nietzschean influence. Fascism may be understood as a toxically masculine response to what fascists regard as the toxic femininity of liberalism.

The point here is not that reading Foucault makes you woke or reading Nietzsche makes you a fascist, any more than reading Marx makes you a communist. The intellectual traditions of critical theory, Nietzscheanism, and Marxism are complex; reading in them can deepen and enrich one's commitment to liberal democracy no less than overturn it. The political projects with which these traditions have historically been associated cannot be reduced to them.

But that said, these traditions lend themselves to certain political projects. What unites woke queer theorists and fascist neo-Nietzscheans with post-liberal religious believers is a shared opposition to liberal-democratic humanism. Woke queer theorists don't like that this tradition has restraints. Fascists and post-liberals don't like that the restraints in this tradition operate against them. Gay fascists and post-liberals may split over the question of homosexuality, but they share an anti-feminism, rooted in their sense of liberalism as excessively feminized. All of these people — woke queer theorists, fascists, and post-liberals — have given up on working out norms around gender and sexuality, or around anything else, that comport with liberal-democratic humanism, as if decency lies elsewhere or nowhere at all.

Viewing this formidable array of opponents to liberal-democratic humanism, you might think that the scholarly humanities, and especially historians, would rally to the defense of their finest traditions, demanding maximal procedural rigor in the pursuit of substantive excellence. You would, of course, be wrong.

The scholarly humanities have momentously decided to join, rather than to try to beat, the forces arrayed against liberal-democratic humanism. As the rhetoric of war against internal enemies has suffused the new right, the humanities have declined to treat their allergy to the study of war and foolishly ceded military history and its larger implications to parochial clique. Instead of fighting under the sign of Clausewitz, whose understanding of war as the continuation of politics by other means expressed his profound humanism, they have chosen instead to fight under the sign of Foucault, whose inversion of the Clausewitzian dictum reflected his equally profound anti-humanism. The Foucauldian inversion — that politics is the continuation of war by other means — is an anti-politics. It replaces the argument, persuasion, negotiation, compromise, and tolerance at the heart of liberal-democratic politics with a brute struggle for power. It is as though ostensible humanists have decided to try to fight what they regard as fascism on fascism's own terms. For people who see themselves as beleaguered resistance fighters, symmetrical warfare is a strange strategic choice — though a more rational one for those who occupy a strong position on the commanding heights of culture.

Wokeness is the most remarked-upon result of this strategy, but it is much more symptom than disease. It could not have ravaged the body humanistic if it had encountered a stronger immune system, one with a greater commitment to scholarly process. Key tenets of wokeness, which draws on multiple branches of critical theory — including both queer theory and critical race theory — are inconsistent with each other and cannot withstand scrutiny. Race, for instance, which has virtually no biological basis, is radically essentialized (trans-racialism is therefore impossible), while gender, which has a stronger claim to a biological basis however mediated by culture, is radically de-essentialized (trans-genderism is therefore a matter of self-identification). But humanists either cannot see these inconsistencies or will not point them out. A collapse of humanistic standards and an epidemic of moral cowardice made wokeness in academia possible, not vice-versa — much as anti-humanism and moral cowardice in the Republican Party made Donald Trump possible. That collapse has deep roots.

Like Trumpism, wokeness is not infrequently compared to a religious cult, and with reason — but if wokeness is a religion, then it is one with a distinctive understanding of the relationship between the human and the divine, of original sin, and of the place of doubt in faith. The Church of Wokeness has no notion of all human beings having been made in God's image. There is no common humanity to hold us all together; there is only a relentlessly atomizing impulse to discover our own intersectional uniqueness, or the bulldozing of individuality by sub-group identities. Hence the Church of Wokeness does not understand original sin to afflict all human beings qua human beings, but only those belonging to particular groups. For those in the wrong identity groups, there is no hope of divine grace or of humanistic self-transcendence through inter-subjective understanding; there is only the purchase of indulgences from the high priests of DEI. Thus indoctrinated, members of the Church of Wokeness oscillate wildly between the two extremes that humanism navigates: on the one hand, absolute certainty in their own virtue; on the other hand, self-abnegating certainty in the impossibility of grace. If the Church of the Humanities had been stronger, it would have denounced the Church of Wokeness as a breakaway sect, but its own faith had grown so weak that it could not recognize the sectarianism.

The historical profession has participated in, perhaps even led, the humanities' turn away from the liberal-democratic politics of scholarly humanism. Its alternative politics can be understood as illiberal politics or as anti-politics, which are functionally similar. On the one hand, the historical profession today indulges in narcissistic, imperialistic presentism, replacing an "I-thou" relationship between the present and past with an "I-it" relationship. A good example of this tendency may be found in one of the statements by the American Historical Association (AHA), prompted by the controversy over the 1619 Project, in which the AHA declared that "knowledge of the past exists to serve the needs of the living." On the other hand, the historical profession invokes its technocratic credentials to deny that it is behaving politically, while adopting a militaristic bunker mentality of being under attack by outside forces. The bunker mentality in turn justifies an ever greater reluctance to find enemies to the left and an ever more intellectually dishonest recourse to the camouflage of technocracy. A good example of this tendency appeared in the previous sentence of the same AHA statement, which declared that "educators must provide an accurate view of the past" and that "professional educators," not "elected officials," should decide what constitutes accuracy. There is a certain tension, shall we say, between those two sentences.

That tension points to the flaws in the prevailing understanding of the role of critical theory in the culture wars. Contra the right, critical theory is not the problem with wokeness, at least not in any straightforward way. In fact, the problem could just as easily be described as an absence of critical theory: people who reflexively invoke their disciplinary credentials ("follow the PhDs!") to defend against attacks from populists are not people who take Foucault's defense of subjugated knowledges as seriously as they claim. Indeed, the anti-Foucauldian behavior of the woke left in academia (and other sense-making institutions) is why so many on the right have turned to critical theory to attack wokeness. For instance, concepts put forward by thinkers on the new right — for instance, the "Cathedral" of Curtis Yarvin (a.k.a. Mencius Moldbug) and the "Iron Prison" of Alamariu, which describe a distributed set of disciplinary technocratic institutions — are Foucauldian to their core. Sometimes critics of wokeness on the right honestly acknowledge their debt to critical theory, like those White House advisors to Trump who, as Geoff Shullenberger has shown, did graduate work on the subject. At other times, these critics plagiarize, *à la* Ron DeSantis, denouncing critical theory even as they draw on its insights into the working of informal cultural, as distinct from formal political, power. The woke left does not call out this plagiarism, despite its crocodile tears over right-wing violations of scholarly standards, because the appearance of total polarity serves its interests no less than those of the MAGA movement. The fundamental problem with wokeness in academia is not that it is left-wing, but that it is anti-scholarly.

All the pathologies of the woke turn — or rather the anti-scholarly turn — in the humanities were on display in *l'affaire* James Sweet. To recap: in August 2022, Sweet, the president of the AHA and a historian of slavery, used his monthly column in the AHA's newsletter to suggest, by way of analyzing contemporary public debates over the history of slavery, that the profession's rampant presentism might not serve its long-term interests or honor its fiduciary obligations to the public. His energetic attempts to bend over backwards so as to avoid offending his woke colleagues made his column rather milquetoast but, predictably, his exaggerated sensitivities availed him not at all, and the usual mob reaction ensued. On "academic Twitter" (a contradiction in terms), he was accused of being racist, of hurting his black colleagues, and of carrying water for the right. Within forty-eight hours he issued an apology, which he insists did not constitute a retraction. (He smoked but he didn't inhale.) Sweet's sin, in the eyes of his critics, was that he had broken faith with wokeness. MAGA has its RINOs (Republican in Name Only); wokeness has its WINOs (Woke in Name Only). Religions don't like heretics, but they hate apostates, who, unlike heretics, do not have the excuse of never having known any better. The Sweet affair demonstrated the inversion of the substantive and procedural commitments at the heart of historical study. Instead of a virtuous feedback loop between humanism and proceduralism, we now have a vicious feedback loop between anti-humanism and anti-proceduralism. The essential connection between method and tolerance has been erased. This degradation of the humanities is driven by the conviction that our issues today are so much more important than whatever happened in the past that we are justified in turning historical subjects into historical objects — making them playthings of whatever contemporary political, social, or other agenda we seek to advance.

This behavior is professionally idiotic and civically tragic. When historians and humanists pooh-pooh their almost invariably left-wing violations of scholarly rules as misdemeanors compared to the felonies of the right, they betray a bizarre and unfounded lack of confidence in the importance of what they do. What is more important than educating the young? What is more important than safeguarding our generational right to be treated with respect by future generations? What is more important than preserving the treasures of the civilization that makes our livelihoods possible? What is more important than protecting the largest database of human behavior we have from cynical instrumentalization? Have we not read *1984*?

One of the crucial ingredients of tyranny in the present is control of historical knowledge — indeed, it is difficult to imagine a tyrant who lacks such control, lest the past afford politically threatening visions of how society should be more justly structured. From the tyrant's perspective, the past is no less potent a rival power center than an opposition political party or an independent judiciary. Why did Stalin erase the victims of purges from photographs? Why does Putin claim that Ukraine has always been Russian? Tyrants weaponize the past in order to crush their opponents in the present. How unutterably self-defeating, how deep a betrayal of their civic duty, for historians to legitimize such weaponization by engaging in it themselves for their own preferred ends! It is an abuse of power. Like tyrants, we are insisting on a right to discipline others while refusing to discipline ourselves. Expertise is meaningless if it is not limited. If we do not respect the limits of our expertise, why should anyone respect our expertise?

It cannot be a mere coincidence that as the historical profession has so largely given up on its commitment to scholarly humanism and scholarly proceduralism, so many Americans across the political spectrum have given up on civic humanism and liberal-democratic proceduralism.

The rising tide of illiberalism on both the hard left and the hard right is characterized by an ends-justify-the-means mentality — a willingness to break the rules in order to secure the outcome they want. This is the political analogue of the narcissistic anti-proceduralism, the rejection of method in favor of ideology, in the historical profession. Just as it is incompatible with humanistic scholarship, so it is incompatible with liberal democracy, which is based on the proceduralist commitment that outcomes reached through procedural violations, however morally appealing their substance may be, are illegitimate.

In liberal-democratic politics as in scholarship, the commitment to procedure has a moral basis. Essentially, it lifts the golden rule — do unto others as you would have them do unto you — to the level of a whole nation. Being enraged at someone is not a sufficient justification to strip them of their right to due process, any more than someone else being enraged at you is sufficient justification to strip you of your right to due process. The substantive moral commitment which grounds proceduralism, as it does the golden rule, is the belief in shared human dignity. That humanistic conviction is why proceduralism prohibits us from violating the rights of our fellow citizens. We may not like them, but we recognize that their humanity has no weaker a claim on rights than ours. Proceduralism thus goes hand-in-hand with humanism.

But the feedback loop between them is now moving in reverse. In politics, as in the historical profession, anti-humanism and anti-proceduralism are feeding each other. On the one hand, across the political spectrum, there is a rampant reliance on caricatures, a refusal to see individuals in their three-dimensional human complexity. The hard right lumps everyone it dislikes into "woke mobs," including those who are neither woke nor mobbish. Meanwhile the hard left sees everyone it disagrees with as white supremacists, transphobes, and so on, seeing no daylight between, say, those who call for the "eradication" of transgenderism and those who would limit the participation of trans-men in women's sports but at the same time believe that transgenderism is natural and that trans people should have full civil rights. Both the hard right and the hard left are intolerant of pluralism and diversity; both are incapable of grappling with nuance and complexity; both are dehumanizing and inhumane. That dehumanization encourages violations of rules, because why bother respecting due process for someone less than fully human. On the other hand, equally across the political spectrum, there is a growing willingness to break the rules. The ur-example, of course, remains the January 6 assault on the Capitol. But there are plenty of more mundane examples, such as attempts to abolish the filibuster and to pass huge spending bills by abusing reconciliation. A nice illustration of the politically protean nature of the rule-breaking impulse was supplied by *The New York Times'* publication of a plea from two law professors on the left "to reclaim America from constitutionalism" — "why justify our politics by the Constitution?" they impatiently asked — and its publication two weeks later of an article about interest on the right in calling a new constitutional convention. Not following the rules makes it easier to dehumanize people, because we no longer have to slow down and try to understand them in all their complex subjectivity.

This mental laziness is excused by a sort of fatalism about the possibility and the effects of empathy. We differ so fundamentally from our opponents, the epistemologists of extremism claim, that we cannot possibly understand them, and we pollute ourselves by trying. Were the historical profession today not itself so fatalistic, it would stand as a stinging rebuke to this fatalism. It is ludicrous to think that the imaginative distance between a Trump supporter and a Biden supporter is greater than the imaginative distance between either of them and a medieval peasant. The historical profession is premised on the idea that, through imagination disciplined by historical evidence, it is possible for a historian in the twenty-first century, who almost certainly believes that the condition of one's birth should not determine one's station in life, to understand how the world looked to someone in the thirteenth century, who saw a society of ranks and privileges as a natural order. It is equally ludicrous to think that there is anyone more evil today than Hitler, Stalin, and the other monsters with whom historians routinely empathize without turning into mass murderers themselves. Historians who deny the possibility and desirability of inter-subjective understanding not only fly in the face of this professional premise but also set a terrible example for all Americans.

The effects of historians' failure to insist on the possibility and importance of inter-subjective understanding are particularly clear in the realm of fiscal and environmental policy. As historians' confidence in this understanding has weakened, so too has their confidence in its possibility across generations. This weakening affects cuts in multiple temporal directions. With no sense of obligation to preserve an inheritance from the past, the present has no sense of obligation to pass on an inheritance to the future. Can its voracious consumption of fiscal and environmental resources, both of which will perilously reduce the freedom of action for future generations, be unconnected to the presentism of the profession most obliged to be anti-presentist?

It is vital for historians to reckon with the flaws of their profession as an institution, not only for their own sake but for the sake of the nation that supports their institution, and to reflect on the ways that they have fed and been fed by the most inhumane and dehumanizing impulses in American life today. It is true that there are forces outside the historical profession that want to destroy it, for reasons that I vigorously disagree with — for instance, for the reason that studying the past is not "useful," with "usefulness" defined in a narrow market-based sense. In reality, there is not much that is more "useful" when it comes to educating free citizens in a liberal democracy than studying the past. Its "utility" is overwhelming. Yet it is also the case that the historical profession has not cared for this "utility" and has not been doing the job properly, and so it has sacrificed the moral high ground to resist the misguided and sometimes malicious calls to defund it.

The historical profession cannot survive without honesty, and it cannot have honesty if it engages in "enemy thinking," to borrow Martin Luther King Jr.'s phrase, about everyone who criticizes it, especially from the right. Put differently, the profession may be in the process of being murdered, but it is also in the process of committing suicide — a characterization true of a number of important institutions in American life.

Scholarly standards, like liberal-democratic standards, exist to protect us from our worst instincts and to encourage us to live up to our highest potential as human beings. As historians and as Americans, we can justify breaking the rules and violating the standards however we wish, but the justification can only ever be a variation on what Milton called the tyrant's plea of necessity, that the ends justify the means. In historical scholarship and in liberal democracy, the means justify the ends. When we forget this, we imperil not only the humanities but humaneness itself.

It is a pathology of the modern United States that Americans require a national-security justification to do almost anything; they clothe everything they do, from the war on poverty to the war on drugs, in militarized language. Obviously they should renew their commitment to rigorous humanism and a liberal democracy because it is the right thing to do, not because it is a national security issue. But it is also a national security issue.

The loss of capacity for methodologically rigorous humanistic thought has implications not only for liberal democracy in the United States but also for its position in the world. It is ironic and tragic that the United States has experienced this loss even as it has become *de rigueur* to narrate the turn of the century as a transition from the "end of history" to the "return of history." History has certainly returned (or rather never went away). Yet a sense of history has not returned with it.

It isn't the 1950s anymore. The United States no longer bestrides a world digging out of the rubble of World War II. The Soviet Union no longer exists, but the United States faces a much more potent challenger to its position atop the global power rankings in China, which has not only the military prowess of the Soviet Union but also far greater economic strength. The United States cannot fritter away its national unity without geopolitical consequence. The principal beneficiary of socio-political dysfunction in the United States and in the Western alliance is, of course, China. By neglecting the humanities, which play a crucial role in nurturing a sense of liberal-democratic unity in a pluralistic nation and alliance, the United States is giving a strategic gift to China.

Since the pertinence of humanistic scholarship to American foreign policy is not obvious, let me explain. Strategy requires a particular kind of thinking. Such thinking will be a condition of American strength in the era of great power rivalry that has now begun. Yet the neglect of intellectual rigor, the decline of its prestige in our culture, will inevitably damage the United States' ability to formulate its strategy amid all the danger and competition. Michael Ignatieff's recent warning in these pages about the importance of understanding what thinking is applies powerfully to strategy:

> We are confused about what thinking is. To think is not to process information. We have impoverished our understanding of thinking by analogizing it to what our machines do. What we do is not processing. It is not computation. It is not data analysis. It is a distinctively, incorrigibly human activity that is a complex combination of conscious and unconscious, rational

> and intuitive, logical and emotional reflection. It is so complex that neither neurologists nor philosophers have found a way to model it, and the engineers of artificial intelligence are still struggling to replicate some of the simplest forms of pattern recognition that human cognition does so effortlessly. We must beware that in our attempt to make computers think like us we do not end up thinking like them.

American policymakers — particularly in the US Navy, which would play the lead role in any conflict with China — think too much like computers. When all you have is STEM, everything looks like an engineering problem with a technical or technological solution. The Navy has reduced the competition with China to a combat problem and is searching for a technological silver bullet with sufficient "lethality" (an insipid term that is to the Pentagon what "disruption" is to Silicon Valley). How else to explain the Navy's failure to articulate how victory in combat ("kinetic") operations against the PLA Navy would advance the strategic end of compelling China to change its behavior? How else to explain its asinine expectation, as noted by Matthew Suarez, that it can leave the tasks of trade protection and interdiction, which have preoccupied the navies of great powers in virtually every maritime war in history, to the tiny navies of "allies and partners"? A war with China would massively disrupt the global economy, and the US Navy will not operate in a hermetically sealed cocoon of combat operations. The American people and neutral stakeholders will besiege it with demands for protection.

The impulse to turn human beings into engineering problems also manifests itself in the instrumentalization of the humanities in the fields of war studies and strategic studies. "Scholars" in these fields, unlike actual scholars in the humanities, are more interested in using findings from the humanities to identify "lessons," discover "principles," and build models abstracted from the particular human (usually historical) contexts to which they belong. In effect, this approach turns the humanities into an instrumental technology. Since the emphasis is on instrumentalization rather than on understanding, the bar for expertise in these fields is low; today's "experts" on economic warfare are yesterday's experts on cyberwar, who were the previous day's experts on Islamic terrorism, who before that were Kremlinologists. (There are exceptions, of course, but they prove rather than disprove the rule.) Human beings are not engineering problems. As John Lewis Gaddis put it, they are molecules with minds of their own. In war, as Clausewitz observed, the will is directed at an animate object that *reacts*. Hence the formulation of strategy requires the ability to interpret the behavior of other human beings. Data alone won't cut it.

Shortages of manpower and material may be excused. Not so shortages of brainpower. The historian Marc Bloch, in reflecting on the reasons for France's shocking fall to the Nazis in 1940, wrote that "the German triumph was, essentially, a triumph of intellect — and it is that which makes it so peculiarly serious." Instead of studying history rigorously, with as much interest in change as in continuity, the French studied it selectively. Bloch recalled a lecture on Napoleonic tactics given in 1910 by Ferdinand Foch, the future Supreme Commander of the Allied forces in World War I, in which Foch "exhibited them as models to be followed irrespective of any changes that might have taken place in the world since Napoleon's time." And this type of intellectual shallowness was not limited to the military. "As a nation," Bloch wrote, "we had been content with incomplete knowledge and imperfectly thought-out ideas," adding that "such an attitude is not a good preparation for military success." Rather, "this mental laziness" led to "a gloomy mood of self-satisfaction." Bloch, who in World War II joined the French resistance and was tortured and executed by the Gestapo in 1944 (*Strange Defeat* was published posthumously), castigated the government for having abdicated its ultimate responsibility for French security: "nothing shed a cruder light on the spinelessness of Government than its capitulation to the technicians."

The great historian's analysis was correct. Those who seek the causes of the French defeat in the technical realm — especially in the realm of armor — merely capitulate again to the technicians. The French actually had more and better tanks than the Germans. What they did not have was an effective way of using them: they made decisions more slowly than the tanks could move. The reason for this slowness was that French command-and-control was highly centralized. As the historian Eugenia Kiesling has shown, the reason for the centralization was that the French army's reserves lacked the training to be entrusted with decision-making responsibility. The reason for this lack of training was mutual distrust between the army and the political left. At the same time, French businesses, on the grounds of liberal property rights, resisted government attempts to prepare the economy for war in time of peace. In short, the proximate cause of the French defeat was that their military could not match the speed of German decision-making; the ultimate cause was the nation's failure to overcome its bitter divisions in the face of an existential threat. This is a social, political, psychological, and economic story, which is the stuff of the humanities. It is not the stuff of STEM, which can get us no farther than the technical nuts-and-bolts of French and German tanks, or of our own missiles.

Bloch's heroism is itself a testimony to the role of historical and humanistic understanding in determining the fate of a society. His post-mortem of a gloomily self-satisfied nation riven by internal tensions in the face of a determined competitor should serve as a warning today. The United States is so self-absorbed that it forgets about the outside world. Steadily we make ourselves weak and irrelevant. The threat of China is growing larger while Americans fantasize about national divorce. If we are broken, it is because we broke ourselves. Yet the sciences cannot fix social and political dysfunction. Only the humanities can; but first they must fix or be fixed themselves.

CASS R. SUNSTEIN

Experiments of Living Constitutionalism: A Manifesto

In constitutional law, there are a lot of isms.

Textualism claims that the Constitution's text is binding. The central idea is that judges are bound by the written words of the founding document. (Reasonable textualists acknowledge that the text is often ambiguous. What, for example, is meant by "the freedom of speech"? That is far from obvious.)

Originalism, which is on the ascendancy on the current Supreme Court, insists that the Constitution should be interpreted in accordance with its original public meaning — its meaning at the time of its ratification in the late eighteenth century, and after the Civil War for the Thirteenth,

Fourteenth, and Fifteenth Amendments. (Reasonable originalists acknowledge that the original public meaning is often ambiguous. What was the original understanding of the constitutional provision granting "executive power" to the president? That is not obvious.)

Living constitutionalism claims that the meaning of the Constitution evolves over time, which means that the document might require states to recognize same-sex marriage now, even if it did not require that before. (Reasonable living constitutionalists acknowledge that judges can go in terrible directions. From American history, you can take your pick.)

Thayerism — so named after the great Harvard law professor James Bradley Thayer — claims that judges should uphold legislation unless it is unconstitutional beyond a reasonable doubt. (Reasonable Thayerians acknowledge that under their approach, school segregation would probably have to be upheld, and freedom of speech would be far less robust than it now is. They respond that if you believe in democracy, you should accept judicial restraint, and take the bitter with the sweet.)

Minimalism contends that judges should avoid abstract theories and go case-by-case, interpreting the Constitution with close reference to the particular facts. (Reasonable minimalists acknowledge that their approach leaves a lot of uncertainty, and also that in some cases they will have to get more theoretical than they would like.)

In view of the proliferation of isms in the domain of constitutional law, there is strong reason to hesitate before proposing yet another. Still, I have one to offer. I do so because it has yet to be identified; because reasonable arguments can be made on its behalf; and because it helps to organize and to illuminate numerous constitutional developments over the last decades. Those developments are otherwise puzzling and unmotivated. At the same time, the approach I sketch suggests a future path for constitutional law that is unlikely to be taken, at least in the United States — but that we would do well to visualize. Constitutional law is full of surprises, and some of the surprises are good ones. In any case, theories of constitutional interpretation sometimes spread through the public, even if they do not get traction in the courts.

Here is the proposal, for your consideration: Experiments of Living Constitutionalism.

The central idea is that the Constitution should be interpreted to allow both individuals and groups to experiment with different ways of living, whether we are speaking of religious practices, family arrangements, sex, romance, marriage, child-rearing, schooling, or work. Experiments of Living Constitutionalism prizes individual dignity. It emphasizes the importance of learning. It cherishes diversity and plurality; it opposes (what it sees as) authoritarianism in all its forms. It is emphatically liberal in character — liberal in its emphasis on freedom and agency, especially with respect to things that people care most about.

The operative phrase — experiments of living — comes from John Stuart Mill, who said this in *On Liberty* in 1859:

> That mankind are not infallible; that their truths, for the most part, are only half-truths; that unity of opinion, unless resulting from the fullest and freest comparison of opposite opinions, is not desirable, and diversity not an evil, but a good, until mankind are much more capable than at present of recognizing all sides of the truth, are principles applicable to men's modes of action, not less than to their opinions. As it is useful that while mankind

> are imperfect there should be different opinions, so it is that there should be different experiments of living; that free scope should be given to varieties of character, short of injury to others; and that the worth of different modes of life should be proved practically, when any one thinks fit to try them. It is desirable, in short, that in things which do not primarily concern others, individuality should assert itself. Where, not the person's own character, but the traditions or customs of other people are the rule of conduct, there is wanting one of the principal ingredients of human happiness, and quite the chief ingredient of individual and social progress.

Experiments of Living Constitutionalists insist on the importance of allowing and encouraging "varieties of character" and on the value of "different modes of life." It does so in part because it values the dignity and separateness of every individual. It does so in part because it sees experiments of living as essential to social as well as individual progress. For those who embrace Experiments of Living Constitutionalism, experiments of living also contribute to the common good. If each of us is able to see what each of us has tried, and is free to experiment, we will have more options to consider; all of us will be able to learn from every one of us. Failed experiments of living may be nothing to celebrate, but they are sources of knowledge and experience and they contribute to both individual and social progress.

As its name (inadvertently!) suggests, Experiments of Living Constitutionalism is a form of living constitutionalism. Its advocates firmly reject originalism. They do not believe that the Constitution should be frozen in time. They do not think that it should be understood in accordance with its original public meaning. If the Supreme Court allows people to experiment with certain forms of speech (blasphemous speech, sexually explicit speech, potentially dangerous speech), it might be going well beyond the original meaning. Nonetheless, Experiments of Living Constitutionalists claim that their preferred approach has deep roots in Anglo-American traditions, and that it can be understood in a way that is faithful to the text of the Constitution. Experiments of Living Constitutionalists value longstanding principles and aspirations in our political tradition, and they try to build on them, even if they do not think that the meaning of the Constitution is forever fixed.

Those who favor Experiments of Living Constitutionalism prize freedom of speech. Indeed, they might prize this freedom most of all. They celebrate Justice Robert Jackson's powerful words in 1943: "Compulsory unification of opinion achieves only the unanimity of the graveyard." They are drawn to Jackson's suggestion: "If there is any fixed star in our constitutional constellation, it is that no official, high or petty, can prescribe what shall be orthodox in politics, nationalism, religion, or other matters of opinion, or force citizens to confess by word or act their faith therein." For that reason, they would protect political speech of diverse kinds. They would also protect art, literature, film, and all the arts, believing that all of these are crucial to consideration of experiments of living.

To be sure, Experiments of Living Constitutionalists do not believe that the first amendment is "an absolute." They know that some speech contributes little or nothing to experiments of living, and they know that some speech imposes serious and immediate harm. They do not think it is a legitimate experiment of living for someone to say, "Your money or your life." They would allow restrictions on bribery, perjury, and fraud, and they would permit restrictions on speech when there is a clear and present danger. They are not at all clear how much the Constitution should protect commercial advertising; they fear that the current Court's keen interest in protecting such advertising is a misadventure. But they are broadly comfortable with existing First Amendment doctrine, which is fiercely protective of free speech, and they would resist efforts to authorize any kind of censorship.

In the same vein, those who favor Experiments of Living Constitutionalism prize freedom of religion. They would allow a plurality of faiths to flourish. They would vigorously protect people of faith, agnostics, and atheists. They would not be reluctant to stand in the way of federal or state efforts to impose secular values, even widely held ones, on people whose religious traditions are inconsistent with those values. (If the Catholic Church does not want to perform or recognize same-sex marriages, that is its right.) Experiments of Living Constitutionalists are especially enthusiastic about freedom of association, whether we are speaking of civic associations, political associations, book clubs, or associations of any other kind. They would be strongly inclined to protect contemporary rights of privacy, including the right to use contraceptives, the right to live with members of one's family, the right to engage in consensual sexual relations of any kind and the right to same-sex marriage. For those who embrace Experiments of Living Constitutionalism, the focus on sexual privacy is not a mistake, a coincidence, or some kind of indulgence. It is entirely appropriate and something to be celebrated, for sex is a domain in which "individuality should assert itself."

Since Experiments of Living Constitutionalists prize individual agency, they take the right to choose abortion seriously. Still, they greatly struggle with this particular issue. For them, it is not an easy question; the moral issue is difficult. (My experiment of living does not allow me to hurt you.) In the end, they might not commit themselves to a right to choose, because of the importance and the value of protecting unborn life. Following Mill, Experiments of Living Constitutionalists enthusiastically agree that the state might interfere with freedom when there is harm to others.

Experiments of Living Constitutionalism is a great friend to federalism, seeing the diversity of the states as an engine for the creation of experiments of living. Mississippi need not take the same path as Massachusetts. Local norms and cultures deserve protection (unless they squelch, through their governments, experiments of living). Those who embrace Experiments of Living Constitutionalism embrace Justice Brandeis' idea of "laboratories of democracy"; they will strongly resist national efforts to override particular values and approaches that are prized by citizens of (for example) California, Georgia, or Wyoming.

At the same time, they will be open-minded on separation of powers questions. The commitment to Experiments of Living Constitutionalism does not entail a particular approach to grants of power and discretion to administrative agencies such as the Department of Education, the Environmental Protection Agency, or the Federal Communication Commission. But Experiments of Living Constitutionalists approach separation of powers issues with Mill's cautionary note in mind: "Where, not the person's own character, but the traditions or customs of other people are the rule of conduct, there is wanting one of the principal ingredients of human happiness, and quite the chief ingredient of individual and social progress."

At this point, you might have numerous questions and concerns. What is the pedigree of the Experiments of Living Constitution? Where on earth does it come from? What are its limits? Justice Oliver Wendell Holmes famously wrote, "The Constitution does not enact Mr. Herbert Spencer's Social Statics." Does the U.S. Constitution enact Mr. John Stuart Mill's *On Liberty*? Wouldn't that be absurd? Why should anyone embrace an effort to understand an eighteenth-century American document by reference to the thinking of a British philosopher over half a century later?

Those who support the Experiments of Living Constitution agree that such questions must be taken seriously, but they think that they can answer them. They point to the distinctive form of liberal republicanism that defined and launched the U.S. Constitution. In brief: liberal republicanism is liberal insofar as it emphasizes the agency and the dignity of all of us; it is republican insofar as it sees government as an engine for collective deliberation about the public good. Experiments of Living Constitutionalists claim continuity with liberal republicanism. They add that to a greater or lesser degree, Mill was essentially summarizing and elaborating principles that predated and informed the American founding.

Experiments of Living Constitutionalists insist in particular that the Fourteenth and Fifteenth Amendments, ratified in the aftermath of the Civil War, are animated by a commitment to individual freedom that fits comfortably with their preferred approach. In their view, the idea of experiments of living has a long tradition behind it; Montesquieu and Locke can be seen as having defended versions of that idea, as can Madison, Hamilton, and Jefferson. Mill was hardly writing on a clean slate. The idea of experiments of living is anything but a concoction, or a bolt from the blue. In American constitutional law, Justice Holmes, Jr. spoke directly in the terms of Experiments of Living Constitutionalism in his great dissenting opinion in *Abrams v. United States*, decided in 1919:

> But when men have realized that time has upset many fighting faiths, they may come to believe even more than they believe the very foundations of their own conduct that the ultimate good desired is better reached by free trade in ideas — that the best test of truth is the power of the thought to get itself accepted in the competition of the market, and that truth is the only ground upon which their wishes safely can be carried out. That at any rate is the theory of our Constitution. It is an experiment, as all life is an experiment. Every year if not every day we have to wager our salvation upon some prophecy based upon imperfect knowledge. While that experiment is part of our system I think that we should be eternally vigilant against attempts to check the expression of opinions that we loathe and believe to be fraught with death, unless they so imminently threaten immediate interference with the lawful and pressing purposes of the law that an immediate check is required to save the country.

Skeptics might ask how Experiments of Living Constitutionalism relates to our existing Constitution, and whether it promises, or threatens, to produce radical reforms. Would government paternalism, understood as the displacement of individual choices by officials who think they know best, be out of bounds? Would motorcycle helmet laws be out of bounds? Would there be a constitutional right to use illegal drugs? Would there be a right to polygamous marriages? To incestuous marriages? To pornography? Which Experiments of Living lack constitutional protection? These are fair and challenging questions. In response, defenders of Experiments of Living Constitutionalism have four things to say.

First, defenders of Experiments of Living Constitutionalism are not fanatics, and they need not embrace everything that Mill says about liberty. Certainly they need not go so far as to accept Mill's Harm Principle (which forbids regulation unless it is justified as a way of preventing harm to others). You can believe in Experiments of Living Constitutionalism without thinking that government paternalism, even of the coercive sort, is always out of bounds. Experiments of Living Constitutionalists should have no trouble with laws that require people to buckle their seatbelts, to wear helmets while riding motorcycles, or to save money for retirement (as through Social Security). They can accept cigarette taxes, even if the goal of such taxes is to prevent people from harming themselves. Nor would they have much interest in the view that the Constitution protects a right to polygamous marriages, incestuous marriages, or child pornography.

One reason is that in some of these cases individual choices clearly impose harm to others (consider child pornography). If your experiment injures someone else, you had better stop experimenting. And even when people are not harming others, Experiments of Living Constitutionalists insist, as Mill did not, on the importance of distinguishing between genuine experiments of living that are fundamental to people's lives (as when people choose to live together in lieu of marriage, or follow a religious conviction of their own) and choices that clearly lack that character (as when people decide to not to buckle their seatbelts, or not so save for retirement). To be sure, there might be some hard line-drawing problems here.

Second, Experiments of Living Constitutionalists emphasize that far from being radical, their approach helps to clarify and support a great deal of existing law. Since the 1960s, the Supreme Court has vigorously protected freedom of speech, including not only political speech but also literature, art, cinema, and much more. (The Court is largely following Holmes.) In the process, it has also protected a great deal of sexually explicit speech. So, too, freedom of association enjoys broad protection. So does religious liberty. As noted, the justices have ruled that sexual privacy qualifies for protection under the due process clause. It is not simple to produce an account that explains and supports all these disparate rulings. Experiments of Living Constitutionalism can provide such an account.

Third, defenders of Experiments of Living Constitutionalism are willing to be respectful of precedent, whether or not they agree with it. They may not agree, for example, with the Court's ruling that the Constitution does not protect the right to physician-assisted suicide. But like almost everyone else, they do not think it appropriate to overrule decisions simply because they believe that they were wrong. You can accept Experiment of Living Constitutionalism while also thinking that any legal system on earth needs to respect *stare decisis*, so as to prevent instability and perhaps even a form of constitutional chaos. A legal system cannot operate if today's decision is in tomorrow's garbage heap.

Fourth, those who embrace Experiments of Living Constitutionalism would give careful attention to the decisions of democratic processes. They are liberals, after all, and liberals are democrats, even if there are real limits on what democracies can do. Experiments of Living Constitutionalists will have to make some difficult choices here, but if Congress or a state legislature has made a reasonable decision, supporters of Experiments of Living Constitutionalism might well be cautious before rejecting it. You can believe in experiments of living without being a fanatic. Everything depends on the details — on the kind of liberty that is at stake, and on the strength of the argument for interfering with it. To this extent, Experiments of Living Constitutionalists might be willing to make common cause with minimalists.

How shall we choose between Experiments of Living Constitutionalism and other approaches to constitutional interpretation? Should we reject it in favor of originalism? Any answer to that question would have to offer criteria of selection, which are urgently needed. I suggest that the only possible answer is another question: *What would make our constitutional order better rather than worse?* That is an admittedly daunting question, but there is no alternative to asking it. It is the only game in town. The Constitution does not contain the instructions for its own interpretation. It does not have an originalism clause; it does not say, "This document shall be interpreted in accordance with its original public meaning." In fact it does not specify any theory of interpretation. The choice of such a theory is inevitably our own.

Some originalists seem to think that their preferred approach follows from the very idea of interpretation, but it really does not. In the end, originalism has to be justified on the grounds that it would make our system better. Many alternative approaches, including Experiments of Living Constitutionalism, can fall within the domain of interpretation, so long as they operate by reference to and within the space of the Constitution itself. It is hopeless to defend a contested theory of interpretation by citing the founding document and pounding the table. The only way to defend such a theory, or to evaluate it, is to ask what it would do for the institutions and rights under which the American people live. Where else can we possibly turn?

It might be tempting to respond that the choice of a theory of interpretation cannot possibly depend on the results that it yields. One might think that that choice has to be made on the basis of some commitment that might seem higher or deeper, or more fundamental. If we focus on results, and choose a theory of interpretation on the basis of results, perhaps we are biased, or unforgivably "result-oriented," and engaged in some kind of special pleading. The problem with such a response is that it rests on an illusion of compulsion. Among the reasonable candidates, judges (and others) are not compelled to adopt a particular theory of interpretation; they must make a choice. One last time: To do that, judges (and others) are required to ask about what would make our constitutional order better rather than worse.

Here is an answer to that question: Experiments of Living Constitutionalism.

MARIO VARGAS LLOSA

The Tranquil Gaze of Benito Pérez Galdós

I consider Javier Cercas one of the best writers in the Spanish language, and I believe that, after oblivion has buried his contemporaries, at least three of his extraordinary books — *Soldiers of Salamis*, *The Anatomy of a Moment*, and *The Imposter* — will still have readers who turn to them to learn what our disordered present was like. He is also a man of courage. He loves his homeland of Catalonia, and his articles inveighing against the secessionist demagoguery of the Catalan separatists are persuasive and incontestable.

In an urbane debate some time back with Antonio Muñoz Molina on the subject of the nineteenth-century Spanish novelist Benito Pérez Galdós, Cercas admitted that he didn't care for the prose of the author of *Fortunata and Jacinta.* As my grandfather Pedro used to say, *entre gustos y colores, no han escrito los autores*, which roughly translated is the old adage that there is no accounting for taste. Everyone has a right to his opinion, and writers do too, but to make such a declaration on the centenary of Pérez Galdós' death, when everyone else was lauding and commemorating him, was certainly a provocation.

I don't care for Proust. For years this embarrassed me, and I kept it under wraps. Not anymore. I confess I read him lethargically; I struggled to get through his interminable novel and its long sentences, its author's fussiness and frivolity. His small, selfish world repelled me, not to mention those cork-lined walls meant to buffer him from the distracting noise of the outside world, which I love so much. Had I been a reader for Gallimard when Proust submitted the manuscript of his first volume, I fear I would have advised against publication, as did André Gide. (He regretted this error for the rest of his life.) All this is to say that, in the polemic in question, I took the side of Muñoz Molina, in opposition to my friend Javier Cercas.

A few months later, in a column in *El País* entitled "The Merit of Galdós," Cercas was far more generous and, I believe, accurate, in his treatment of the writer. He admitted that in the immense vacuum in Spanish literature that followed *Don Quixote*, Pérez Galdós had embarked upon "a literary project of unprecedented ambition and breadth in an attempt to consolidate a novelistic tradition conspicuously absent in Spain." And he affirmed that neither Pio Baroja's *Memoirs of a Man of Action* nor Ramon Maria del Valle-Inclán's *The Carlist War* were conceivable without the *National Episodes*, the extraordinary corpus of forty-six historical novels about Spain that Pérez Galdós produced between 1872 and 1912. I could not agree more.

It is unjust to say, as many did in his day, that Benito Pérez Galdós was a bad writer. He was not a genius, but he was the best Spanish writer of the nineteenth century, the most ambitious, and probably the first professional writer that the language had. In those days, whether in Spain or Latin America, it was impossible for a writer to live from royalties. (Many journalists, instead of receiving a salary, wrote solely for the purpose of making themselves known.) Pérez Galdós had a prosperous family that admired him and kept him afloat for a long time, letting him exercise his vocation, granting him the independence that he needed to write freely. His novels and his essays were brought out by different publishers (sometimes even by himself) under contracts that he did not always believe were honored. And yet he became famous, and soon set to writing the *National Episodes.*

For a long time, I wanted to read Pérez Galdós from beginning to end — as a student I had read *Fortunata and Jacinta,* of course, but I was ignorant of his work as a whole — and it struck me that the coronavirus pandemic would provide a fine occasion to do so. After eighteen months, having finished the plays, the novels, and the *National Episodes,* I was impressed by the tranquil, wounded world that he invented. I have yet to read all his essays and articles: they represent an immense labor, and I am still making my way through them. I doubt that more than a few scholars have tackled them all. The reason for this is simple: Pérez Galdós was not a great thinker, like Ortega y Gasset or Unamuno, and though he did compose a few interesting essays, the better part of his journalistic work has been rightly unremarked upon, being transient and superficial. There is little point in devoting so much time to literature of so little weight, even if there are a few nuggets of value in the lot.

Pérez Galdós was born in Las Palmas de Gran Canaria, or the Canary Islands, on May 10, 1843, the son of Lieutenant Colonel Sebastián Pérez, the military leader of the island and a landholder who devoted much of his time to his assorted businesses. Benito was the youngest of ten siblings, and his mother, Dolores de Galdós, a woman of great character, was known to wear the pants in the family. It was she who decided that Benito, apparently in love with a cousin she disapproved of, should go to Madrid at the age of twenty to study law. Yolanda Arencibia, a great promoter of Galdós and the author of what is far and away the best (and most voluminous) biography of him, has tried to determine whether his love affair with his cousin Sisita was the true cause of his departure from Las Palmas. But she ran up against a wall. In that family, secrets were not to be broached.

Pérez Galdós used his first vacation period in Madrid to return to his home island and see her. But, according to Arencibia, Sisita was soon to depart for Cuba — she was a native of its most beautiful colonial city, Trinidad — to marry the landowner Eduardo Duque, who would give her a son, Sebastián, who lived only a few years. After the death of her first husband, Sisita married a relative, Pablo de Galdós, but died at the young age of twenty-eight of a postpartum infection, which in those days was known as puerperal fever. Some believe that Pérez Galdós was forevermore in love with her and remained single to honor her memory, but this is pure speculation, as neither he nor those close to him ever addressed the subject directly or allowed pertinent details to come to light.

Obedient to his mother, Benito attended the Complutense University in Madrid, but soon became disenchanted with the law. Journalism was more attractive to him, and he devoted a great deal of time to it — and to bohemian Madrid, the vitality in its coffee houses full of painters, scribblers, reporters, and politicians, which he abundantly described in his writings. He turned increasingly toward literature, starting with theater, his first passion, writing comedies in verse and prose. According to his own account, none of them made it to the stage, and one day he burned them all. He would return to the genre years later.

He loved Madrid extravagantly, more than any other writer before or after. He was the most faithful and refined connoisseur of its streets and dive bars, its shops and boarding houses, its salons and gossip mills, its human types, its customs and professions and businesses, the errors in spoken Spanish common to its less cultured citizens, and, of course, its history. As an example of the depth of Pérez Galdós' love for and acquaintance with Madrid, it suffices to read the first two chapters of *Prim*, one of the best of the *National Episodes*; the streets and their residents seem to come to life as though touched by a magic wand — the author's prose — as the character of Santiago Ibero, a fervent young admirer of General Prim, prepares the two men's vertiginous escape to Mexico. The same novel includes also a wonderful description of the Atheneum, where Pérez Galdós studied and read voluminously; the passage is splendid for its prose and its measured summary of Spanish politics in April 1862. The writer's vision is tranquil, patient, serene, and diligently portrays a world immobilized by religion, which possesses the virtue (or the fault?) of holding it in an almost painterly stasis, but which at other times is its tragedy, its doom.

The hostility that Pérez Galdós awakened in his country in the years when he was writing his novels, his plays, and the

National Episodes now strikes us as hard to believe. Of course he had his supporters, but his adversaries were apparently more numerous. It was said that his books "stank of pork stew," that he wrote vulgarly and inelegantly. Famously, in 1924 in his play *Bohemian Lights*, Valle-Inclán insulted Pérez Galdós and his naturalist style with the nickname *garbancero,* or "the chickpea man," which he was never able to live down. This animosity became particularly evident in 1912, in the widespread opposition to the then-seventy-nine-year-old writer's nomination for the Nobel Prize in Literature, which had been proposed by some five hundred writers, journalists, and artists with the support of the Spanish government. The Swedish Academy is said to have received more petitions against his candidacy than for it, with the objections coming principally from far-right Catholic circles that saw in him a republican and an extreme freethinker. No man is a prophet in his own country, and in the Spain of the time, dominated by narrow and sectarian Catholicism, Pérez Galdós was considered a fiercely anticlerical liberal. This was never quite true: his liberalism and his republicanism were scrupulously tolerant. With typical logic and clarity, the poet and writer Andrés Trapiello said of the conspiracy against Galdós, "It was the triumph of Spanish mange and meanness in the face of liberal principles."

In his works, Pérez Galdós described primarily the middle classes — or so it is said; but he did not ignore the aristocracy or the humbler fringes of society. As a writer he climbed up and down the social ladder at will, and one of the late *Episodes,* entitled *A Coterie of Imps,* begins with a splendid description of Madrid at its poorest, "one of its most destitute and hideous streets, the one called Rodas, which rises and falls over the hill between Embajadores and the Rastro," where a village woman, Lucila Ansúrez, lives. She has taken refuge with Captain

Bartolomé Gracián, a man she loves who is being persecuted by the powers that be.

Photographs depict the huge crowds in Madrid that accompanied Pérez Galdós' mortal remains to the Almudena Cemetery on January 5, 1920. According to the press, at least thirty thousand people came to pay homage to him in death. What was the source of this popularity? Above all, the *National Episodes*. He did what Balzac, Dickens, and Zola had done for their countries, and what he admired them for doing: telling, in fiction, the history and the social reality of their nations. Though as an artist he did not surpass the first two (with some of his novels he may have exceeded Zola, only three years his elder), his *Episodes* exist in the same line, and convert the lived past into literature, putting within reach of the broader public an even-handed, pleasurable, wise, and well-written version of the nineteenth century, with living characters and solid reportage — and this was a decisive period for Spain, encompassing the French invasion, the independence struggles against Napoleon's armies, the reactionary absolutism of Ferdinand the Seventh, the invasion of Morocco, the Carlist Wars (a series of nineteenth-century conflicts over the legitimate heir to the Spanish throne which laid the ground for the legitimist and traditionalist forces of twentieth-century Spanish fascism), the short-lived First Republic, and finally, the Bourbon Restoration. Unlike other European countries such as Germany, France, and England, Spain cannot be said to have experienced the industrial revolution, and much of its time was wasted in these years in anachronistic wars of religion, which left it fatally backward after centuries as the supreme power on the continent.

Pérez Galdós' merit lies not only in documenting this period in his novels, but also in his way of doing so: with objectivity, with a comprehending and generous spirit, without taking sides ideologically, putting the ethical above the political, separating idealism from fanaticism, seeing the generosity and the misery in the hearts of both sides of the debates of the time. This is what stands out most when we read the plays, the novels, and the *Episodes*: a writer struggling to remain fair and impartial. His approach seems to freeze the Spain of his time in a sure objective gaze, immobilizing his subject to give a more faithful account of its nature.

This is the furthest thing imaginable from the obstinate, peremptory caricature of Galdós that we have come to know. He was a civil man, a liberal who in his old age supported the Republic; but more than a politician, and a representative in the Cortes, he was a decent and thoughtful man. When narrating a tumultuous period in Spain's history, he strove to do so equitably and with detachment, singling out the good from the bad and recognizing the presence of both in friends as well as foes. The exception to this, perhaps, was his view of the frivolity of the upper and middle classes, particularly at the time of the Restoration; about this he was often implacable. Yet the general absence of moral censure confers an air of justice upon the *National Episodes*, from *Trafalgar* to *Cánovas*, and brings his readers very close to the writer.

He wrote as he did because he was a man of substance — *muy buena gente,* as we say in Peru. Not all writers are like that; some are quite the opposite. The differences in temperament have nothing to do with differences in talent. Pérez Galdós' temperament was enriched by a spirit of fair-mindedness that made him lovable and credible. His remarkable composure gave his tales a certain stillness easily confused with immobility, as if his narratives were photographs.

Something similar was the case in his private life. He was a lifelong bachelor, but his biographers have noted the presence of three long-term lovers and many other fleeting ones. The first, Lorenza Cobián González, a humble Asturian who gave birth to his daughter María (whom he recognized and made his sole heir), was illiterate, and he taught her to read and to write. His affair with the writer Emilia Pardo Bazán, a woman of passion (except when she wrote her novels), was rather torrid. "I will crush you," she says to him in one of their letters. This may not have been only poetic license: this feminist writer appears to have been a devilish libertine in her private life. The last of the three was an apprentice actress, a good deal younger than him, named Concepción Morell Nicolau. Pérez Galdós supported her career in the theater, and to all appearances he behaved very badly toward her. It must be said that she was a difficult woman, and something of a cadger. Their breakup, which involved numerous friends, was drawn-out but diplomatic.

His great defect as a writer was his pre-Flaubertian idiom: his failure to grasp that the first character that the novelist invents is the narrator, whether he realizes it or not. This is true whether the narrator is omniscient or implicated in the action of the story; as a figure, it is he (or she) who grants independence and autonomy to the fictional creation. Despite his vast literary production, this is something that Pérez Galdós never grasped. And so the omniscience of his characters is of the classical sort, and his Gabriel Araceli and Salvador Monsalud have an impossible awareness of the thoughts and the feelings of other characters, in this way detracting from the realism of the novels. As the narrator of the *Episodes* and other novels, Pérez Galdós — in *Amadeo I,* for example, from the fifth series of the *Episodes,* where he appears under the name of Tito Liviano, a caricature of Titus Livius — attributes this awareness of the contents of other minds to historians and eyewitnesses or, still worse, to fantastical occurrences narrated in the realist mode, which gives an unnatural and artificial air to those otherwise naturalistic works.

In the later volumes *The First Republic* and *From Carthage to Sagunto,* which tell of the chaos and disorder of the First Republic in Spain — with constant crises in the ministries, the siege of Cartagena during the Cantonal War, the threats of putsches, and the Civil War against the Carlists — the historian Tito Liviano, shyster, dwarf, and tireless fornicator, will fall in love with a teacher, Floriana. She will turn out to be a nymph and will drag the historian into a subterranean passageway full of magical surprises, such as monumental bulls that serve as mounts for the delicate feminine figures populating underground Madrid. This is, of course, an imaginary recreation of ancient Greece — a dream. It interrupts the plot arbitrarily, introducing an obtrusive and far from convincing element of fantasy. With time, such embellishments vanished from the *Episodes*, but attentive readers must make their peace with such backsliding into the fictional styles of the past, aware that Flaubert had already put forward a revolutionary conception of the narrator as a central, if invisible, character in the narrative — an idea that he worked out in the letters he wrote almost daily to Louise Colet as he fashioned and re-fashioned *Madame Bovary*.

In *From Carthage to Sagunto*, the second-to-last of the *Episodes*, there is a description of the siege of Cuenca by the Carlist army at the orders of a woman on horseback, María das Neves, wife of Alfonso of the House of Bourbon. Here reality mingles with the diabolical in ferocious battles, beheadings, pillages of indescribable cruelty and savagery. It is proof that at times the mild Pérez Galdós' narrative may be wild and brutal, but this is an exception. In general his tales proceed serenely, in quiet prose that moves with unruffled steps.

In 1887, *Fortunata and Jacinta*, the novel that his critics and his posterity consider Pérez Galdós' masterpiece, was published in four volumes. It originally had a subtitle, suppressed in certain editions: *Two Stories of Married Women*. He devoted two years — interrupted by a trip to France and Germany — to the composition of this ambitious tale, which many regard as the great Spanish novel of the nineteenth century. Others feel that this accolade should go to *La Regenta* by Leopoldo Alas, which appeared in two volumes in 1884–1885, but such a debate is rather absurd, given the eternal difficulties of fully describing the achievement of two first-rate novels representative of the entire era of the Spanish nineteenth century. The nineteenth century has generally been considered the zenith of the European novel, characterized by such crowning glories as *Les Misérables, War and Peace, The Brothers Karamazov*, and the works of Dickens and Balzac, of which Pérez Galdós was an enthusiastic admirer. All debates aside, *Fortunata and Jacinta* is without a doubt Pérez Galdós' most significant and ambitious novel.

Of particular importance in this *chef-d'oeuvre* is his perspective on Madrid, where the main episodes of the story take place. *Fortunata and Jacinta* elaborates a comprehensive vision of the city, describing its streets, its squares, its buildings, and especially its cafes, integrating them brilliantly into the action, and encompassing all of the city's social strata, from the cream of the aristocracy to the middle classes and the very poor in a totalizing vision distinct from, but in no way inferior to, that presented in other works. I have now read this massive work three times, and the story has captivated me every time, from the first words to the last, demanding an absorption and commitment characteristic of the finest novels that I have known.

Its story is quite simple, but Galdos' way of telling it is not: there is a wealth of subtlety and detail, and a deftness in its prose, both in the descriptions and the dialogues, not present in anything Galdós wrote before or after. Here again the story is told in the first person by a narrator apparently well-informed about the matters at hand, but eventually this artifice vanishes, and without the reader realizing it the narrator-as-party-to-the-events is displaced by a more conventional omniscient narrator. Like virtually all nineteenth-century novels, *Fortunata and Jacinta* tells the story of a romantic passion. Where it differs from its counterparts is in the duration of the passion recounted, and in the humble young woman who embodies it and who experiences passionate love — by which I mean a total surrender to a kind of love that becomes the essence and purpose of an entire life, a kind of religion — long before the Surrealist invention of the idea of *l'amour fou*.

Fortunata lives this in the flesh, and in her abandonment displays a generosity without limits, until her devotion to her lover becomes the core of her existence. She gives herself completely to the young and wealthy Juanito Santa Cruz, making him her reason for living and the lodestar of her heart. Despite the obstacles and the neglect that she endures, her love will never flag, not for a single day, convinced as she is that he is everything for her. In her pledge, she does not expect reciprocity; her constancy, her stubbornness, attest to what is, in the end, her own obsession; and she is prepared to suffer humiliation and disgrace from friends and family. In a way, she meets a triumphant end, departing this world as events follow the very course that she had foreseen.

A village woman — her proclamation that "I'm village through-and-through" has become a prominent theme in critical discussions of the novel — Fortunata is illiterate when she first meets Juanito. He is at once attracted by her beauty and repulsed by the sight of her eating a raw egg, which we must imagine dripping through her fingers. The girl lives hand-to-mouth in Cava Baja (where a plaque was recently placed in memory of her on the centenary of Galdós' death).

Fortunata's epic passion is a bit difficult to explain — but is an explanation of love even possible? — because, though he is handsome and elegant, Juanito Santa Cruz hasn't much to offer. He is a social parasite, sponging off the fortune of his parents, Baldomero and Barbarita, who toil and save their whole life as cloth wholesalers, while he lives an epicene life of leisure, devoted to his conquests and his frivolous entertainments. In the course of the novel Juanito frequently leaves Fortunata for one of his paramours, and each time she just goes on with her life. She confesses to taking lovers herself — "eight or so," she guesses — but they mean nothing to her, and she has no doubt that she will drop them as soon as Juanito appears, because he is the one true love of her life. She is happy with him, especially in the beginning, when he sets her up in an apartment where he can visit her alone, but soon he will abandon her. They will have a child before death takes her away. Fortunata's love is total, composed of countless sacrifices, while Juanito's is superficial and transitory, and has room for other affairs. And even for his wife Jacinta: their honeymoon in Burgos, Zaragoza, Barcelona, Valencia, and Seville is recounted in the first chapters of the book.

Jacinta, the other heroine of the novel, is a graceful young woman whose life is shadowed by tragedy. She loves children, but she cannot have any. The pain of this lack will follow her until she comes to care for the newborn Juan Evaristo, Juanito and Fortunata's son. Just before dying, Fortunata leaves the boy in Jacinta's hands for her to raise as her own. This is a great boon to Jacinta, who had taken Fortunata to be her moral superior, following her conviction that a woman incapable of giving her husband offspring had no right to be his legitimate spouse.

This is a brief synopsis of the central thread of the novel, which is otherwise densely peopled in a Dickensian way, with representative figures from every social class in nineteenth-century Madrid appearing and reappearing. Their ranks include a proud and unforgettable woman, Mauricia the Hard, so-called for her zealous, irascible character and her physical resemblance to Napoleon. She is one of Pérez Galdós' finest and most striking creations, and whenever she shows up, she showers her companions with violence and rhetorical excess. Mauricia is a woman of humble origins, perpetually at war with the rich and noble. No one can tame or cow this natural born anarchist who, apart from being a rebel by nature, is subject to fits of genuine madness, one of which leads the nuns of the convent of Micaela — where penitent Catholic women go to be reeducated — to expel her.

No less notable is Maximiliano, whom Fortunata marries but does not love, knowing that she will deceive him whenever Juanito Santa Cruz comes calling. An ugly, sickly boy of scant education, he is bowled over by Fortunata, falls deeply in love with her, and is ready to do anything for her, marrying her and pushing her toward the Christian ideal of goodness, with no success to speak of. Later, in desperation, the poor devil goes mad, raving, dreaming of murder, inventing a personal religion designed to free all humankind from the demons that torment it.

Apart from its descriptions of representative types, the pages of *Fortunata and Jacinta* abound in detailed and historically accurate descriptions of Madrid in the second half of the nineteenth century, with fine-grained illustrations of almost every street, neighborhood, and house, as well as the political and social life of the city and the customs governing it. Particularly significant here is the portrayal of its cafes, which were centers for the literary world and for society; great attention is devoted to them in the third section of the novel, when we meet Juan Pablo, one of Maximilian's brothers and yet another marionette in the story, who wiles away his days in them. The author gives the impression at times of omniscience, as if nothing that occurred in the Madrid of the time escaped his vision, which brings together all sorts of incidents and experiences, minor and major. His empathy seems infinite, and he knows and explains everything with precision and concision.

Though the prose is exemplary throughout, the dialogues are superior to the descriptions, apart from those occasions when Galdós indulges his old vice of aping the malformed expressions of the less cultured. Often he manages to do so with grace and good humor, wishing to gently point out the errors and malapropisms of those whose grasp of language is less than firm, with an attitude less disrespectful than amused; but at times the attempt falls flat. Some have praised Galdós' enthusiasm for documenting the jargon of certain of his characters, such as José Izquierdo, who receives the nickname "Plato" in the novel. But unless a writer aims for a thoroughgoing reconstruction of spoken language, this way of letting characters speak in uncultured argot seems like caricature, and contemptuous of them — the work of a condescending but entertained middle-class gentleman who delights in the barbarisms of country folk, with their lexical infractions and their mangling of words whose meaning they do not know.

What Pérez Galdós does is not re-creation: there is no labor of literary correction in his solecisms. His novels simply reproduce the speech of these people as he hears it. In this way, he does indeed ridicule his uneducated characters, who talk as they do because they know no grammar, and whose twisted speech serves only to divert an audience of people of the better sort. This is very different from, say, Faulkner, whose novels, situated in the heart of Mississippi, recreate the speech of poor whites and blacks without caricature. He can do this because his novels and stories involve a true act of literary reconstruction, whereas Pérez Galdós, the documentarian novelist, is a mere collector of expressions that distort proper and well-spoken Spanish.

Such disruptions are thankfully kept to a minimum in this great novel, as is the fustian prose of some of his other works. Everything is subordinated to the story itself, and the characters rarely depart from the frame of action proper to them, pushing the novel forward at a slow and steady pace. Even the secondary characters fulfill very precise functions. Consider the magnificently rendered Placido Estupiñá, the eternal chaperone of ladies out doing their shopping — we would call him a walker — with his almost clinical need to talk and be heard. Without such people, the novel would not be what it is. Another unforgettable creature is Doña Guillermina — the saintess, as she is known — a woman of aristocratic origins who has dedicated her life to doing good, that is to say, to squeezing every wealthy person she knows for funds for a building under construction where wayward youth will be put on the right track. In her spare time, she goes around offering counsel and aid to victims of poverty. Generous and selfless, she gives her life to the cause of helping others, doing good in the Christian sense of the term.

The novel is rich with evidence of its author's human sensitivities — for example, in a chapter called "A Visit to the Slums," we have this, in Agnes Moncy Gullon's translation, about the defeated Izquierdo:

> The most peculiar thing is that in his sadness he heard a sweet voice whispering: "You're good for something.... Don't let yourself be dragged down...." But he couldn't be persuaded. "If a man could tell me," he thought to himself, "what the hell this mess of a man is good for, I'd love 'im to death, love 'im more than my own father." The unfortunate man was, like many other beings who spend most of their life out of place, drifting, drifting, without ever stopping in the square on the chessboard that fate has marked for them. Some die never reaching it.

But "Plato" finally finds his place and achieves success as a model for contemporary historical painters. And Pérez Galdós comments: "There is no human being, no matter how despicable he may have been, who cannot stand out in something."

Or consider the fineness of this passage about the inner volatility of Fortunata:

> During the first few days she went through hours of intense melancholy in which her conscience, together with her memory, vividly presented to her all the wrong things she had ever done, particularly getting married and committing adultery only a few hours later. But suddenly, without a clue as to how or why, everything

> turned inside out in the unknown depths of her soul, and her acts seemed clean, and clear, and firm. She judged herself and found that she was guiltless, innocent of all the evil that had ensued, as if she had acted on impulses dictated to her by some strange, superior entity.....Her conscience spun on an axis that showed her first the white side, then the black. At times this abrupt rotation depended on a word, a whimsical thought that flew into her head like a bird whisking across the immensity of the sky. Fortunata stopped thinking of herself as an evil monster and suddenly felt like an innocent, unfortunate creature. A leaf falling from an already withered stalk and landing silently on the rug could cause the change, or the neighbor's canary starting to sing, or an unidentified carriage rumbling noisily down the street.

There is a general mood or atmosphere in *Fortunata and Jacinta* that reveals the character of its author: comprehending, tolerant, always looking to understand rather than to judge the conduct of others, the moral sphere they move in, their beliefs, fixations, and obsessions, softening their defects while emphasizing their virtues. And so, despite the horrors that it recounts, the novel is no more pessimistic or dark than life itself. Notwithstanding the hopelessness and the pain that appear in its pages, *Fortunata and Jacinta* portrays existence as full of light, comprising more happiness than sorrow. The author's temperament seeps into the characters — all of them, with the exception of Mauricia the Hard — who remain optimistic about life throughout the harsh situations that they find themselves in. This is one of the great merits of the book, and of Pérez Galdós' novels, plays, and essays in general.

The description of Spanish society that emerges here is

one of decadence in comparison with the European nations which, at the time, were undergoing an industrialization that would change the nature of capitalism, raising incomes and promoting workers' rights even as Spain was left behind, its antiquated economy still the fruit of agrarian exploitation and a commerce that depended on inherited wealth, state-backed speculation, or — in the case of Torquemada, who will appear briefly here but will take a starring role in future novels — outright usury. Missing out on the industrial revolution that would propel its neighbors toward the future, Spain remained mired in a gargantuan bureaucracy packed with well-connected layabouts who only showed up to their respective ministries on payday. Spain's decadence, which many trace to the seventeenth and eighteenth centuries, truly took root in the nineteenth century, as Pérez Galdós' vast novel shows. In it, he points out, among much else, the antiquated nature of Spain's political system, its social anachronisms, how far the political and economic elite have strayed from the common people who form the crux of the novel, and the country's underdevelopment in relation to many of its European neighbors.

In such circumstances, it was inevitable that the venerable Spanish Empire would cease to stand at the head of Europe, as it had for centuries, becoming — and this, perhaps, is the central lesson to be drawn from the political and social standpoint that dominates *Fortunata and Jacinta* — a backward picturesque land, a reminder to European artists and travelers of "beautiful and ancient" customs, with bullfights, flamenco, and Andalusian bandits: an exotic vision of Old Europe appropriate for literary fictions, such as Prosper Mérimée's *Carmen*, which was read far and wide.

Oddly, the critics were silent when *Fortunata and Jacinta* appeared. This stung Pérez Galdós, who complained in a letter to his friend Leopoldo Alas: "By then I had forgotten ever having written such a work, given the dreadful silence that befalls every product of the imagination here that is not *La Gran Vía,*" referring to the main thoroughfare, the Broadway, of Madrid. Time, however, put paid to that silence, so much so that the sole rival to *Fortunata and Jacinta* in the scholarly study of Spanish literature is *Don Quixote* itself.

Was Pérez Galdós a great writer? He was. It would be too much to compare him artistically to Cervantes, nor was rivaling Cervantes his ambition; but in the nineteenth century, and even into the beginning of the twentieth, none among his compatriots had the dedication, the inventiveness, the enthusiasm, the powers of observation, and the literary gifts of Pérez Galdós. Not to mention his stamina and his persistence: not one of his contemporaries has left behind a body of work as monumental as his.

It is true that, with the exception of Valle-Inclán and Azorín (the *nom de plume* of Jose Martinez Ruiz), there were no great writers in Spain during this period, but this dearth in no way undermines Pérez Galdós' achievement. Even if, like all writers, he had his low points, these only draw one's attention to the grandeur of his successes, particularly in his best novels and plays. That said, he was not an innovative writer, one who opened roads through which other writers could discover their voice. He was, rather, a hugely talented follower of the great serial novelists of France and England in the nineteenth century. Pérez Galdós would not have existed without Balzac, Zola, Hugo, Dumas, or Dickens, whose *Pickwick Papers* he translated into Spanish.

As I have noted, the most surprising and unexpected defect attributable to him is not having assimilated Flaubert's lessons about the function of the narrator in the novel. This limitation makes many of Pérez Galdós' novels stretch on too long. In presenting himself as the narrator, he must append an autobiographical thread that runs on and on and on; and at times he forgets his own comments about the sources of the story that he is telling.

He was uneven, as most writers are, particularly as he refused to rework his texts, preferring superficial corrections and the hasty deletion or insertion of the odd word. The fate of his manuscripts was to be published or put aside; there was no middle point, no question of extended reconsideration and revision. And yet he produced a series of classics: *Fortunata and Jacinta, Misericordia, Doña Perfecta, Torquemada at the Stake, Our Friend Manso,* and others that even today can be read and admired. And he was no less accomplished a playwright, even if his theater, too, followed his rhythm of alternating masterpieces with works that may be entertaining but are of little or no consequence. It does a writer no dishonor to boast of great successes and great failures. Few escape this curse; most hit the mark sometimes and sometimes miss it wildly. In truth, it takes only a single instance of greatness to mark one's place in the history of literature. And Pérez Galdós managed it several times over.

Nor ought Pérez Galdós be judged like other authors of his era. With the *National Episodes*, his art turned in a specifically historical and pedagogical direction that none of his contemporaries followed, and it is to his enormous credit that he brought many significant historical events into the grasp of the broader public in the manner of Hugo or Dumas. He did so with verve, and this makes the best of the *Episodes* stand tall over many of his other writings. He helped to create an integrated society in which people from different regions, with different customs, came to feel themselves heirs to a common past. Pérez Galdós was the only Spanish writer of his time to contribute to the sense of homeland. In doing so, he carried on the legacy of Cervantes, whose great book has been read and reread by virtually all who have the good fortune to read and write in Spanish, making us all legatees of a common origin, a community epitomizing the greatest virtues of the Spanish and Latin American people, not to mention some of their more visible vices. The solitary Pérez Galdós helped to cement this brotherhood across the seas.

His polemics regularly hit the mark. Spain's great problem was its strictness, the implacable character of the Catholic Church with its grim prohibitions and intolerable prejudices. Unlike others in his time, Pérez Galdós seems not to have been a dyed-in-the-wool rebel, let alone a revolutionary. He could even be called a believer in the modern mold, well-versed in the teachings of the church but unable as a matter of liberal principle to accept its intolerance or its high-handed interventions in private and public life. Often his work proposed solutions to social matters that are out of place in a novel or a play — for the rich to redistribute their fortunes to the poor, for example. These critical interpolations speak well of him, even if his solutions themselves were extraordinarily unrealistic.

Pérez Galdós was typical of the liberals of his time, who had no interest whatsoever in economic realities and proposed solutions to social ills that invariably hinged somehow on religion, and to this degree were divorced from matters as they actually stood. Spain was not the country that would produce the most profound and rigorous notions concerning the elimination of poverty. It did not dream of the equality of opportunity that distinguishes the most advanced societies from the rest. In this regard, British, American, and Austrian economists contributed more than any French or Spanish writer. Pérez Galdós was ahead of his time, though, in being an "engaged" writer, clearly disturbed by the problems of his era and bold enough to plunge before any of his colleagues into the marrow of his country's tremendous flaw: namely, the immense material difference between the poor and the rich, which he examined in numerous writings.

He traveled widely in Europe, and of course across Spain, gathering material for his *National Episodes*, and he knew a few languages — Italian, a smattering of French and English. He wasn't much of a reader of foreign literature, and he failed to notice, or to see the significance of, the revolution in the novel initiated by Flaubert that would produce — passing through Joyce on the one hand and the great Russians on the other — something utterly different from and superior to what the genre had been before. He lived until 1920, but there are no traces of modernism in his work. We must read Pérez Galdós as a representative more of the classic novel than of the modern.

His limitations are those of the country in which he lived
more or less his whole life. He never seriously considered leaving Spain or writing about realities beyond its borders. In his most fertile years as a writer, Spain was isolated from the literary world, and this is reflected in Galdós' work, in the limitations of his style and his themes. His preoccupation with Spanish history and Spanish tribulations are the source of his reputation, but they show also a certain narrowness, and even symptoms of provincialism.

His rejection or ignorance of literary experimentation, of the avant-garde that existed, for example, in Paris, limited the diffusion of his work outside his country. He did contribute to the daily *La Prensa* in Buenos Aires, and he published a few articles elsewhere in Latin America, but what leapt inevitably to his eyes, what he read every day in the paper at home, what he talked about with his friends, was Spain, and it was natural that this would come to dominate his literary production.

Yet all this is not to say that he was a conventional writer. Pérez Galdós wrote against the grain, he was calm but not complacent, and he endured attacks from all sides, some of them quite brutal. Years would pass before their intensity would wane, making him a respectable figure and, eventually, a source of pride, someone who would bring honor to Spaniards everywhere. I do not doubt that, among the thousands who attended his funeral, there were many who had attacked him in his younger days. And I do not doubt that some of them regretted it.

MARK EDMUNDSON

Good People: The New Discipline

"But Mark, you don't seem to understand, these are good people. These are all *good people.*"

My interlocutor was a long-time administrator at my university, and an accomplished scholar. In his genial way he was trying to set my straight on some important facts. I had just learned that there would be a new aspect to our annual reports. We would be asked to tell our overlords how each one of our activities contributes to Diversity, Equity, and Inclusion.

Teaching? How did it advance DEI? Scholarship? How did it help speed DEI on its way? If you get an honor or an award, you are to say how it contributed to Diversity, Equity, and Inclusion. Outside consulting: did it do any DEI duty? And what does the university mean by Diversity, by Equity, by Inclusion? The university doesn't say. There are no official definitions out there to consider.

So I had a lot to tell my friend about administrative interference with academic freedom. I didn't want the university deans and DEI enforcers setting the agenda for my teaching or my scholarship, or for anyone else's. At the same time, I couldn't really argue with my friend's observation: the people in the dean's office and the DEI enclaves are decent sorts. I like them. Was asking us to apply DEI standards to every aspect of our work a radical piece of over-reach? I think it was, and is: I fought against it at its inception and still do.

But I also see the move as part of a larger pattern of enforcing discipline, and that pattern may be more important than any single program or initiative. The good people who came up with this notion are — without knowing it, I suspect — softly tyrannizing us. They are also softly tyrannizing themselves. And what they are up to isn't only a university matter. It is happening in corporations, medical centers, primary and secondary schools, foundations, and NGOs. Surveillance and discipline, carried out almost exclusively by *good people,* are becoming pervasive. In this case, the terms employed in that discipline were, ostensibly, progressive. The fact that most faculty members call themselves liberals or progressives makes the exercise more palatable to them. It makes it all seem virtuous. But it's possible that the terms in play mean less than the process of ever-tightening scrutiny and control that is becoming a part of almost every enterprise that is administered by the good people of the world. They are "squeezing our shoes," to borrow a phrase from David Foster

Wallace, and getting their own shoes squeezed in the bargain.

The deans are good people, the DEI office is full of good people, the HR building's no doubt populated by decent characters. And all these people are not ideologues. OK, some of them are virtue exhibitionists who put those In-Our-Family-We-Believe-That signs in front of their houses. And some get all misty when they say the word "black," but probably not many, and even those who do have their virtues.

Reactionaries think that a major plot, a real conspiracy, is afoot in the universities, and in the corporations too, to turn everyone into a lockstep leftist. There's a tablespoon of truth in that. But I think that indoctrination to an ideology may not be the main issue here, not quite. People tune out professional droners. They make stuff up to fill in the Diversity square on the application. They mock the literal-minded hacks who spew institution-speak into the air like sterile seeds. When questioned they obtain services from the consulting firm of Duck and Hide. Subtly, quietly, you can evade the ideological indoctrination. But that is not the end of it. There is a dimension to institutional life now that is probably more consequential (and more pernicious), and that you cannot evade. You *must* participate in this part of the endeavor, as both subject and object.

"I hate the builders of dungeons in the air."

That is Ralph Waldo Emerson gently venting his disapproval at knee-jerk pessimists. He is not enamored of those who build castles in the air either, but Emerson, who has a predilection for hope, has no time for the born and bred nay-sayers. I have for some time put Michel Foucault in the category of the airy dungeon builders. He is the pessimist's pessimist, the well-known theorist who sees no hope, or very, very little. Foucault believes that the world has changed markedly since, say, the early twentieth century, and that we are now beset with a different and relatively novel kind of oppression. It is an oppression, one might say, administered by "good people."

In his person, Foucault was a bit of an enigma. His photos display a man with a shaved dome, techy glasses that give him something of a fiendish face, and an x-ray glare. He comes off as the post-human anchorite of scholarship, a creature of sub-basement archives, yellowing manuscripts, and discarded record books. He looks like an unforgiving android. In person, however, matters seem to have been different. His friend Simeon Wade, who wrote *Foucault in California,* clearly adores Foucault, but is also prone to candor. The master, he says, was giggly, naïve, especially about sex; and rather scared of women and girls.

Me? I have greatly admired his major work, *Discipline and Punish,* though the admiration has faded a bit over time, and generally I find his programmatic pessimism distasteful. The problem is that, however distasteful Foucault's vision is, just now it is coming true. Something has changed to make Foucault's vision far more applicable than it was when he published his work thirty and forty years ago. Foucault knows the good people — in academia, in business, in the foundations, in the museums — a good deal better than they know themselves.

My libertarian friends, my one-time hippie friends, seethe at the imposition of the DEI regulations, the diversity workshops, the mandatory displays of righteousness in which nothing is righted. They hate it. They see a lot of it as moral exhibitionism and pointless pseudo-reform. The formidable Marxist writer Adolph Reed has observed that the effect of the recent "racial reckoning" in America is to diversify the top ten percent income earners. And maybe he's right. The black kid who didn't get a breakfast before the reckoning is probably still not getting a breakfast. My friends see the new dispensation as purely gestural, as a protracted pantomime, shoe-squeezing to no purpose at all. I sympathize with their view, but I part company in my growing conviction that it's more than a pantomime, quite a bit more.

How does power work? In the eighteenth and nineteenth centuries we thought we knew. Freud knew, Marx knew, the American revolutionaries knew. Power comes from the top down. Power come from the king, the nobles, the bourgeoisie. Or alternately, power comes from the punitive super-ego, the agency within the psyche that tyrannizes the individual with impossible demands, then punishes him for not fulfilling them. The super-ego stands metaphorically atop the hapless ego — power from above.

But maybe things have changed. In an interview in 1979 called "Truth and Power," Foucault declares that we still need to cut the off the king's head — in political theory that still has not been done. His remark doesn't mean exactly what it seems to mean. He is not thinking of doing away with top-down power, he is telling us that we need to forget that kind of power, because it is obsolete. There is no more taking the king to the guillotine, no further need to storm the Bastille.

Instead, we find ourselves within a web of power whose influence is everywhere and whose center is nowhere. And who administers this power? Not the king, or the duke. And not even — this will matter in what's coming — the president. Power is now administered by everyone in what we might call an administrative position. They are the ones who design, vet, and disseminate the mandatory work surveys; the ones who have a hand, or just a finger, in getting the annual reports out to the workforce, whether a faculty or a corporate population; the ones who evaluate the students for intelligence, grade them for performance, collect data on their likes and dislikes. These administrators of power include marketing people and advertising people and public relations people — all the people who count and characterize, and whose work manages to shape the lives of their subjects.

All these people — most of whom are no doubt good people — are watched and counted and measured in turn. Do some have more disciplinary power than others? Do some have more surveillance power? Maybe — but it probably doesn't really feel that way to any individual. They are just doing their jobs. A certain amount of such bureaucratic calculation and observation is critical to the functioning of a mass society, certainly. Yet I think the collective effect of these jobs done by good people is more discipline. The collective effect is less freedom. One is observed more. One is judged more.

The goodness of these good people is of a rather limited sort. When I was a boy, getting a Catholic education at the Sacred Hearts Church in Malden, Massachusetts, I learned that there were two kinds of sins. First there were sins of commission. These were bad deeds that you enacted and told the priest about at confession. "I lied"; "I cheated"; "I stole." But there were also sins of omission. You missed mass; you neglected to be kind to an aging parent or grandparent; you didn't share what you had. It seems to me that most "good people" now excel at avoiding sins of commission. They don't drink to excess. They don't have affairs. They don't cheat (much) on their taxes. They never use the terrifying "n-word," and are reluctant even to say "Negro," lest someone somehow might take offense. But I think you'll find sins of omission among them in plenty: turning their backs on a maligned friend; not standing up against administrative over-reach at work; not saying the necessary, unpopular word. In our on-line culture it is easy to be busted for stepping forward at the right-wrong time. Good people tend to avoid doing so. Could you achieve grace by simply avoiding sins of commission? The word at Sacred Hearts church was that you could not.

When you read Foucault's interview, it seems like he must have been speaking during the flourishing of Internet culture. For there is no device that augments discipline in the way that the Internet does. Here's another form — fill it in, get it back fast — repeat *ad nauseam*. But this is not the case. Foucault seems to have taken his teacher Derrida's view of signification, a web without a center, and applied it to social control. One is inclined to say that Foucault simply got lucky in securing his prophetic status — but intuition does count in intellectual life and Foucault, who seemed to be about as non-intuitive a person in everyday life as one can imagine, simply nailed it. We may have thought that we had assimilated all of Foucault's thinking, but the truth is that reality has now caught up with him, to the extent that he is fully relevant, and painfully so, again.

Does everyone exert discipline? Does everyone not only exist in the web but also do the work of the web? I think there is a simple answer to this important question. The answer is no. If you went to college and have a job, you probably do the work of the web. If you didn't go to college, you may do web work with your small business, but probably you don't. If you did not attend college and if you do not sit down every day at a computer to do your web work, then you are probably an object of discipline and surveillance, but not a frequent practitioner. (You probably also voted for Trump, but more on that anon.) Those who work the web are also its objects—that goes without saying. The observers are observed.

What are the terms of observation — what are the terms of discipline? I think we can confidently say that they have grown exponentially since Foucault's time, but what he saw and said still has its validity. Michael Walzer once observed that much of Foucault's work can be considered as an elaborate pun on the word "discipline." In its first sense, discipline means controlling people; it means determining the shapes of their lives: where they can live and how, where they can go and where they cannot. It means getting them to show up and sit with their legs beneath their desks and to pay attention. But it also means letting them know who and what they are and getting them to believe it.

That's where the second denotation of discipline comes in. Those branches of knowledge that we broadly call the human sciences — sociology, medical science, criminology, psychology, the study of sexuality, certain varieties of historical scholarship, and the rest — are all about establishing norms. The criminologist will tell you who the delinquent is, and how the criminal comes to be; the psychologist will offer portraits of aberrant behavior; the sociologist will tell you how relatively socialized people behave in groups. These definitions and characterizations have a couple of dimensions: they are subtly prescriptive in that by telling us what unorthodox behavior is and how it comes into existence, they also tell us what orthodox or normative behavior can and should be. The disciplines help to discipline. They also point a scientific or pseudo-scientific finger at the outsiders. They stigmatize the ones who cannot or will not conform.

Foucault, who is claimed as a paragon of gay liberation, would detest the process by which one becomes identical with one's sexual practices. Sexuality is not identity. Or to put it better, affirming someone's sexual identity, even one's own, as a central aspect of human essence is a form of coercive discipline. All forms of identity that draw on the intellectual disciplines are at the very least suspect, and some are outright anathema.

In Foucault's day, the chief means of extending discipline was through institutions. You were shaped and sized by the school, the church, the prison, the military, the government, and they did an effective enough job of it. Now power disseminates itself also through the Internet. It's much harder to run, much harder to hide. You've got to fill out those forms, take that test, be the objective of a given assessment. Internet discipline can be far more effective, comprehensive, and unavoidable than pre-Internet discipline ever was. And the powers who are not really powers, the good people, can demand much more of you (and have more demanded of themselves in turn). My annual report used to consist in a typed page. Now it is about fifteen electronic pages. I will now be rated on a scale of one to ten in nine different categories. And I, as a professor, abide in one of the freest jobs there is.

It will become more confined and confining over time, for those who are paid to enforce discipline must justify their positions by making ever more disciplinary demands. If they simple left matters as they were, the computers would do their work, and they would be replaceable. In time, discipline will make its way into every interstice of life, for that is the logic of network power. The regulations for sexuality within institutions, say, will become more comprehensive, detailed, and bizarre. A preview of coming attractions can be found in my own university's rules about sado-masochistic sex undertaken by members of our community. "When parties consent to BDSM 3, or other forms of kink, non-consent may be shown by the use of a safe word, whereas actions and words that may signal non-consent in non-kink situations, such as force or violence, may be deemed signals of consent." No, I did not make it up. And yes, the combination of liberal tolerance for apparent erotic extravagance and disciplinary control by the institution are emblematic of the present, and of things to come. There is virtually nothing that the Internet and the good people, acting in consort, cannot observe, discipline, and attempt to control.

And yet these new developments will seem liberal, even liberating. The fact that the idiom of the corporation is now rhetorically progressive — Diversity! Equity! Inclusion! — is not without meaning. The enlightened words blur and confuse our perception of what is really going on — the incontrovertible fact of using these terms to exert not freedom but discipline. Someday the terms may be Family, Flag, and Faith. That, too, will matter. The diffused structure of contemporary power is compatible with many worldviews, or with none at all. What will matter more is the use of these terms to measure, evaluate, and "understand" people. What will matter will be the power of discipline, to curtail freedom.

Perhaps you truly think that Nike and Apple and Google deeply care about progressive policies. You are wrong. What they care about is gaining control over their workforce and making as much money as possible. If the terms of art were Family and Flag, they would pretend to endorse them, too. The employees in HR and some of the idealistic young may think that they are doing social good in the world. They are wrong. They are using the terms of liberation to bring more and more free people closer to mental serfdom. Some day they will awaken in a cage of their own devising, so harshly confining that even they, drunk on their own virtue, will have to notice how their lives are the lives of snails tucked in their shells. By that time, there may not be anything to do about it. They will be the once willing slaves of the new super-rich; they will be the principals of their own subjection, the masters of their own enslaved selves.

My neighbor a little less than a half mile down the road has a Confederate flag fastened to the side of his house. The flag is so old and worn now that it is hard to identify, but I have seen it there from the start, even before the election of Trump. My neighbor drives a pick-up truck, a little rusty, with his dog, an agreeable mutt, riding shotgun, hanging his tongue out the window to taste the air. I walk along our dirt road sometimes, and I see him, and we talk. He hates the government; he hates Washington; he hates what America has come to. We agree on nothing — I'm Bernie 2016, 2020, 2024 and '28 if his lips are still moving — so we disagree on a good deal.

When he drives slowly, careful not to fill my face with road dust, I see the lines that he has painted on the back of his truck by hand: "Don't let goddam liberals, run your fucken life." My neighbor doesn't have email, he doesn't use a cell phone as far as I know, and he wouldn't be likely to pump anything approximating personal information into a computer. Still, he knows what we all do: he is on the grid, under discipline, an object of power. When he tells the world not to let liberals run your life, he means what he says. Don't listen to Biden and Ocasio-Cortez and don't take cues from the *bien pensant* gang at the university. What he wants, it seems, is to reclaim the country.

If so, he's not alone. Many people on what is called the right want to recapture the center of power and get things straightened out. Trump may have been on the way to doing that, they think, but he probably didn't have quite enough time. What we need now is to repossess the center of power. We tried to do it on the sixth of January — or at least half-way tried — and it just slipped through our hands. Soon, soon, we'll possess the palace, and all will be well, or at least a whole lot better.

Some people, maybe my neighbor included, want to see the January 6 attack on the Capitol as something akin to the storming of the Bastille. They see it as an attempt to reclaim a node of illegitimate power — in fact, it is *the* node of illegitimate power, akin to Pandemonium, the palace that Satan built in Milton's hell. The rebels, or pseudo-rebels, seem to believe that they are living in the eighteenth or nineteenth century, when you could depose the king or the czar and achieve real freedom. They think that replacing one chief executive with another will transform their lives and make them free — free from the chickenshit liberals who are always finding new ways to deploy their computers and their techniques of discipline and surveillance to run and ruin the lives of ordinary people. I am far from saying that it does not matter who the president of the United States is, but it may not matter nearly as much as the characters waving Trump flags, wearing MAGA hats, and fuming about the stolen election imagine.

For really, there is no center of power to take possession of. If Trump wins the next election, the forces of discipline, which are deployed by no one, in the interest of no one, will continue to compound themselves. The college-educated will get to push more of the buttons, but they too will be subjects of discipline, constantly evaluated, scrutinized, regimented, and regulated. At least they will feel as though they possess some power and some dignity. The non-college group, by contrast, will stroke many fewer keys and see that their lives are being run, though they will think they are being run by those goddam liberals, not by the disciplinary regime. They will not recognize the power that expands for its own sake and functions, finally, for nothing and no one. Its only interest is its own blind growth. And they will continue with a pre-Foucauldian sense of how power works, as will the college-created crowd, though they will probably think less about it, feeling as though they are in some measure in charge, and being well remunerated for it. If you jockey the computer, you are enslaved by the matrix; and if you do not computer jockey you are also enslaved, though you may have a more developed sense that something is way off.

In *The Age of Surveillance Capitalism,* Shoshana Zuboff shows how corporations have not only collected data from us all but used that data to influence and shape our behavior. And they have done so, according to Zuboff, in search of profit. Maybe so. But it seems to me that the constant exercise of disciplinary power beyond a certain point profits no one. Rather, disciplinary power expands with what seems a will of its own. Socialism, communism, communitarianism, environmentalism, what have you: no alternative to capitalism would inevitably unseat disciplinary power.

Journalists spent a lot of time trying to figure out what the people who stormed the Capitol had in common. Education — yes, but not much college; more or less of rural and suburban origins. But there was something else, too, something that I find illuminating. Many of them, perhaps half, had experienced financial troubles. They had lost a house, gone bankrupt, had the loan company's wolf at their door. Now in America, given the power grid, you cannot run and hide from debt. If you owe, you will pay, or you will pay for not paying. Your interest and fees will compound and compound. You will be chased from post to pillar and back, and the stringent bankruptcy laws will keep you in play. You may not go to debtors' prison, but other forms of confinement will find you. Once the machines are onto you, once they have all your account information, they will never let up. And this is so especially if you are maladroit online.

The explosion of conspiracy theories on the right may be a loud literalization of the feeling that something is out to get us — that it is invisible and weird and knows where you live. Run afoul of the disciplinary regime in its financial guise and you are righteously screwed. The good people will have you in their power, though of course the good people are out oppressing each other to beat the band. The stolen election trope restores a sense of assurance about who the enemy is and what might be done about it. This sense of assurance is spectacularly false.

Now is the time for a set of bracing solutions to the ever-clenching disciplinary web that we live in. I haven't got any. Still, I do have a prediction that is not entirely pessimistic. In time, people will begin to sense that there is something rotten in the disciplinary regime — that power is growing and growing and serving nothing but itself. They may never become articulate about this perception — they may experience it on a gut level and that's all. But slowly the cultural weather will shift. Those who spend all day on their computers will begin to be derided as dupes. Walking down the street fooling with your iPhone will mark you out as a clown. People will leave the glowing, sterile silver world of their computers for the green world out their windows. They will spend a day, then a week, then a month, barely stroking a key. They will find better things to do. And the dragon will begin to starve for want of what feeds it, which is our time, and our willingness to watch and be watched.

This will not happen tomorrow, but I believe it will happen. During the height of the plague many people left their jobs, skipped their appointments with the physician and the shrink, stopped answering their phones, fumbled, accidentally on purpose, their Zoom accounts, and without knowing it consciously said no to discipline. Some of those people simply never came back. Soon, but alas not too soon, many of the rest of us may well be joining them.

MOSHE HALBERTAL

Two Concepts of God

For Moshe Idel

Since the very inception of their discipline, scholars of Kabbalah, or Jewish mysticism, have tried to define the object of their study based on its supposed relationship to myth. Gershom Scholem viewed the rise of Kabbalah in the Middle Ages as the return — with a vengeance — of myth. After having been repressed by Biblical and rabbinic traditions, it reemerged, cloaked in mystery and veiled in esotericism, to insinuate itself into the heart of Judaism, from which it would dictate the future of Jewish thought and history. Another school of thought, led by Moshe Idel and Yehuda Liebes, has denied that myth had ever been absent from Judaism, and has traced lines of continuity from the kabbalistic mythos to elements already present in the canonical texts of ancient Judaism. Whatever the precise relationship between myth and Kabbalah, medieval Jewish philosophy has been presented in no uncertain terms as Kabbalah's nemesis. Under the influence of Maimonides, who defined much of its agenda, Jewish philosophy sought to purify God of any trace of anthropomorphism and to systematically eradicate any mythic elements from Jewish tradition. According to this account, then, the twelfth and thirteenth centuries saw the rise of two movements with diametrically opposed relationships to myth: Kabbalah and Jewish philosophy. The kabbalists are said to have had the upper hand because they tapped into the primordial wellsprings of myth and irrigated every corner of Jewish existence from it, while the philosophers uprooted Judaism from its source of vitality and turned it into an alienated and abstract religious culture.

Scholem conceived of this contest as a medieval precursor of the great cultural clash between Romanticism and the Enlightenment in the nineteenth and twentieth centuries. The conceptual framework that he used to analyze Kabbalah borrowed considerably from the way Romanticism imagined itself in relation to the Enlightenment — that is, as a more authentic and exciting alternative to the aridities of reason. In this way, a broad cultural conflict from modernity was projected backward onto medieval Judaism and considered to be the key to elucidating its driving forces.

This historical account has become the dominant way of thinking about Kabbalah, even as the debate over the connection between kabbalistic myth and earlier strands of Jewish thought continues. There is no question that its broad outlines are well grounded in the sources and that it has contributed greatly to our understanding of Jewish intellectual and cultural history. But it is not the whole story. It seems to me worthwhile to present another way of thinking about these issues, an alternative conceptual framework that will help us get a fuller view of the Kabbalistic phenomenon itself, and will situate Kabbalah's relationship to medieval Jewish philosophy in a different and added context. Indeed, the implications of this different view extend beyond the confines of Jewish religion to the more universal and fundamental question of how we may think about the nature of divinity itself.

I would like to propose a contrast between two conceptions of the deity: God as a personality and God as a being. Each one provides utterly different ways of accounting for existence and for the religious posture. When categorizing the two medieval Jewish movements according to this criterion, a surprising result emerges: philosophy and Kabbalah, hitherto regarded as spiritual and intellectual opposites, turn out to be part of the same massive conceptual and religious shift. Together they reject the notion of God as personality for that of God as being. To put it another way, they replace God with the Godhead. One may have personal relations with God, but not with the Godhead, which in Kabbalah is a multifaced and dynamic structure, a system of divine reality.

In the biblical tradition, God is a relational subject who enters into a covenant with the Israelites. The history of this people, with all its ups and downs, is interpreted in terms of the straining and strengthening of a complicated relationship between the divine personality and Israel, which is marked by love and tested by betrayal. (The Biblical conception of God as a personality was most richly explored by the late Yohanan Muffs.)

Similarly, for all its vastness and its multiplicity of genres, rabbinic literature everywhere exhibits the same basic perception of God as a personality entangled in a web of relationships with humans and the Jewish people. Not only does the biblical anthropomorphic conception of God not trouble the Sages, but they broaden and deepen it.

A midrash in *Mekhilta de-Rabbi Yishmael*, an ancient collection of rabbinical commentaries on the Book of Exodus that was redacted in the third century CE, helps to highlight the monumental disparity between the concerns of the ancient rabbis and those of their medieval successors. It concerns verse twenty-one in chapter thirteen, "The Lord would go in front of them by day [in a pillar of cloud, and by night in a pillar of fire]," about which it remarks:

> Is it possible to say this? But it already says, "Do I not fill heaven and earth — declares the Lord" (Jer. 23:24); and it is written, "And one called to the other and said, 'Holy, Holy, Holy [is the Lord of Hosts], His glory fills the entire earth'" (Isa. 6:3); and it says, "Behold, the glory of the God of Israel came from the way of the east; and His voice was like the sound of many waters; and the earth was illuminated by His glory" (Ezek. 43:2). What is the meaning of "The Lord would go in front of them by day"?
>
> Rabbi [Yehuda Ha-Nasi, or Judah the Prince] said: Sometimes the Emperor Antoninus would hold court on the dais until it grew dark, and his sons would remain with him. After leaving the dais, he would hold the lantern and light the way for his sons. Imperial dignitaries would approach him and say, "Let us hold the lantern and light the way for your sons." But he would say to

> them, "No. It's not that I have no one to hold the lantern and light the way for my sons, but that I am showing you how dear my children are so that you accord them honor." Thus did the Holy One show the nations of the world how dear Israel is, so that they would accord them honor.

At first glance, this midrash seems troubled by the kind of metaphysical problem that exercised medieval Bible commentators: How can a deity who fills the entire world be constricted to a cloud or a fire? In the twelfth century, Abraham Ibn Ezra sought to defuse the problem by claiming that God was not actually within the cloud or the fire, and that Scripture only makes it seem so because those phenomena are manifestations of His power.

A closer look, however, reveals that Rabbi Yehuda's parable about the Roman emperor — the ancient Jewish tradition frequently compares divinity to kingship — is addressing another question altogether. Instead of wondering how an infinite deity can be confined to a finite physical space, the midrash wants to know why almighty God decided to lead the Israelites in a pillar of cloud and fire, when He could have sent any of his hosts of messengers to do His bidding or gone forth Himself in all His resplendent glory. Rabbi Yehuda answers that God, like the Emperor Antoninus, chose to show His children the way Himself, not because He had no capable agents but to demonstrate His burning love for His children. And if he had brought His royal retinue, the message would have been lost on the overawed observers.

To elucidate the parable, let us consider a more contemporary story. A country is hosting a foreign president, and instead of booking him a presidential suite at its most luxurious hotel, it puts him up in a hostel. The resulting scandal about the country's treatment of the president does not broach any questions of metaphysics; it's not as if they tried to defy the laws of nature and squeeze the president into a matchbox. It is, rather, the unseemliness of it that makes headlines. As far as the above midrash is concerned, God can obviously manifest Himself in any way that He deems fit, even in a pillar of cloud or fire. It is asking instead about the appropriateness of the chosen form. One would think that a god whose glory permeates the cosmos would make more of an impression. This is the difficulty that Rabbi Yehuda's parable addresses.

Mekhilta de-Rabbi Yishmael raises a similar question about God's revelation to Moses through the burning bush. Again, the Sages desire to know why God would reveal Himself to Moses through a homely, prickly bush in the wilderness instead of in a more grandiose display befitting His majesty. One of the answers given is that God wanted to convey that He, too, suffered the pain of slavery experienced by the Israelites, like a bird caught in a thorny thicket:

> Moses was tending the flock... And the angel of the Lord appeared to him in a blazing fire out of the midst of a bush" (Ex. 3:1—2). Rabbi Shimon b. Yohai says: Why did the Holy One reveal Himself from on high and speak to Moses out of the midst of a bush? Just as this bush is more brutal than every other tree, so that a bird which enters it cannot escape intact, having been cut to pieces, so too the slavery of Egypt is more brutal for God than every other slavery. A different interpretation: "Out of the midst of a bush" (Ex. 3:2). Rabbi Yehoshua says: Why did the Holy One reveal Himself from on high and speak to

> Moses out of the midst of a bush? For whenever Israel is in distress, it as is if He is distressed, as it says, "In all their troubles He was troubled" (Isa. 63:9). [...] And thus would R. Yehoshua say: Come see how great are the mercies and beneficences of the Holy One upon Israel! They went down to Egypt, and the *Shekhina* (divine presence) was with them, as it says, "I will go down with you to Egypt" (Gen. 46:4); they went up [from Egypt], and the *Shekhina* was with them, as it says, "and I will bring you back up" (ibid.); they went down to the sea, and the *Shekhina* was with them, as it says, "And the angel of God traveled" (Ex. 14:19); they came to the wilderness, and the *Shekhina* was with them, as it says, "and in the wilderness, where you saw how the Lord your God carried you" (Deut. 1:31); until they came to the Temple. They experience suffering, and He, as it were, experiences the suffering with them, "out of the midst of a bush"; they experience relief, and He experiences relief with them, as it says, "To behold the prosperity of Your chosen ones, to rejoice in the gladness of Your nation, to glory in Your inheritance" (Ps. 106:5).

This midrash contains one of the important innovations in the anthropomorphic religious thinking of the ancient sages: God suffers when the Jewish people suffer. Attuned to the nuances of divine self-revelation across Scripture, the midrash discerns in the unusual appearance of God in a scrubland bush an expression of divine empathy for the Israelite plight.

The Bible maps the relationship between God and humans onto a few hierarchical human relationships: father and son, husband and wife, judge and accused, king and subject. The Sages then contribute new relational categories to this anthropomorphic foundation, including teacher and disciple, homeowner and laborer, patron and client. These capture and accentuate subtleties in the religious relations. Even more so: while in Scripture, God is the more powerful figure in the hierarchy and Israel the less, at times the Midrash brazenly reverses the balance of power in its human analogies, so that Israel or a human is the master, husband, or judge and God the servant, wife, or accused. In addition, the midrashic imagination does not limit itself to the Bible's verticality. It envisions horizontal relationships that are non-hierarchical and intensely intimate, such as exist between twins or friends. The sheer creativity of the Sages is not evidenced, then, by exegetical acrobatics to minimize God's anthropomorphism, but by the endeavor to look exhaustively at all relations between human beings to better grasp and give meaning to the religious relationship with God.

This core religious sensibility of the Bible and the Midrash, which perceives God as a relational subject, met fierce opposition in the Middle Ages. The Maimonidean philosophical concept of God denounced as idolatrous any attribution to God of emotional states and personal characteristics. In this account, God's transcendence defies any analogy to the human realm, a transcendence that reaches its height in the denial of the capacity of language altogether to serve as a proper medium for the attainment of any knowledge concerning God. This philosophical conception of God, which was tremendously influential among Jewish thinkers (and non-Jewish thinkers too, such as Aquinas) had the effect of usurping a robustly personal God with an austerely metaphysical God. Dramatic narrative was replaced by abiding ontology. What has not been sufficiently documented, and what I will try show below, is that the dramatic shift from God-as-personality to God-as-being was also the hallmark of medieval Kabbalah. This is true, to borrow Moshe Idel's broad characterizations, both of ecstatic-prophetic Kabbalah and theosophical-theurgical Kabbalah.

Ecstatic-prophetic Kabbalah focuses on the development and use of mystical techniques to attain unification with God. As Idel has shown, the pinnacle of this kabbalistic striving is the experience of *unio mystica*, the absolute assimilation of the individual into the Godhead, to the point of ontological identity. The aspiring mystic achieves this by shedding his individuality and personality, by turning the ego (*ani*) into naught (*ayin*). (The Hebrew words are anagrams of each other.) In the Kabbalah of Nahmanides in the thirteenth century in Catalonia, union with God depends on a complete negation of the human will, because the will is what individualizes a human as a being separate from God. In other traditions, the negation of the ego is achieved by completely emptying the consciousness of certain particularizing elements. And to match the mystic who strips himself of all personal qualities, the deity with whom he merges is not a personality but an all-encompassing being. The crowning attainment of the ecstatic kabbalist is the dissolution of the ontological distance between humans and God, the very space necessary for interpersonal relations to exist. For this reason, in his moment of spiritual ecstasy, as he is enveloped by God, the mystic does not — cannot — interact with God in any human sense.

These mystical traditions that reject the conception of God as a personality clothe their longing for union with God in the traditional notion of *devekut*, or "cleaving" to God — but this never before meant a nullification of the self or a complete melding with the divine being. In Scripture and in classical rabbinical literature, cleaving to God entails limitless devotion to the word of God and following in His footsteps. Drawing close to God, for the Sages, means being on the most intimate terms with God, but it certainly does not mean overcoming the ontological gulf that separates humanity and divinity. Note how the Midrash interprets the verse in Numbers about the human who drew as close as humanly possible to God:

> "Not so with My servant Moses; he is trusted throughout My household. With him I speak mouth to mouth, in a vision and not in riddles, and he beholds the likeness of the Lord" (Num. 12:7—8). Rabbi Pinhas said in the name of Rabbi Hoshaya: "And he beholds the likeness of the Lord" — it is comparable to a king who reveals himself to a member of his household in his linen garment.

Moses' extraordinary closeness to God is expressed in the language of familiarity and intimacy. He is like a member of a royal household who is privy to see the king in his undershirt, divested of the trappings of royalty and with his guard down. But the kabbalistic notion of cleaving, in which one cannot tell where the mystic ends and God begins, does not allow for intimacy, because intimacy is something that exists between distinct persons. (Many centuries later this preference for being over personality was reversed by Martin Buber in his dialogical account of human interaction with the divine.) The fact that the ultimate religious attainment for these kabbalists has changed from intimacy with God to losing oneself in Him perfectly encapsulates the reconceptualization of the divine personality as an apersonal being.

A similar and no less significant transition occurs in

theosophical-theurgic Kabbalah. This school of mystical thought introduces two new fundamental ideas about God, both of which end up effacing the divine personality. The first is a dualistic conception of God: the hidden and unknowable *deus absconditus*, and the manifest divine potencies emanated from the former's innermost depths. The concealed dimension of the Godhead, which is termed "Absolute Privation" (*ha-afisa ha-muchletet*) in Nahmanidean Kabbalah and "the Infinite" (*Ein-Sof*) in other kabbalistic thought, is utterly apersonal and has no characteristics. It is being so pristine and pure that the particularizations of language and the categorizations of cognition slip right off it. It is important to stress that this aspect of the Godhead, which scholars generally identify with Maimonides' philosophically purified God, is nowhere to be found in rabbinic literature. The ancient sages consider God a personality through and through; they posited no apersonal dimension in His being.

A fine illustration of this significant gap between the rabbinic Midrash and the understandings of the Middle Ages can be seen in their respective interpretations of the very first words of the Bible: "In the beginning (*be-reshit*), God created" (Gen. 1:1). One would expect God's book to begin with a reference to Himself: God created, in the beginning,.... So why, the question is asked, doesn't God appear first? According to the kabbalists, this semantic ordering signifies that the true Creator God, the hidden dimension of the divine Naught, cannot be expressed in language. Out of this infinite Nothingness the *sefirot,* the elements of the godhead, emerge, and the first word of the verse, *be-reshit,* is actually an allusion to the first knowable *sefirah* called *Chokhma*, or Wisdom. The rest of the words in the verse allude to the other *sefirot* according to their order of descending emanation and increasing particularization. A critical step in transforming God from a personality to a being is the positing of a hidden, unfathomably pure existent of *sui generis* oneness, which serves as the primordial substrate of all existence. Yet the Midrash, by contrast, knowing nothing of this divine schematic, uses this as yet another opportunity to glean insight into the divine personality:

> "In the beginning, God created" (Gen. 1:1). Rabbi Yudan in the name of Aquilas: It is befitting to call such a one "God." The common practice is for a king of flesh-and-blood to have his praise proclaimed throughout the city without having built them public works or baths.
>
> Shimon ben Azzai says: "You have increased Your humility for me" (2 Sam. 22:36). Flesh and blood mention their name and then their praise: so-and-so followed by their title. But the Holy One does not. Only after creating the needs of His world does He mention His name: "In the beginning [created]" and after that "God."

The Sages do not read the absence of God's name from the opening of the verse as an ontological statement about any Absolute Privation that grounds the rest of the Godhead and the universe. They take it instead as a reflection of God's humility — of an aspect of the divine personality. In stark contrast to the self-important emperors, God declares His primacy only after doing something for humankind.

The effacement of the divine personality can also be seen in the manifest aspects of the Godhead, which brings us to the second major innovative doctrine of theosophical Kabbalah: the emergence from the divine Naught of a complex of divine potencies variously called attributes, existents, utterances, or, most familiarly, *sefirot*. These potencies are the manifest aspect of the Godhead and mediate between the hidden dimension of the Godhead, on the one hand, and the universe and humans, on the other. In this picture, the complexity of God's qualities and attributes found in Scripture and rabbinic literature are reconceived as distinct existents or hypostases. God is remolded into the Godhead, a being that elaborates itself into particularity via a process of emanation, and the potencies that emerge therefrom form a complex, quasi-organic association with one another.

The ancient rabbis coined many epithets for God that signify qualities of the divine personality, but they have been transformed in kabbalistic literature into the discrete entities of the Godhead. The names that the rabbis created — for example, *Gevura*, signifying God's omnipotence, and the feminine name *Shekhina*, signifying God's immanence — did not refer to separate dimensions that exist side by side within the Godhead. The *Shekhina* in Rabbinic literature is not an ontological dimension forming part of the totality of the divine structure; it is God's name. And therefore, when the rabbis describe the *Shekhina* going into exile with the Jews, they mean that God accompanied them. For the kabbalists, however, the *Shekhina* going into exile meant that the "lowest" *sefira* was pulled away from the rest of the divine structure. The *Shekhina* in rabbinic literature is not God's female companion; it is God's totality perceived as feminine. By externalizing God's qualities and names into discreet dimensions emanating from the divine naught, the kabbalist deconstructed the divine personality into a schematized system of ten nodes of divinity that can be visually represented, often in the form of a kabbalistic tree.

It bears noting that despite this fixed order and arrangement, the *sefirot* remain dynamic and in flux, because the manifest part of the Godhead yearns to return to its concealed source. The configuration of the *sefirot* exists as a fragile unity and separation. This dynamism of the kabbalistic Godhead is incompatible with Maimonides' Unmoved Mover, a perfect and disengaged deity of the Aristotelian kind, and its internal multiplicity runs counter to the strict and simple unity of God insisted upon by Maimonideans. And yet, in spite of these tremendous theological differences, both Kabbalah and medieval Jewish philosophy fundamentally consider God as being. By depersonalizing God, the two medieval movements catalyzed a transformation in the religious consciousness that would remake the face of Judaism.

Theosophical Kabbalah gained sufficient traction because it endowed Jewish rituals with theurgic meaning. The precarious unity of the divine configuration must constantly be maintained, in order for the *sefirot* to be properly nourished by the divine efflux that emerges from the depths of Naught, and to transmit it thence to the entire universe. Safeguarding the balance and unity of this multifaced system is entrusted to humans. Performing positive commandments unifies the divine structure, and transgressing negative commandments disunifies it. This notion, which scholars term theurgy, views the observance of the commandments as fulfilling a divine need. While the religious act can still fulfill the goals delineated in rabbinic literature, such as improving human nature or appeasing God, the theurgic explanation attributes to the doer a causal effect on the foundations of all existence. The rabbinic explanation of commandments takes for granted that there are two persons, the one giving orders and the one carrying them out, whereas the theurgic reason is distinctly impersonal, it is not a relational activity but rather a casual act on a complex being on a dynamic and manyfold entity.

And so the doctrine of theurgy further drove a wedge between the old and new conceptions of God. Consider the rabbinic and kabbalistic interpretations of Moses' role in the Israelites' battle against Amalek. The Biblical verses report:

> Whenever Moses held up his hand, Israel prevailed; but whenever he let down his hand, Amalek prevailed. But Moses' hands grew heavy, so they took a stone and put it under him and he sat on it, while Aaron and Hur, one on each side, supported his hands; thus his hands remained steady until the sun set. (Ex. 17:11—12)

The Mishna — the earliest codified work of rabbinical teachings which was edited in the end second century CE rejects this straightforwardly magical account of the event and raises an incredulous objection:

> "Whenever Moses held up his hand etc." Do the hands of Moses make or break a battle? Rather, it tells you that whenever Israel would look upward and make their hearts subservient to their Father in Heaven, they would prevail, and if not, they would fall.

According to this mishna, when Moses lifted his arms heavenward, it signaled that the people were rededicating themselves to God and looking to Him for salvation. This reading explicitly rejects any causal explanation — magical or otherwise. Turning to and pleading with one's Father in Heaven is, of course, a deeply interpersonal act.

In kabbalistic thought, though, matters are reversed. In his Biblical commentary, Nahmanides doubles down on the causal explanation:

> By way of truth, he raised ten fingers to the Height of Heaven to allude to the ten *sefirot*, in order to make it cleave to the Faith that fights for Israel. This explains the matter of the uplifted palms during the priestly blessing and its secret.

By raising his hands, Moses was not praying. He was performing an ontological action and influencing the configuration of the Godhead: he induced the cleaving of the *sefirot* to "Faith," another name of *Shekhina*, the lowest *sefira* that is most prone to detachment from the rest of the configuration. When Moses lifted his hands, he caused a unification of the upper *sefirot* with the *Shekhina*, which was doing battle for Israel, so as to energize it with the divine efflux. The impact of his action was felt cosmically, not humanly. The phrase "by way of truth," in Nahmanides, denotes an esoteric kabbalistic reading. According to Nahmanides, the same theurgic technique lies behind the commandment for the Kohen, or Jewish priest, to raise his hands during the priestly blessing, as is still commonly done in traditional synagogues. Thus, an interaction between the sons and their Father turns into the metaphysical operation of a technician cranking up the power of the divine machine.

There is perhaps no better example of this change in the meaning of the religious act than prayer. In the history of Judaism specifically, and of world religions more generally, prayer is the ultimate relational encounter between humans and God, an intimate moment pregnant with vast interpersonal potential. The supplicant's attitude towards God can vary widely based on their perceived relationship with God and their life circumstances. Prayer can be a humble entreaty, a cry of despair, a brazen demand, a fierce protest, and much more.

When the kabbalists turn prayer into a theurgic act, demanding a heightened focus on each word to intend it to act on a specific *sefira*, they strip this encounter of its dialogical and relational quality. When one examines the massive collection of kabbalistic prayers with their manifold techniques and "intentions," one is left to wonder, where is the son pleading with his Father? There is indeed a good reason why one of the earliest critiques of Kabbalah, penned in fourteenth-century Spain by the renowned jurist Rabbi Isaac b. Sheshet, touches on prayer:

> I have also informed you that my teacher, Rabbi Peretz Ha-Kohen, would neither speak about nor give prominence to the *sefirot*. I also heard him say that Rabbi Shimshon of Chinon, who was the greatest rabbi of his generation, ... would say, "I pray with a mindset of a child." That is, to the exclusion of the kabbalists, who pray one time to this *sefira* and another time to that one.

Now, Shimshon of Chinon was not a Maimonidean philosopher who considered kabbalistic prayer an unconscionable contradiction to God's absolute unity. He was an exceptional jurist and legal authority from Talmudist circles (known as Tosafists) in France, for whom Maimonidean philosophy was as foreign as kabbalistic doctrine. His objection to such complex and technical prayer "intentions" is that they remove the personal quality from the prayer setting; the abstract hyper-awareness that they require necessarily stanches any natural outpouring of emotion. While the kabbalist intently sends off every word to its appropriate supernal destination, Shimshon prefers to pray with the blissful innocence of a child.

This analysis of the shift from God as personality to God as being within the two central streams of Kabbalah offers a new perspective on the meaning of Jewish mysticism. Like any general observation, however, it overlooks the sheer diversity of kabbalistic thought. The ascription of a personality to God was part of the fabric of the canonical Jewish tradition that the kabbalists inherited. The concise, systematic character of Nahmanidean Kabbalah is worlds apart from the sprawling and dynamic Kabbalah of the Zoharic literature. And yet, even in the sections in the Zohar (the canonical medieval work of Jewish mysticism composed in Spain in the thirteenth century but attributed to Rabbi Shimon bar Yohai of the second century CE) known as the *Idrot,* which are considered the most anthropomorphic texts in Zoharic literature, the effacement of the divine personality is apparent. The *idrot* provide a detailed depiction of God's facial physiognomy. They zoom in on the divine skull, forehead, eyes, nose, mouth, cheeks, facial hair, and beard. It is important to note that the depiction of God in a human form shows a strong lack of any aversion to an embodied vision of the divine, but such a vision is common in Kabbalah. Yet what marks God as a personality is not having a body, but being a relational subject with a complex emotional life. A body does not necessarily imply a personality. An early medieval text called the *Shiur Komah,* or "Dimensions of [His] Stature," records the fantastically large measurements of God's body. ("The soles of his feet cover the whole universe....") The author is clearly in awe of the vast dimensions of the deity, but one sees little evidence of any personal connection to this entity. What relationship can there be with a body that spans light years in the vast emptiness of space?

In the *Idra Rabba, or* the "Great Assembly," a mystical text incorporated into the Zohar, the gigantic face of *Arikh Anpin*, or the Long Countenance, pours down mercy unceasingly, and yet it is a completely static face. A face with no facial muscles; white eyes with no pupils, no eyebrows, no eyelids. Can one humanize a shining face that never changes its expression? Can one engage it? The divine face has an iconic, inanimate quality to it. Compare this to the simple meaning of the second verse of the priestly blessing, that God should illuminate His countenance for His people (Num. 6:25). The hope is that God's countenance will glow radiantly for His people, in the way that someone's face lights up when they meet or are reminded of someone they love. But the divine face of *Arikh Anpin* in the *Idra* is always shining — without intention or interruption, without prior prompting or pleading. This "face" has far more in common with the Sun than with anything living.

In the *Idrot*, God's interiority is translated into external existents. The Thirteen Attributes of Mercy said to be aspects of *Arikh Anpin* are attributed to various regions of the divine beard. Whereas human compassion and empathy are psychological and emotional states that move a person to help someone else, divine compassion and kindness in the *Idra* are a liquid essence that flows from the divine skull down through the strands of the wondrous beard to sustain all of existence. The elite kabbalists who have convened in this "great assembly" do not relate to this immutable and unmoved divine countenance as the face of a person. For them, it comprises yet another collection of divine facets in need of mystical rectification. They are a maintenance crew whose job it is to ensure that the conduits of the divine efflux are in good working order, that the strands of hair have no split ends, so to speak.

Unlike *Arikh Anpin, Ze'er Anpin*, (or the "Lesser Countenance") can change, but its range is severely restricted to only two states: fury and grace. The default setting is the red face of fury, but when it is mixed with the whiteness of grace that flows from *Arikh Anpin*, the face changes. Be that as it may, the members of the mystical assembly still do not address *Ze'er Anpin* directly. They work theurgically to try to align *Ze'er Anpin* with *Arikh Anpin*, so that it can receive the divine efflux that will dilute the anger.

Even this anthropomorphic God is not a personal God. Without a doubt, the *Idrot* represent one of the most imaginative products of the medieval kabbalistic imagination, and there is no denying that they humanize aspects of the Godhead. But it is hard to shake the feeling that the *Idrot* grafted an apersonal Neoplatonic worldview, in which a monad emanates existence to a multiplicity, onto the received biblical-rabbinic tradition of God as a personality. They turned the subjectivity of an engaged God into an objective metaphysical structure and process.

Later stages of Jewish mysticism also exhibit this turn towards God as a being in their thinking about God's presence — what scholars call immanence. A person's presence is acknowledged by his attentive care or sensed by his physical proximity. In rabbinical literature, the *Shekhina* ascends or descends, moves away or draws close. But when God is depersonalized, His presence means something completely different: the embeddedness of the divine entity, or aspects thereof, in our world. This can be expressed in varying degrees of ontological blending. Some doctrines talk about divine "sparks" captive in or sustaining our reality, while others, especially those espoused in the modern era by Habad Hasidism and Rabbi Abraham Isaac Hacohen Kook, posit a greater and somewhat pantheistic identity between the Godhead and reality. For our purposes here, there is little difference between pantheism (the doctrine that God and the universe are the same) and panentheism (the doctrine that the universe exists in God but that God is still greater than it), for in both the Godhead is an entity, a "thing," thoroughly entwined with the universe, such that there is no place devoid of His existence. Such a presence does not entail attentiveness or proximity. It is for this reason that in these systems of thought the theurgic religious act is aimed at being in touch with the segments of the Godhead enmeshed in this world for one of two purposes: to collect them and to gather them, so as to make the fragmented divine entity whole again, or to cleave to the divine realm through the contact with its spark within mundane world. This is a conceptual revolution in and of itself, but it generates new types of religious experience and action that are inconceivable under a personal God. This is not a God one addresses or quarrels with.

The transition from God to Godhead, from a personality to an array of potencies, became more and more elaborate with time, to the point that one could only attempt to navigate what had become a divine labyrinth with immense erudition in kabbalistic lore. The God to whom one could turn as a son or servant had been lost in the mammoth engines of Lurianic Kabbalah in the sixteenth century and later; its God was a kind of secret to be rediscovered. Yehuda Liebes has argued that the esoteric religious doctrine of Shabbetai Zvi, the false messiah of the seventeenth century, was that there is in fact a personal God who can be communicated with directly, and with whom he claimed to be in unique intimate relationship. His secret theology sought to rehabilitate the personal God known to any elementary school pupil who is versed in the Jewish tradition. The disappearance of this personal God into an esoteric teaching has been due to the rise of Lurianic Kabbalah, and in response to it Shabbetai Zvi tried to resurrect the personal God. As Liebes says:

> Understanding the meaning of Shabbetai Zevi's behavior requires us to delve into the essence of his *Mystery of the Godhead*. Rather than limited ability, his conscious opposition to the technical and impersonal style adopted by Lurianic Kabbala — in which an advanced, multifaceted machine had replaced the personal God — guided Shabbetai Zevi. Replacing the Lurianic machine with a personal God led Shabbetai Zevi to abandon Lurianic devotional prayer and pray "as someone who prays to His King," as attested by his fellow student R. Moses Pinheiro.

The romance of Shabbetai Zevi, the manic mystical messiah who traumatized his people when he converted to Islam, deserves to include the poignant fact that he sought to replace the vast systems of doctrine about the Godhead with the experience of a personal God like the God of Abraham, Isaac, and Jacob.

It would appear, then, that conventional view of Kabbalah as a reinvigoration of myth, which has significantly contributed to our understanding of Kabbalah, somewhat obscures a monumental shift in Jewish religious consciousness. The shift is away from the Biblical and Rabbinic religious consciousness, and it took place in both principal types of Kabbalah. The distinction between philosophy and Kabbalah is not to be located in their respective relationship to God as a personality. Both movements perceived God first and foremost as a being rather than as a relational subject; the great difference between them focused on what kind of a being God is. Of course, each one's concept of God was informed by the epistemological methods that they considered valid: philosophy relied on strict logical reasoning, while Kabbalah was nourished by visions and mystical speculation.

In the twelfth and thirteenth centuries, the great Jewish esoteric movements emerged, and they all shared discomfort with the personalist perspective of the Bible and rabbinical literature. The source of this discomfort is in the rejection of the understanding of the fate of humans as a reflection of their lived relations with God. Personality was replaced by being as part of the dominance of the idea of nature, an idea that perceives causal structures as the ground of being and as the guide to human action. The search for the specific causal model was shared by all the major Jewish schools of thought that burst onto the scene in the Middle Ages: Kabbalah, philosophy, and astrology (of the variety propounded by Abraham Ibn Ezra). They favored different causal models, including the Neoplatonic, Aristotelian, and Hermetic-astral, but they all shared the same basic account of nature, causality, and a divine entity. Each in their own way effaced God's personhood.

The deeper one probes into the most esoteric strata of these doctrines, the more one finds that God's personal features are shed and God turns into the Godhead. If the contest between Jerusalem and Athens is between a personal

God and a natural causality, then Athens won the hearts and minds of the great medieval Jewish esotericists. The only figures to remain faithful to Biblical and Midrashic traditions were those who did not propound esoteric lore, who in their interpretation of the canonical Jewish texts did not identify a realm of hidden secrets which they have the spiritual privilege to uncover. Rashi is a perfect example. Throughout his renowned commentary on the Bible, God's personhood is plainly evident. No wonder that it was one of his disciples' disciples, Shimshon of Chinon, who would pray like a child — with wonder, with petulant demands, with ordinary intention behind the words — to show that the master-bearers of the secrets had it wrong.

LESLIE WILLIAMS

Meditation with a Gash in the Natural Order

I like parking at the big box store, watching people come
 out and go in.
Swaying winter grasses in the median, sky that brigand
 Saturday blue.
I'm waiting to pick up my son from his guitar lesson.
 Already masterful,
he doesn't quit. Even Jimi Hendrix continued with a
 vocal coach,
up to the very day he died. I have so much useless knowledge.
Like what the monk said about meditation: if while sitting
 on your cushion
you have the best idea you've ever had — stunning, complete —
you mustn't get up to capture it. Also, a lot of what we
 call miraculous
is just the way things work: a monarch always emerges from
 its chrysalis
as a radically different worm. A *miracle* is living flesh
 restored to reeking
corpse. It's the man sitting calmly, shaved and dressed,
 after he'd raved

at city gates for more years than anyone who stepped
around him
could remember. The monk said: when wondering what
to do in life,
do what will cost you the most. Commit to watching
the gorgeous
bubble evanesce. That's the only way this works.

Large Empty Bowl

sitting in the bower
after lunch with
my sadness

like unto Magdalene
our defectiveness known all around
the town

(a passion for extravagant apology)
(flimsy promise to do better from now on)

I knew the crowd had stones
heating the hollows of their hands

(the teacher has always shown me
the underlying structure of

a situation, though often
years after I no longer cared, was
no longer there, at all)

stone and bread are alike
in the hands of the just

bread and stone the same

An Occasion

Our bones will touch in the water
one day after the supernova,
or maybe it'll be an Electromagnetic Pulse
we bought the old Volvo to outsmart—

we escaped the need for computers
to govern coffee makers,
and made our own kombucha—
but one by one the streaked coyotes,

wimpled foxes picked off
the rooster and our stupid hens. A cascade
of tiny choices to occasion
an implosion.

The mushroom log left wildly fruiting
in the hand-hewn springhouse afternoon.

On Seeing Old Skis in the Garage

So many slopes they touched, and once
leaned outside while I tromped into the parlor
of an alpine monastery, clattering boots, my bluster
welcomed to dine silently with the brothers
who had also vowed to get to the powder
of what is daily fused with life: to glide, to carve,
to schuss and float with what the spirit clamors for —
even though my body's sluggish, slow, it remembers
mountains, glory in the snowfell
hill, its bluebell kindred skills — a rough jouissance
is what I brought, in all my choices good
and not so good, the might-have-beens
and new offerings from the range
I'm entering, something milder — I'd still strive
for the milk of kindness, hold out my simmering
so the fat might rise like broken proteins
to the top, to be skimmed off.

ELLIOT ACKERMAN

The American Strategic Imagination: An Agenda

Depending on how history is written, Russia's invasion of Ukraine may be looked back on as the beginning of a third world war. President Zelensky's government, along with its advocates in allied governments, has been making this argument since the war's inception. They frame Ukraine as one battlefield in a larger global struggle, one that pits a growing axis of authoritarian nations against the Western-oriented liberal democracies that have dominated the post-Cold War world order. In this version of history, the war in Ukraine is not the Ukrainians' war alone but the West's war, too, an existential struggle for all freedom-loving peoples. There is plenty of evidence that lends credence to this argument. Had Putin's initial invasion gone according to plan, a year later we would be talking about a similar invasion of Taiwan — as we anyway already are envisioning — and then the question of whether we were in the midst of a third world war would hardly merit debate.

Conditions remain ripe for an upheaval of the global order of the type induced by a world war. These upheavals, in the modern era, have occurred approximately every century. The First and Second World War should more properly be categorized as a single conflict with Versailles more of a ceasefire than a peace, and the twenty years of the Napoleonic Wars that birthed a century of continental stability certainly qualify as a world war. One indicator that we might already be in a world war — or that one is imminent — is that the generation that can remember the last one has died. Without memories to restrain us, we become reliant on our imaginations, not only to prevent war but, if one begins, to help us navigate its exigencies, and to win.

Whether the war in Ukraine is part of a third world war, in which liberal democracies must beat back a rising tide of authoritarianism, or whether it is an isolated territorial-philosophical conflict, is not a question of semantics. Defining a war's scope is essential for any war planning, and for any victory. The role of imagination in the making of strategy has too often been under-appreciated. The conclusions that planners and officials will draw from analysis and data will always be circumscribed by the limits of what they can imagine about the future, by their sense of historical possibilities. If it is true, as the old adage has it, that generals always fight the last war, that is in part because they have not trained their imaginations to picture the next one. Inspired by its disgust with the

Iraq war, the Obama administration drew the conclusion, and enshrined it in Pentagon doctrine, that land wars are a thing of the past. Tell that to the tank officers in Ukraine.

Innovation — of concepts and weapons, of everything — always involves imagination. And the imagination of future warfare is essential also for another reason: it forces us to conceive of the war from our adversary's point of view as well as from our own. The strategic imagination is a significant deterrent to the other side's greatest advantage, which is strategic surprise. While the strategic imagination can certainly run wild — remember General Buck Turgidson — the greater danger is that it not run at all.

In the past fifty years, America's two great military defeats —Vietnam and Afghanistan — were the result of misunderstanding the scope of the wars that we were fighting. In the former, American policymakers believed we were engaged in, as President Kennedy put it in his inaugural address, "a long twilight struggle" against transnational communism, when in fact the Vietnamese were fighting a war of national liberation. In Afghanistan, we believed we were fighting "a different kind of war," as President Bush said to Congress ten days after September 11, a war against transnational terrorism. Yet like the Vietnamese, the Taliban were also fighting a war of national liberation with no objective greater than expelling foreigners from their homeland so that they could impose their theocracy upon the population. Their sympathies with al-Qaeda were nauseating, but not their reason for being. In both incidents, a failure to imagine our adversary's psyches and define the true nature of their objectives and of the very war we were fighting led us to disaster.

Although it would be easy to discount the Kremlin's absurd narrative of the war in Ukraine — one in which Zelensky is a Nazi, the West is the aggressor, and there is a genocide against ethnic Russians — it would be a mistake to ignore this narrative entirely, no matter how ridiculous, both when formulating a strategy to defeat Russia and when creating an agenda for our own strategic imagination. The first item on this agenda must be a robust understanding of the conflict from our adversary's point of view. Data alone may not be able to depict our enemy. The specifics of such an understanding will be fluid, it will involve imaginative interpretation, and it will consistently clash with our own narrative.

A war is like a coin. It has two sides, and what we call the *casus belli* is really a debate as to what side of the coin we are on: whether a revolution is in fact a civil war; whether an invasion is in fact a liberation. Irreconcilable political narratives — or imaginaries, to use the academically popular term — are not a contradiction. The war itself becomes the very process through which these narratives will be resolved. But any strategy that does not consider an adversary's counter-narrative — no matter how odious that narrative might be — is destined to fail.

Although war is waged in the consciousness of peoples and nations, it is also a craft that requires a tradesman's skill. Both the Napoleonic Wars and the world wars of the twentieth century resulted in societal and technological advances that few could have predicted. Perhaps the greatest innovation of the Napoleonic Age was the *levée en masse*, in which Napoleon crafted a new citizen army from a body politic mobilized for military service. His new army, which few could have imagined before the popular revolutions of the eighteenth century, supplanted the long-serving professional and mercenary armies that had dominated the continent for centuries. The primacy on the battlefield of the citizen-soldier, which cemented national identities, would have implications well-into the twentieth century and even into our own, as both Ukraine and Russia adopt strategies to keep their societies mobilized for war.

The issue of how to keep a nation — and allied nations — mobilized has direct bearing on what we now call influence operations, a discipline which must sit atop any strategic agenda. Influence operations — sometimes known as psychological warfare or disinformation — are as old as war itself. Clausewitz's renowned dictum that "war is a continuation of politics by other means" is an articulation of the first principles of influence operations. Politics do not stop when the bullets start. Nations at war must target popular opinion in their adversary's country as well in their own to achieve victory. This does not mean that a government should lie to its own people.

Authoritarian nations possess an intrinsic advantage over open societies in the control of information, but this does not mean that they will ultimately succeed in swaying popular opinion, particularly over the course of a long war. Eventually the truth has an almost miraculous way of getting under the door. Speaking about information warfare during the Cold War, Adlai Stevenson once described our preferred policy toward the communist powers this way: "When you stop lying about me, I'll stop telling the truth about you." But the truth must be aggressively deployed — for our adversaries, inconveniently and damagingly deployed — in influence operations. Truth may be the first casualty of war, but it is also one of its most potent weapons. Unfortunately, current American attitudes toward influence operations often seem analogous to Secretary of State Henry L. Stimson's attitude a century ago to the then-evolving discipline of espionage: "Gentlemen don't read each other's mail."

Today we can ill-afford misplaced decorum when crafting policies around influence operations. One of the greatest restrictions placed on American influence operations is a fear of blowback, in which propaganda or other forms of influence or disinformation disseminated beyond our borders filter back into the United States. Although different U.S. government agencies, such as the Department of Defense, the Department of State, and our intelligence services, have varied risk tolerances for blowback, when operations targeting foreign audiences also find American audiences it violates current programmatic statutes that govern the scope of information operations.

Government protections of the American population against its own propaganda extend back to the aftermath of the Second World War. The Smith-Mundt Act of 1948, which regulated State Department broadcasts such as Voice of America, was one of the first pieces of legislation to restrict American propaganda efforts. This was due to concerns over empowering government agencies to disseminate ideological materials to the American people. In 1975, after the Church Committee Report revealed Operation Mockingbird, a large-scale multi-decade CIA program to manipulate domestic American media, other restrictions soon followed. These included Executive Order 11905, signed by President Ford, which brought the intelligence agencies to heel on a variety of covert programs, to include assassination and covert influence; and Executive Order 12333, signed by President Reagan in 1981, according to which the president outlines the duties of America's intelligence agencies, those responsible for American propaganda efforts where the hand of the

United States government must remain hidden. Such covert efforts are where the threat of blowback is greatest. It is also where our risk tolerances are lowest, and where we are being overtaken by our adversaries who harbor little to no concern for blowback against their own populations. The question still needs to be asked whether the abolition of covertness for various purposes is strategically wise. It is undeniable that our national obsession with the evils of covertness has made us look away from a more important aspect of our influence operations, which is its robustness.

In the past decade, both Russia and China have used influence operations and propaganda against the United States to great effect. In 2014, the Russians deployed soldiers in unmarked uniforms during the invasion of Crimea and the Donbas. Disinformation, like cancer, requires only the presence of a single malignant cell to metastasize, and Russia's "little green men" in their unmarked uniforms allowed the Kremlin to propagate a narrative that their soldiers were homegrown Ukrainian separatists. In the United States we have seen the potency of Russian disinformation firsthand, in our own elections. ("Cut it out," Obama once scolded Putin about Russian hacking. It didn't do the trick.) Russian interference in the campaign of 2016 proved catalytic, yielding an exponential result that played out over years, creating a firestorm in American politics with few parallels. As is often the case with well-placed disinformation, the targeted society will do your work for you if you let it.

The Chinese Communist Party understands this. For the past two decades, the CCP has effectively used the American profit motive as a tool of American self-censorship. During the Cold War, when the Soviet Union posed the greatest threat to global freedom, American culture articulated that threat, particularly in Hollywood. In the past twenty-years, however, during China's rise, American cultural institutions have remained largely silent. Unlike with the Soviets, American and Chinese financial interests are intertwined. The Chinese have used this codependence as a tool to silence American critiques. In 2022, as American producers agonized over whether to include a Taiwanese flag on Tom Cruise's leather jacket in *Top Gun Maverick* for fear of offending CCP censors and eroding the film's Chinese box-office, Chinese producers had their biggest box-office hit of all time, *The Battle at Lake Changjin*, which glorifies the Chinese slaughter of Americans during the Battle of the Chosin Reservoir. The previous box-office champion had been the second installment of *The Wolf Warrior* franchise, in 2017, in which a Chinese former soldier battles against the arch-villain, a bloodthirsty former U.S. Navy SEAL named "Big Daddy."

Chinese influence operations extend far beyond Hollywood. Their sway over global governance bodies like the World Health Organization has quashed any consensus as to how the Covid 19 pandemic began. A parade of international administrators with their timid "investigations" and non-sensical public statements have proven quite willing to carry China's water on this issue. All that was needed was to sow some doubt. If Russia's brand of disinformation — little green men in Ukraine, election tampering, claims of American biological labs in Ukraine — seems more absurdist than the means employed by the CCP, both are plenty effective in obfuscating the truth.

The sheer volume of propaganda, manipulation, and disinformation dispensed by authoritarians would seem impossible to counter. An American strategy that would seek to reform government agencies so that they could dispense the same type of propaganda as their authoritarian counterparts is certain to fail. An open society — even if flawed — cannot compete on the field of lies with the authoritarians. The only propaganda strategy that we can consider is one that aggressively propagates the truth. There is nothing that more weakens the hold of dictators and autocrats on their populations than the truth and its ruthless strategic proliferation.

If one holds the cynical view that the truth is subjective, a matter of competing narratives, then this and all truth-based strategies are doomed to failure as authoritarians will always outmatch us. (But if the relativists and perspectivists are right, on the other hand, then we should be less inhibited in our propaganda!) The Biden administration's handling of Russia's troop buildup in the days leading up to the invasion of Ukraine presents a refreshing and encouraging example of how information operations based on the truth can outmaneuver those based on lies.

As the Kremlin massed its divisions, it continued to insist that these troop movements were part of a military exercise and that war remained avoidable. At the same time, the Biden administration had intelligence that Russia was in the process off coordinating a false-flag operation — a type of psycholog- ical ploy in which a military attacks itself or others under a flag that is not its own — to instigate a war. At a press briefing three weeks before the invasion, John Kirby, the Pentagon spokesman, preempted the Kremlin's plan: "We believe that Russia would produce a very graphic propaganda video, which would include corpses and actors that would be depicting mourners and images of destroyed locations, as well as military equipment at the hands of Ukraine or the West, even to the point where some of this equipment would be made to look like it was Western-supplied."

The Biden administration adopted a strategy of flooding news outlets with sensitive intelligence, on everything from the false-flag operations to the movements of Russia's frontline trauma hospitals and command centers, all of which proved that despite Russia's claims to the contrary their intention to invade was clear. The Biden administration adopted this strategy over the objections of Zelensky who, at the time, remained concerned about inciting panic inside his own country. Although this strategy did not prevent a Russian invasion, it did limit the Kremlin's ability to further claims that Ukraine was the aggressor. And just as important, it prepared us mentally, and our allies too, for what was coming. In this instance, the Biden administration skillfully shaped the American strategic imagination. The international condemnation and economic isolation that followed Russia's invasion is due in no small measure to the Biden administration's strategy of preempting Russian disinformation.

Although a strategy of preemption proved effective in Ukraine, no similar strategy was deployed against the Chinese government as they restricted and manipulated studies around the pandemic's origins. Three years later little consensus exists as to the virus' origins, though theories abound. The issue itself has become politicized, with views so entrenched it seems no amount of evidence can now sway beliefs; the creation of irreconcilable narratives is, of course, the purpose of a disinformation campaign. In the pandemic we may have lived through a dress rehearsal of the future of biological warfare, a discipline which must sit firmly atop any agenda for our strategic imagination.

In recent years, biological warfare has taken the form of gas attacks visited by Bashar al-Assad on his population in Syria and assassinations ordered by Putin against his political enemies. These tactics — in which individuals are poisoned, and armies and civilian populations are shelled or rocketed with gruesome agents — have evolved little since first appearing a century ago. They are designed to induce fear and are typically limited in scope to the area in which they are deployed. A pandemic, if ever weaponized, would auger in a different type of warfare, and we would be naïve — we would be catastrophically unimaginative — to believe our adversaries are not imagining ways to do exactly this.

In Ukraine, we have seen the critical importance of economic sanctions in modern war. In the pandemic, we saw how a virus brought the global economy to the brink. The grisly nature of traditional biological weapons will likely limit their use in the future; politically, they cost more than they deliver. But a biological catastrophe — of the kind that we have already lived through — would surely be a feature of any future world war, not simply due to the human toll but also the economic toll.

Imagine the United States along with its allies was fighting a peer competitor, an authoritarian nation such as China with the capacity to exercise significant control over its population. We would, of course, do our best to exercise economic pressure on them, and they would do the same to us. As in wars past, our national means of production would prove decisive to the war effort. Now imagine that this authoritarian nation possessed a virus like the coronavirus and that it had already developed its own vaccines. As people grew sick that country would be able to implement a vaccination campaign, isolating its citizens from the deadly effects of the virus. Without the vaccine in our possession, America's war effort would be crippled. Our adversary would, of course, claim no knowledge of how this new virus spread. They would deny its origins and have no moral obligation to share vaccine technology with a nation they are at war with.

The costs would be profound. Our most recent pandemic saw the largest drop in American manufacturing in seventy-four years. Aircraft carriers such as the *USS Theodore Roosevelt* were forced into port due to outbreaks of virus among the crew. A healthy army facing a sick one possesses an obvious advantage, and the same advantage extends to the economies supporting those armies. The United States would eventually develop its own vaccine, but the disruption would prove significant and could provide a peer-level adversary with a decisive edge.

After living through the Covid 19 pandemic, the way we think about biological warfare must change. It should still include the acute nerve agents and chemical weapons that we have seen in the past, but it also must incorporate a view of biological warfare that includes man-made pandemics and accounts for how such events could be deployed as tools of economic warfare when laundered through the very same types of disinformation campaigns that have, thus far, obscured any global consensus and accountability regarding the origins of Covid 19. The moral case to abolish chemical and biological weapons is obvious. But, as with nuclear weapons, there is the unpleasant but effective matter of deterrence. Even if weapons of mass destruction do not deter conventional or cyber weapons, they have so far deterred other weapons of mass destruction. A balance of terror, that Cold War doctrine and Cold War reality, is existentially hideous but strategically wise.

If discussions of a third world war echo another era, it is because *this* war long existed as part of the Cold War's vernacular, a time when students cowered under desks for bomb drills, when families constructed fallout shelters in the backyard, and when nuclear winter was the most well-known definition of climate change. To imagine a third world war means to update our conception of it, but also to redefine its terms. And one of these terms, deterrence, has unfortunately fallen out of use. During the Cold War, deterrence (particularly of the nuclear kind) evolved into an entire discipline, with strategists on both sides of the Iron Curtain relying on game-theory to ensure that humanity did not annihilate itself with its newly discovered nuclear weapons. The result of this deliberate approach to deterrence was decades of relative peace, and certainly nuclear peace, between the two superpowers. Also, we were lucky.

We still possess that destructive capability though deterrence, as a tool, is discussed far less. In the decades immediately after the Cold War, we lived in a unipolar world, in which deterrent strategy lacked its previous relevance because the United States enjoyed a significant power imbalance over any would-be adversary. In recent years, the unipolar post-Cold War world has yielded to an increasingly Hobbesian multipolar world. And in a multipolar world strategies of deterrence become increasingly complex, with so many competing actors involved that it is virtually impossible to arrive at elegant deterrent solutions such as "mutually assured destruction," which prevented a nuclear war between the Soviet Union and the United States for decades.

Yet it is not simply the proliferation of actors that makes deterrence strategies complex, but the proliferation of threats. Unlike in past decades, nuclear weapons are not the only means by which societies can annihilate one another. There are the biologicals and the chemicals. And there is another new dimension of warfare. The end of the Cold War coincided with the creation of the Internet.

As deterrent strategies became a thing of the past, every modern nation — indeed, every nuclear-armed nation — was undergoing a decades-long project of taking its infrastructure online. Thirty years later, we have awoken to a multi-polar world in which the United States faces peer-level competitors that not only possess society-ravaging nuclear arsenals, but also cyber capabilities that could wipeout our infrastructure. The chaos that follows a significant infrastructure strike would lead to civilian deaths as planes crash, hospitals lose power, and cities descend into darkness. The economic and social havoc would be immeasurable. And even though cyber-attacks shut down critical infrastructure with the flip of a switch, that infrastructure cannot be brought back online with a second flip. The damage is often permanent.

For this reason, our strategic imagination requires a thorough education in the new vulnerabilities, the new possibilities of destruction. One of the challenges of creating deterrent strategies around cyber-warfare is that it is difficult to envisage such destructive capability. Most of this work gets done in films and science fiction. At the end of the Second World War, at Hiroshima and Nagasaki, the world witnessed the destructive capabilities of nuclear weapons. We never needed to imagine a mushroom cloud over a city, we had witnessed it, and it required scant imagination to know that, no matter one's nationality, there would be few winners if the great powers of the world chose to unleash their nuclear arsenals.

Cyber is different. The world has yet to witness the full destructive scope of a strategic cyber-attack, and because the threat is largely intellectualized, and not yet experienced, the likelihood of a misstep is greater. One of those potential missteps, for example, involves the permeability between cyber war and nuclear war. Whereas a cyber-attack may justify a cyber-counterattack, are there circumstances of crisis in which it would justify an escalation — a breaking of what nuclear strategists used to call the firewall? A nation crippled by a cyber-attack could very well respond with a nuclear attack, particularly if an adversary has compromised their ability to respond in kind. Even if a cyber-attack is designed with a limited scope, it is often difficult to control the spread of the attack, resulting in collateral damage that could lead to an unanticipated escalation. This was the case with Stuxnet, the American- and Israeli-designed malware that targeted Iran's Natanz uranium enrichment facility in 2010. Although Stuxnet proved successful in crippling Iranian nuclear infrastructure, the Americans and the Israelis failed to contain the spread of the malware. It has since attacked industrial capability across Iran and in other Middle Eastern countries.

Over the past thirty years, American and Russian conceptions of the use of strategic weapons have evolved in opposite directions. While the United States created security strategies that minimized the role of strategic weapons in future conflicts, Russia pursued new concepts and capabilities to expand their roles. Whereas it is unlikely that Putin would resort to a tactical nuclear weapon, his nuclear saber-rattling is not merely rhetorical. It is based upon the current Russian doctrine of "escalate to de-escalate." The latest version of this doctrine, titled *Basic Principles of State Policy of the Russian Federation on Nuclear Deterrence,* was released in June 2020. It declares that Russia "reserves the right to use nuclear weapons to respond to all weapons of mass destruction attacks." A strategic cyber-attack would certainly qualify as a "mass destruction attack," but it remains vague as to what else might fall into this category. It also classifies "aggression against the Russian Federation with the use of conventional weapons when the very existence of the state is in jeopardy" as warranting a nuclear response, but this seems a subjective standard, particularly with an authoritarian like Putin who abides by the dictum *l'état, c'est moi.* When it comes to effective strategies of deterrence, ambiguity is sometimes an advantage but sometimes not. A psychological truism teaches that all ambiguous behavior is interpreted negatively, and Russia's current strategic posture places a premium on unpredictability, which makes deterrence the more challenging.

Since invading Ukraine, Russia has been tempting a mass destruction event. The shelling of Europe's largest nuclear power plant at Zaporizhzhia was particularly reckless, though it would be a mistake to believe that Russia — and its authoritarian allies like China — are behaving irrationally. Russia has its reasons and its worldview; some of its thinking is characteristic of great power *raison d'etat*, some of it is peculiar to Russia and its view of its history and is less rational. If today we are at the outset of a third world war, this is because our adversaries are fighting to upset and then redefine the global order. There is no clearer way to upset that order than by mimicking the act of creative destruction that created it: the use of a weapon of mass destruction.

This could be a nuclear attack, a cyber-attack, or even a biological attack akin to another pandemic. If such an attack occurs, it will be accompanied by a narrative propagated by the authoritarians who launched it. The attack itself will matter, but what will also matter are the myriad taboos that it will break, jolting us out of one strategic imaginary and into another. The immediate destruction wrought by a low-grade tactical nuclear weapon would be of less relevance than the raw fact that it would be the first nuclear weapon used since the Second World War. This would upset the global order and so would be a logical step for those authoritarian nations whose goal is to destroy the long-enjoyed global dominance of liberal democracies.

Ample opportunities exist to avoid these grim scenarios. By understanding the intentions of our adversaries, we prepare ourselves to counter their strategic agenda with our own. Our agenda must account for challenges in information operations, biological warfare, and cyber warfare, but it must never lose sight of the truism that armies win wars, not weapons alone.

In Ukraine, an authoritarian Russia along with its allies hopes to prove that the sun has set on liberal democracy. Thus far, what has stopped them is a fully mobilized society and a highly motivated army. The fighting has been a hybrid of low-tech (infantry, artillery, armor) and high-tech (drones, precision missiles, artificial intelligence). The heart of any battle, according to Clausewitz, is "slaughter." A people's will to endure that slaughter has always and will always prove a determinative factor in war.

In the world wars fought since the Enlightenment, authoritarian armies have performed poorly. I do not mean to downplay the military achievements of the authoritarians: Napoleon certainly knew how to fight a battle, and the Germans invented the decentralized, mission-style tactics that the Ukrainians have used to outmaneuver the Russians. But war is a human endeavor, a contest of wills. A society's will to remain free will always prove stronger than those who compel them to obey. As we imagine the future, we must not lose sight of this.

JAMES WOLCOTT

Come Dressed as the Sick Soul of Late Capitalism

[Innocent wayfarers, beware. This essay contains what are vulgarly known in the trade as "spoilers," so if for some unfathomable reason you've yet to view Succession, Glass Onion, and The White Lotus, tread gingerly and try not to gasp.]

It may be the most famous and chewed-over exchange in American literature that never actually took place, at least not in real time. In 1936, when the country was still in the hold of the Great Depression and in no mood for mooniness, *Esquire* magazine published Ernest Hemingway's cinematic story "The Snows of Kilimanjaro," a meditation on mortality and the beautiful consoling desolation of a cathedral mountain, all that. Amid the flashbacks and the regrets, the narrator couldn't resist sneaking in a catty sideswipe: "He remembered poor Scott Fitzgerald and his romantic awe of them and how he had started a story once that began, 'The very rich are different from you and me.' And how someone had said to Scott, 'Yes, they have more money'."

That "someone" was of course Hemingway himself, unable to resist puffing his chest at "poor Scott"'s expense. Earlier the same year *Esquire* had published Fitzgerald's revelatory confessional "The Crack-Up," so it was understood that he was in a precarious state. Fitzgerald's understandable ire at being mocked and misrepresented — he complained to their mutual editor, the Solomonic Maxwell Perkins — forced Hemingway to soften the passage later for hardcover publication and substitute the weak-water name "Julian" for "poor Scott." Didn't matter. Sophisticated readers knew the real score. For decades, the original back and forth in print was patted down and packed into a tidy conversational anecdote, with Hemingway's snappy comeback considered by many (most?) the definitive retort — a bull's-eye reality check — to Fitzgerald's dreamy, minty-green Jazz Age romanticism.

The verdict has been reversed over time. Is there any doubt today that Fitzgerald, swimming in the aqua sparkle of his own perceptions, had it right and Hemingway was talking out of his pith helmet? It was Lionel Trilling who defended the Fitzgerald case most elegantly. "The truth is that after a certain point quantity of money does indeed change into quality of personality: in an important sense the very rich *are* different from us..." It was true then and it is even truer in this millennium. The evidence pimp-slapped in our faces is that the rich are more different from the rest of us than ever before — they are evolving into a mutant species.

As the middle class is increasingly whittled thin — witness union jobs being replaced by a gig economy, the coronation of corporate executives, the premature knighting of Palo Alto wunderkinds, the emergence of Davos Man, and saturation bombing of the airwaves with ad blitzes for online sports gambling and mega-millions lottery draws — the chasm is widening yearly between the have-somethings and the have-it-alls. It has only gotten worse since Covid, only widened. Tech billionaires, hedge funders, private equity predators, Saudi princes, Russian oligarchs, the former president who besmirched the office, and similar excrescences of turbo-charged late-stage lift-off capitalism have top-loaded this century into a second Gilded Age, one that even the ongoing global recession hasn't been able to dent.

A second Gilded Age might seem to be a bonanza opportunity for novelists, for some young, hip, penetrative Gen X/Gen M/Gen Z/Gen-whatever Edith Wharton to train her spy glasses or AR goggles on. But perhaps the spectacle of the mega-rich is simply more than contemporary novelists (a more inwardly investigating crew) can consolidate. The traditional big social novel of manners and disturbing flutters in the drawing room may be too antiquated an undertaking. The pursuit of great wealth and the cruel delight of writing the little ingrates out of your will largely disappeared from serious fiction, as serious fiction itself has been eased into the infirmary. The strenuous toils of Theodore Dreiser (*The Titan, The Financier*) belong to an iron age. The stately mansions of later John O'Hara lie empty and neglected. Inherited money inhabited the background of Louis Auchincloss' novels, but it was a listless resource, carpet-worn.

The contemporary remakes and invocations of *The Great Gatsby* — will we ever be rid of them? — offered retro cosplay that's unable to capture the lyrical lift of the prose, the goosy thrill of Puritan restraint being kicked to the curb and the human body flowing free as if for the first time. The field was left to commercial pop fiction to project fantasies of the rich, virile, fertile, and resplendent in potboilers whipped to a mad fandango by Jacqueline Susann, Judith Krantz, Harold Robbins, Shirley Conran, and other pagan immortals of the airport paperback rack. Some of the anecdotes in these concoctions may have been pinched from honest gossip but the overall effect was of escapist make-believe.

For a brief fun time, before everything got engorged, the true signifiers of American wealth required a keen acquisitive eye to spot. They didn't call undue attention to themselves, but were hostessy and understated, niblet-sized and exquisitely prepared. Truman Capote, who prided himself on being the keenest double agent inside the velvet folds since Marcel Proust, informed an interviewer that what separated the rich from the rest of us primates was their serving of tiny vegetables: "Delicious little tiny vegetables. Little fresh-born things scarcely out of the earth. Little baby corn, little baby peas, little lambs that have been ripped out of their mothers' wombs." Tom Wolfe's *New York* magazine account of Leonard Bernstein's fundraiser for the Black Panthers — "Radical Chic" — introduced us to the party with a rapture over the *hor d'oeuvres*. "*Mmmmmmmmmmmmmmmmm.* These are nice. Little Roquefort cheese morsels rolled in crushed nuts. Very tasty. Very subtle. It's the way the dry sackiness of the nuts tiptoes up against the dour savor of the cheese that is so nice, so subtle." Not that there wasn't the occasional representative of wealth with more democratic taste buds. William F. Buckley, Jr., whose sailboats were stocked with wine and champagne before they embarked into distant latitudes, was addicted to a grocery store brand of peanut butter called Red Wing. But this seems to have been more of a quirky personal indulgence, not something he'd slather on Triscuits when Mrs. Kempner came calling.

Prime time television, bless its bionic heart, filled the void left by serious fiction and classic Hollywood films and then, as television inevitably does, overfilled it. On network TV, extreme wealth was often troweled out as a bestowal of the golden promise of Southern California on the fortunate few, whether they be oil-rich lucky-strike yokels (*The Beverly Hillbillies*) or crime-solving playboys (*Burke's Law*). The Reagan era became the heyday of the rich clan soap opera that had the swoosh and swoop of a pink poodle Ross Hunter production: *Dallas, Dynasty, Flamingo Road,* and *Falcon Crest,* where the matriarch was played by Ronald Reagan's first wife, Jane Wyman. The storyline from *Falcon Crest*'s debut episode: "Wealthy vintner Angela Channing feels threatened when her nephew Chase Gioberti returns to Falcon Crest for his father's funeral." Angela Channing — a name that could ring church bells — was well advised to be on guard. On all of these soaps, barely a season went by when there wasn't a misplaced nephew or niece or illegitimate son or daughter popping out of the topiary to demand his or her rightful due. It was also the era of the lavish mini-series adaptation, such as *Lace*, based on Shirley Conran's bestseller, and remembered today for Phoebe Cates' sneering icebreaker, "Which one of you bitches is my mother?"

To complement the fictional exploits of the coiffed, avaricious, and scheming no-gooders, there gurgled up a new genre of reality television, pioneered by the guided tour through *Lifestyles of the Rich and Famous*, which premiered in 1984 and ran for over a decade. The popularity of the series ratified that in the 1980s it was no longer enough to be rich or famous, you had to be rich *and* famous, for that was the new American Dream. Each syndicated episode of *Lifestyles* was like a fawning vacation brochure or magazine spread with a bumptious, trumpety voiceover supplied by its irrepressible and uncharacteristically effusive British host Robin Leach, whose catchphrase motto "Champagne wishes and caviar dreams!" was like a wedding toast. *Lifestyles of the Rich and Famous* might have been relegated to the slag heap of a period novelty if it hadn't inspired copycats such as MTV's *Cribs* (2000 to present), documentaries about the palatial lives of fashion designers (*Valentino: The Last Emperor*, in 2008), and, most infectiously, the "staged reality" extravagant lunches and battle royals of Bravo cable's *Real Housewives* franchise produced by Andy Cohen, the David O. Selznick of Ryan Seacrests. It is hard to keep track of how many cities have rich *Real Housewives* emerging from limos and going Godzilla. Every urban squad of prancing, feuding divas takes valuable time out from babying their tiny pedigree dogs to attend restaurant openings, disparage their frenemies, fling drinks in each others' unreal faces, and point menacingly long fingernails as they trade heavily bleeped-out trash talk. The campy, pool-splashing, hair-pulling catfight between Krystle and Alexis in season three of *Dynasty* was the precursor for every "Real Housewife" dominatrix match.

Cementing fan loyalty and tabloid fever between seasons are the real-life headline scandals that leave cracks in the fake-real facade, as with the arrest and imprisonment of Jen Shah (*Real Housewives of Salt Lake City*) and Teresa Guidice (*Real Housewives of New Jersey*), and the commotion on *Real Housewives of Beverly Hills* over "powerhouse attorney" Tom Girardi, the then-husband of ice-blonde aspiring disco goddess chanteuse and BH housewife Erika Jayne, who was accused of stealing money from clients, some of them desperate and destitute, and the roiling undercurrent of suspicion that Jayne, hardly a spotless lamb, had to be aware of what hubby was up to — the old fool had been bankrolling her vanity career. It made for many squinty, tense pauses and spitfire moments on *Real Housewives of Beverly Hills*. In relating this, I acknowledge that to the uninitiated it may sound as if I'm speaking Romulan — as when I tried to explain *Buffy the Vampire Slayer* for the dubious enlightenment of the late John Simon — but this is the streaming canal in which some of us oar.

Although *in toto* these reality TV fishbowls reveal sociological glints of how we live now — or rather how *they* live now — their blatancy appeals to low-information, viral-clip viewers in need of incessant cheap kicks. For an immersive experience of how the richy rich think, act, behave, misbehave, maneuver, socialize, enjoy their toys, ignore their children, speak in code ("like real Americans, they always talked in code," to adapt an insight from Norman Mailer), maintain the pecking order, monitor the perimeter, and forge a phalanx whenever they move in concert, only high-budget, hierarchy-obsessed, mission-driven dramas and satires will do. Only they can muster the necessary resources of screenwriters, directors, actors, costume designers, location scouts, etc., to evoke and enter the distortion field of spoiled monsters and damaged psyches.

For a curated verisimilitude, Tom Wolfe-worthy signifiers are strategically implanted in the most fanatically detailed film and television chronicles of the super-rich, whether it's the strictly-business black "stealth wealth" (as if there is such a thing) baseball caps that the male Roys wear screwed tight on their heads in HBO's *Succession*, which has concluded its triumphant four-year run, or the Audemars Piguet Royal Oak Offshore Camouflage timepiece and Randolph Engineering Aviator sunglasses that Bobby Axelrod (Damien Lewis) sport in Showtime's *Billions*. These accouterments of killer cool seem to have been issued by the murders and acquisitions division to princelings and upstarts who compare themselves to modern-day pirates, gangsters, apex predators, and fighter pilots, and pride themselves on their agile wits, their mastery of Machiavelli, Sun Tzu, and Jedi moves (yet have a spaz if their favorite bottled water arrives a tad lukewarm). Underachievers are kept under constant notice. The trading floor at Bobby Axelrod's Axe Capital is a glassed pavilion dojo where only the top survive and flushed-out schmuckos take the walk of shame carrying their belongings in a box. Unreluctant to deploy blackmail and hardball tactics, Bobby Axelrod is Michael Corleone with a bouncier step. Neutralize your foes with extreme prejudice and the gormless boards of directors will fall like dominoes. The scope of the wealth and global designs of Axelrod and his rival plunderers make "the masters of the universe" in Tom Wolfe's *The Bonfire of the Vanities* look like tiddly-winkers.

Tom (Matthew Macfayden): "Umm, do you want...a deal ... with...the devil?"
Cousin Greg (Nicholas Braun), after a pause: "What am I going to do with a soul anyway? Souls are boring."

SUCCESSION, SEASON 3, EPISODE 9.

Succession is less of a bro fantasy than *Billions*, more of an acid bath where illusions and ideals are dissolved and sentimentality separates from the bones, which is why many deem the series cold, heartless, and intractably cynical. As if Jonathan Swift was some sweetheart. Created by Jesse Armstrong, *Succession's* line of attack fuses the scabrous, scorpion invective of *The Thick of It, In the Loop,* and *Veep* with the infighting, stylized lingo, and devious subterfuge of peak David Mamet. No series has consistently shown greater gunslinger skill with caustic sound bites while keeping tabs on the chief imperative. In Mel Brooks' *Silent Movie*, in 1976, the Hollywood studio modeled on Gulf & Western was named Engulf and Devour, which could double as the corporate handle for *Succession*'s Waystar Royco conglomerate, with its portfolio of theme parks, cruise ships, and troubled film division. (All film divisions are troubled.) Its crown jewel is the innocuous sounding American Television Network, or ATN, a red-meat, right-slanted "bigot spigot" cable news operation capable of driving the national dialogue, dictating the next president, and dragging even the loftiest reputations through the muck. Any resemblance to Fox News and the Murdoch family is strictly intentional and the ATN lineup struts its own Tucker Carlson/Sean Hannity anchor stud, a Nazi-flirting smug vacuity who bears the perfect evil name of Mark Ravenhead.

Clinging to the throne and constantly chaffing in irritation and fury at the fools around him, many of them family members, is Royco patriarch Logan Roy (Brian Cox, an aging lion who can inject menace into a simple "Uh-huh"), an old school analog-bred media magnate who minimizes mind games to go for the throat or the groin or, preferably, both. Logan Roy possesses an animal cunning for reading situations and subtle momentum shifts; like HBO's other iconic anti-hero, Tony Soprano, Roy has an animal cunning — a psychological sniffer — for who's with him, who's against him, who's wavering, and who needs to be gang-planked. Animal is the word. "Boar to the floor!" is Roy's sadistic idea of a parlor game, and he vows to go "full fucking beast" on his foes. When he prowls the floor of the ATN newsroom in ominous sunglasses, one character says, "It's like *Jaws* if everyone in *Jaws* worked for '*Jaws*.'"

Seeking to extricate itself from its attachment to old media (newspapers, local television stations, basic cable, movie production), Waystar Royco, mighty as it is, fears being gobbled up in a single gulp by some digital baron "Zucker-fuck." The younger tribe of Roys — primarily sons Kendall (Jeremy Strong) and Roman (Kiernan Culkin), and daughter Siobhan, better known as Shiv (Sarah Snook) — angles to divorce itself from the doom and chaos they've done so much to sow and join the newer species of super-rich that originated in Silicon Valley or some other incubator of myth-hype, red pill hubris, and algorithmic domination. This gnawing awareness of the vexing gap between the traditional 1% and the top 1% of the 1% is rawly laid out plain in *Succession* when Roman, in one of his conversations with his sexty, executive mommy-figure Gerri Kellman (J. Smith-Cameron) promises that if their scheme pays off, "You will get properly 'fuck you, fuck *you* I-don't-even-care-about-climate-change I'm-in-New-Zealand-with-my-own-private-army' rich. Not like some pathetic asshole beach house on the Vineyard rich." A beach house on Martha's Vineyard, so lame.

The New Zealand reference in Roman's spiel alludes to Peter Thiel, whose plans to build an extensive luxury lodge alongside a mountain-surrounded lake as part of his apocalypse insurance policy have been thwarted by local authorities. Thiel is not alone in preparing blueprints for when everything goes kerflooey. Douglas Rushkoff's recent

Survival of the Richest: Escape Fantasies of the Tech Billionaires is an allegory about an elite group of doomsday preppers who intend to live out the coming social disorder and pestilence in scenic, remote compounds that will be self-sustaining, impregnable to zombie invasion, and offering the utmost in civilized comfort as the earth bakes. In times of trouble you can always count on the rich. The undying wet dream of wealthy anarcho-libertarians has been for their own Galt Gulch, the mountain hideaway in Ayn Rand's *Atlas Shrugged* where society's elite doers, makers, and dissenters isolated themselves from the shabby ranks of takers, losers, and liberal simps with their meeching platitudes. Some of the Gulf States are planning glass-domed mega-cities in the desert powered by wind and solar that will contain their own amphitheaters and five-star hotels. "The plan, distilled, is to become the global headquarters for the mega-wealthy," Scott Galloway writes in his newsletter *No Mercy/No Malice*. That will do for most, but for a few visionary billionaire survivalists the world is not enough, to borrow the title of a James Bond film. Elon Musk, as everyone knows, has made it his mission to colonize Mars, and Amazon's Jeff Bezos and Virgin Atlantic's Richard Branson are competing astro cowboys with their satellite launches and dreams of orbital tourism.

Since space colonization is going to take a while and underground compounds lack eye-candy and are indistinguishable from the underlit subterranean nerve centers in Marvel movies and dystopian sci-fi, the preferred getaway in movies and TV for rest, relaxation, and inviolable refuge is a private secluded island that combines the fortress capabilities of Dr. No's Crab

Key with the lush splendor of a tropical paradise. Guests arrive by invitation only, their presence a privilege extended by the host, who cloaks an ulterior motive or two beneath the too-hearty bonhomie. Everything is arranged to perfection, the hospitality staff seamlessly appearing and reappearing as if on winged feet. Or smooth rollers. Robot sherpas serve as the luggage conveyors in *Glass Onion*, Rian Johnson's successor to the improbably successful *Knives Out*, once again centering a tangerine-skinned Daniel Craig with a preposterous Southern gumbo accent trying to solve an Agatha Christie-ish whodunit where clues appear and vanish like magic coins. As in Christie's *And Then There Were None*, the great-grand-mommy of this elimination game, a group of unsuspecting strangers have been summoned for a remote outing only to find themselves at the mercy of machinations that produce many a scream and squeal.

Here the host is billionaire Miles Bron, played with vapid gusto by Edward Norton and blatantly modeled on Elon Musk, a purported galaxy brain tech visionary who has hoodwinked the press and the public into believing that his company's innovations all sprung from his fecund brow. Bron's guests are fellow futurists and disruptors — "Disruptors have assembled!" he cries, as if hailing the Avengers — but there is no question that he is the alpha dude disruptor supremo, its Tony Stark. (One of the many Twitter nicknames hung on Musk is Phony Stark.) A culture-philistine (to use Nietzsche's term) whose Rothko painting is hung upside down, Bron has come into possession of the actual Mona Lisa, which he hopes to deploy as an ace card to impress world leaders and broker global peace or something equally grandiose. The Mona Lisa in its translucent case is just a MacGuffin to keep everyone's eyes off of the misdirection.

As in the later, glossier Hollywood adaptations of Agatha

Christie (the original *Murder on the Orient Express* and *Death on the Nile*, not the clomping Kenneth Branagh remakes), *Glass Onion* unfurls a bright tapestry of brittle pleasantries, shadowy motives, fidgety gestures, ominous foreshadowings, and devious mind games, heightened by the showy entrance of an unexpected intruder — Janelle Monae, who is tasked with projecting old Hollywood Rita Hayworth/Ava Gardner-ish glamor and delivering a flat tire. Old Hollywood homaging as well is Johnson's penchant for peppering the film with amusing cameo pop-ins: Hugh Grant, Jared Leto, and, making his final screen appearance, Stephen Sondheim, whose co-written script for *The Last of Sheila* was an inspiration for the *Knives Out* enterprise. The dolled-up cast seems to be having a grand time, which is part of the Easter egg attraction of these films for entertainment buffs and makes them a harmless exercise in slumming for those of us observing from the sidelines.

Meanwhile HBO's *The White Lotus* miniseries — two seasons thus far, with a third season under construction — also stacks its cast with familiar movie-TV faces but it mixes in provocative newbies to freshen up the entourage and add cosmopolitan flavor. Created, written, and directed by Mike White, whose métier is the comedy of creeping unease, *The White Lotus* pulled off the feat of formulating its own aesthetic from the outset, a cushy ambiance that provides its own commentary on the action. The affluence on display is a confluence of air and attitude, a state of grace soon to come unpeeled. The new wealth — generated by crypto, software, apps, Tik-tok and Instagram product endorsements, sponsorships, and celebrity appearances, OnlyFans stardom, and new sluices for money laundering — seems to have been conjured from nothing, with no apparent effort from its beneficiaries. It seems to flow wherever they go, and for these surfers of invisible, undulating currents, expensive possessions (art, rare wines, diamond tiaras, *Architectural Digest* interiors) are less existentially desirable than the supreme ease of movement. They've come to expect everyday life to be a series of seamless transitions, like a single gliding Steadicam shot from beautiful dawn to beautiful dusk, not that they pay much attention to either. They are too busy contemplating the wonder of their being and why it doesn't make them happier, more receptive.

One of the ingenious aspects of *The White Lotus* is how it reveals how narcissists become not just spoiled but infantilized by their idyllic lifestyle fantasies. The slightest hiccup in service or hitch in itinerary and they turn into crybaby complainers, offended by every unscheduled raindrop. It is also the series that has most ingeniously incorporated the incel as a human pathogen and negative-energy capsule. Integral to the series' sensibility is a pervasive, nullifying affectlessness — a cool, glib, eyes-shaded anomie that comes across as so Californian. Caring about something or someone risks being considered uncool; just breathe in and out the moment, dude. Practicing mindfulness only staves off the demiurges for so long, however. Those looks your spouse is giving you when she lifts her Ray-Bans — they spell trouble.

The plot intrigues of *The White Lotus* stress-test the vacationers until they shed their protective coating and expose how their wiring really works under crisis or when temptation beckons. Jungian shadow elements can be teased out most tantalizingly for prestige-TV viewers in a balmy picture-postcard getaway where the characters' inhibitions and self-defenses melt away. This is the overriding advantage that serial television has over feature film: revelations can be hinted at and winkled out over the course of several episodes rather than blurted out in a single bolt. Pressure becomes more systematically applied. *The White Lotus* also devised its own clever variation on the Agatha Christie formula. Its first season opens with a coffin being loaded on a plane and the question becomes, Who, among the vacationers we're about to meet, leaves in a box? Who's the mystery corpse?

Jorma (Henrik Dorsin): I'm very rich. Yes, let's not beat around the bush. I'm very rich.
Ludmilla (Carolina Gynning): How rich are you?
Jarmo: Oh, I'm so fucking rich!

—SHIPBOARD CONVERSATION, *TRIANGLE OF SADNESS*

Ruben Oslund's *Triangle of Sadness* — the title, not as portentous as it sounds, refers to a geometrical frown patch that can appear between the eyebrows — takes place on a luxury yacht where a soiree of privileged wankers are being feted by an infinitely patient crew. (Luxury yachts are for the depraved-rich genre what opera houses were for Balzac.) Their party is joined by a pair of bodies beautiful, Carl (Harris Dickinson) and Yaya (Charlbi Dean Kriek), he a male model, she an Instagram influencer — a matched set of dollhouse cliches to go with the other loaded stereotypes lounging on the deck. For all of its auteurist mojo handjive (individual chapter titles, a long introductory scene that exhales documentary dead air, a distended running time, a subverting Ironic Twist), the film is a self-pleased demonstration of shlock instincts and facile follow-through. Its cavalier knowingness thinly camouflages a rather sophomoric class struggle on a Ship of Fools (or, if you prefer, a Love Boat of the Damned) which coarsely degenerates into a duel of capitalism vs. Marxism quotation-mongering during a raging storm between the socialist Captain (who doesn't need a proper name in the credits, given that he's portrayed by an instantly identifiable Woody Harrelson) and a Reagan-idolizing Russian oligarch (Dimitry, bellowed by Zlatko Buric).

As the yacht is buffeted to and fro, their audio chatter counterpoints the passengers' volleys of projectile vomiting — pea-soup geysers that outdo *The Exorcist*'s Linda Blair in spray radius and velocity. After the boat goes down, sparing us any further shots of Harrelson slovenly smacking his lips, a few ragged survivors wash ashore on what appears to be a deserted island. A power reversal ensues as Abigail (Dolly De Leon), the yacht's lowly cleaner and "toilet manager," takes charge, and the catered-to have to fend for themselves and barter for favors. Roughing it doesn't come easy to these softies. This dictatorship of the proletariat seems destined to meet a premature end when it is disclosed that a spa resort lies nestled on the other side of the mountain — who knows, possibly another *White Lotus*. No matter how far away and Robinson Crusoe-ish an island may seem, cabanas spring up like toadstools and beach umbrellas are planted like victory flags. Global capitalism will not be denied.

Where *Succession, Glass Onion, Triangle of Sadness*, and *The White Lotus* have their slapstick, farcical sides, their jarring pratfalls, *The Menu* is staged with the solemnity of a Passion Play, which gives its flashes of dark humor far more incision. Directed by Mark Mylod, who has honed his needlepoint precision directing numerous episodes of *Succession, The Menu* presents a sacrificial rite disguised as a unique dining experience — a masque of the red death with impeccable table arrangements and flawless plating. As with *The White Lotus, Triangle of Sadness*, and *Glass Onion*, the experiencers in

The Menu are a group of achievers and hangers-on who fancy themselves inside dopesters of discernment. They're ferried to a remote island — but of course, where else? — for a special multi-course meal prepared by chef *assoluto* Julian Slowik (Ralph Fiennes) and his ninja staff. Before each course the chef offers a brief introduction to the dish and a homily intended to add their appreciation of the thought, the finesse, and the distinctive and locally sourced ingredients. "A course of a single raw scallop perched on a craggy rock and surrounded by carefully tweezed seaweed and algaes is virtually indistinguishable from an actual dish at Atelier Crenn, a San Francisco restaurant with three Michelin stars," *The New York Times* helpfully reported. Authenticity in details adds to the absurdism of what transpires, the flattering foreplay for *la grande bouffe*.

Although the cult of the (male) chef has taken a deserved blow in recent years with the sexual harassment allegations against former numerous television cooking-show celebrities, the mystique remains, which Fiennes wears like an untarnished crown. His Chef Slowik is impresario, emcee, choreographer, wizard, and samurai of the cutting board. His authority radiates from a tight core of *uber*-willpower, a testimony to Fiennes' gift for containment and slow release. It's frightening how his tight smile sometimes lingers a beat too long, surveying the room. Slowik's control only begins to betray hairline cracks when some of the feeders, instead of accepting their roles as congregants, begin to behave like customers. They ask for additional seasoning, request substitutes, or get overly chatty and show-offy. He declines to alter the menu with a Caesar-like smile that tenses as the evening proceeds and his patience snaps. In his furious pride and concentration in preparation that goes into his dishes, Slowik resembles an five-star extension of Seinfeld's Soup Nazi. But where the nicknamed Soup Nazi was satisfied to boot and permanently banish annoying customers from his establishment, Fiennes' Slowik metes out the punishments of a Lord High Executioner. One of the victims, a past-his-prime action star named Georgie Diaz, played by John Leguizamo (and based, says Leguizamo, on Steven Seagal), is condemned for appearing in a film that Slowik saw on his day off, hoping to be entertained. He was not entertained. He was most disappointed. For this, Diaz must pay. It is a tribute to Fiennes that he makes this explanation sound eminently reasonable. Anyone who has sat stonily through an Adam Sandler comedy can sympathize.

Like the passengers in *Triangle of Sadness* and the vacationers in *The White Lotus,* the A-listers in *The Menu* have become so accustomed to telling others what to do that they don't know what to do when they have no one to boss around — when they're the ones being bossed. Even the wait staff doesn't indulge their piques. The guests' inner resources have so shriveled from neglect that most of them are unprepared for the impact of what the critic Marvin Mudrick once called "life direct," and by the time their instincts kick in it's too late — they're fodder. The interesting twist in *The Menu* is not how feebly the diners resist and how quickly they capitulate, but that they and the staff start to accept that perhaps they have earned their place on the pyre. They whimper, they plead, they submit. This is the price for not having lived the right life. This makes for neat allegory, and the tidy violent end — a choreographed die-in — panders to an audience's yearning for retribution that real-life villains and greedheads seldom face.

The sole escapee from the bloodbath and conflagration is Anya Taylor-Joy's Margot, who munches a simple cheeseburger that Slowik has made for her with care and devotion. By her unpretentious all-American taste and cheeky insubordination, Margot is spared the bonfire of the vanities. She is also granted absolution because no one wants to see Anya Taylor-Joy killed off, just as no one watching season two of *The White Lotus* would have wanted to have Aubrey Plaza get the tarp pulled over her. In a difficult, perilous time, Hollywood needs a few unexpendables to keep audience identification from being irreparably severed. Leave all-out nihilism to the mad-hatter satirists.

The problem with most extreme movie satire is that it has nowhere to go but into overkill. From *Dr. Strangelove* to *Don't Look Up*, the nerviest expeditions rely on a cataclysmic finale to spike their message in the end zone. The depiction of class warfare in *High-Rise*, from 2016, adapted from J. G. Ballard's novel, descends into chaos, anarchy, orgiastic stabbing, and the roasting of a dead dog's leg. It's that kind of film. *Glass Onion*, after preening its insouciance through reams of repartee and exposition, climaxes in a giddy orgy of glass sculpture smashing and the fiery destruction of the actual Mona Lisa, a priceless touchstone of Western art torched because of a billionaire's vainglorious ego.

The largest discharge is not blood or fire or showering debris but vast deposits of *merde*. When push comes to shove for the ultra-rich, all crap literally breaks loose. It is almost a psychoanalytical banality, these filmmakers' preoccupation with this conjunction of wealth, shit, and mortifying incontinence. "'We [know] about the superstition that connects the finding of treasure with defecation,' Freud wrote in

"Character and Anal Eroticism," to reinforce the point that, on the subconscious level, "feces have always been understood as a form of currency." (I owe this to Simon van Zuylen-Wood's jaunty, punny essay on "Feces and the Gold Standard: A Psychological Explanation of Goldbuggery" in *The New Republic* in 2012.) *The Magic Christian*, the novel written in 1959 by Terry Southern and adapted into a now-forgotten film a decade later with a mind-boggling cast (Peter Sellers, Ringo Starr, Laurence Harvey, Roman Polanski, and Raquel Welch are among the duped), ends with desperate, greedy saps fishing for pound notes scattered in a large tub filled with urine, fecal waste, and other unpleasantries. The burly Russian oligarch in *Triangle of Sadness*, who has made his fortune in fertilizer, proclaims himself "The King of Shit!" He keeps crowing the word as if to rub his fellow travelers' noses in it. The film soon rubs our face in it, too. Its key punchline edit comes when Harrelson's Captain extols the $250 million craft being pummeled by the elements and the next cut is to a miserable passenger crouched on a soiled toilet. Freud also hypothesized that misers were those held in their stool as children, hoarding money in adulthood, which may support the revelation in *Succession* that Logan Roy died while trying to fish his iPhone out of a clogged airplane toilet. The symbolism is almost too much.

This scatological imperium may have been foretold in a Hollywood film that many of us scoffed at in its day, and rightly so. In 1974, at the weary end of the disaster epic *The Towering Inferno*, the disillusioned architect played by Paul Newman proposed that the burnt-out, windows-shattered one-hundred-and-thirty-five-story hulk be left standing as "a kind of a shrine to all the bullshit in the world." Even in our Watergate-era cynicism, what naifs we were then. We little suspected how much worse would be in store. The world's bullshit supply was still in its developmental stage, amassing its resources to achieve full sentience, establish free-market capitalism as the undisputed queen of the ball, and extend privatization into every sphere and cranny of endeavor until much of mankind would be superfluous and disposable, supplanted by intelligent machines.

It is in the nature of satire to go too far, but now "too far" scarcely feels far enough, given the enormity of the wealth accumulating to those at the top of the diamond pyramid and the social fissuring below. If there is something punitive and body-horroring about so many of the films and series about the super-rich, it may reflect the frustration that no matter what the crimes and excesses of the Moneygods, karma isn't coming for them — the fix is in. Their escape pods are loaded up and at the ready. So karma has to be dealt out on screen, with as wicked a hand as necessary and a wham-bang finish. Rough justice may not be real justice, but you take your reckonings where you can get them.

NOGA ARIKHA

After Neurocentrism

Some thirty years ago, with the launch in 1990 by the Bush administration of the "Decade of the Brain," neurocentrism took hold in the Western world — America, Japan, and Europe. It held on well into the aughts. Neurocentrism is the belief that the brain is the seat of the mind, that they are in some sense the same entity, and that therefore one can understand mental and psychic life by understanding the brain, which is often dubbed the most complex object in the universe, with its estimated eighty-six billion neurons and hundred trillion or so synaptic connections. As a consequence of discussions about the brain already underway in the 1980s between upper-level American science agencies, councils, and associations, the government awarded generous funding for research in neuroscience, psychology, and neurology. It aimed in large part to address the staggering cost of neurodegenerative diseases, which was (correctly, as it turned out) predicted to increase massively over the next decades, as well as to study the aetiology and the effects of neurological disorders and accidents.

An underlying assumption of the program was that it would constitute one of the ultimate achievements of humankind to unravel the brain's functioning. A similar hope was pinned on genetics, with the Human Genome Project launched in 1990, with a similar equivalence posited between genomes and selves. If one came to grips with the biology, in short, one would finally understand the nature of life, identity, and consciousness. There was an essence that one could seize. Science would yield ultimate truths. In those years a reductionism of mind and life to their constituent parts prevailed; it was galvanized and encouraged by the optimistic ethos of the time. Popular books about the brain, and also about genetics, flourished. To be sure, there existed corners of resistance to reductionism, in the name of phenomenological complexity, with philosophers of mind exploring the nature of consciousness — for instance, a *Journal of Consciousness Studies* was founded in 1994, which provided a forum for collaborations between philosophical speculation and empirical data, and interdisciplinary conferences on the major topic started taking off then. But this resistance took place within rarefied academic spheres. Neurocentrism was easier for non-specialists to comprehend.

Meanwhile the fields of mind sciences grew, and multiplied, separately from biological neurosciences, insofar as the term "mind" designates not a physical entity but the abilities that allow organisms to function in and interact with the world. A "Decade of the Mind" was announced in 2007. The cognitive sciences yielded modular models of the mind, represented for a while as subdivided into mechanisms supposedly developed during the Pleistocene. Importantly, these cognitive sciences were a formidable and fertile response to the behaviorism that had preceded them, insofar as they supposed, in contrast to behaviorist assumptions, that there was indeed such a thing as a mind that could be studied. The association of the cognitive sciences with neuroscience then gave birth to cognitive neuroscience, which made use of imaging technologies to explore mental functions.

The appearance in 1991 of functional magnetic resonance imaging (fMRI) — a technology that allows one to observe the brain in action — was a historical revolution whose impact on the imagination was not unlike that of the moon landing. It seemed to announce a bold, bright future when one could finally peer into places that had never before been visible. The first steps into this future were taken, however, with a measure of presentist and materialist hubris, and often at the cost of philosophically informed subtlety. Now, three decades later, research and funding continue, and rightly so — but the mood, the priorities, and the assumptions have radically changed. And so it is time to take stock of where the mind sciences are today, and what place these sciences now hold in the collective imagination, especially in light of the bewilderingly rapid evolution of computer science and, most recently, of artificial intelligence — an expression whose assumptions also need parsing.

At its height, neurocentrism in its excitement generated countless claims about the cerebral location of mental functions, delivered in the media as so many revelations about the "place" of the deepest aspects of human experience — cognition, language, volition, emotion, and even artistic and religious feeling. Experience was "in the brain" and therefore, somehow, better understood, or so went the claims. In this respect, the historical moment was structurally at least reminiscent of phrenology, popular in the early decades of the nineteenth century until it was dismissed as pseudoscience some years later, according to which the brain's divisions determined personality, qualities, and faults, and mental functions had specific, visible locations and could be measured by bumps of the skull. The neurocentrist excitement was also reminiscent of the older urge to posit a "homunculus" inside the organism to account for its operations — no matter that this created an eternal circularity, since assigning functions to some agent or structure in the brain begs the question of how that agent or structure works in the first place. It begs the question, too, of how one can determine a causal link between the structure and the function. Extracting indubitable causal connections out of a myriad observed correlations remains, as it happens, a central puzzle and problem for brain science, as indeed it is for all sciences.

The excitement that was provoked by fMRIs is understandable. Thanks in part to these and other novel imaging technologies, highly important work has emerged since the 1990s, in all fields of neuroscience as well as neurology, in brain anatomy and physiology. A focus on neural networks replaced the erstwhile localizationism, and the identification of the functions of decidedly interconnected brain areas became, and continues to become, more and more fine-grained. Advances in neurophysiology fed into the development of neuropharmacology and of second-generation targeted medications for psychiatric disorders — though the functioning of these pharmaceuticals remains inadequately understood and their use can be controversial. New tools such as optogenetics were born, to study the behaviors of individual neurons. There developed, and there continues to develop, a better understanding of the etiology of various dementias, despite their continued intractability. Since 1990, there has also been the invention of deep brain stimulation (DBS) to counter some of the symptoms of Parkinson's, and of transcranial magnetic stimulation (TMS), a non-invasive technique that acts upon and helps to decode neural activity during specific tasks, such as recall or attention. The genetic basis of some devastating neurological diseases, such as ALS or Huntington's Chorea, emerged out of these significant studies. The use and applications of computational neuroscience grew tremendously, allowing for the refinement of our understanding of attention, orientation, and vision, or for the creation of brain-computer interfaces that allow paraplegic patients to move again — and the tools and concepts that it deploys grow in sophistication every day.

The various imaging technologies, moreover, are growing increasingly refined, in some part because awareness has also grown of how complex it is to interpret the images that these technologies yield. Indeed, it is much more of a cultural given today than it was in 1990 that there are no readable maps of any kind without signposts, nor without readers who know the signposts — and that neither signposts nor readers are devoid of bias. A map is never a one-to-one rendering of what it represents. Studies of the brain are not limited to the interpretation of images, in any case. They can provide support for studies that take place at multiple levels — genes, molecules, neurotransmitters, single neurons, and neural networks — and within numerous interconnected subdisciplines, such as neurophysiology, developmental neuroscience and psychology, social psychology, cognitive and affective neuroscience, computational neuroscience and robotics, all of which converge by now with the many fields pertaining to the cognitive sciences and psychology. With the development of epigenetics, the impact of the environment on infants' and children's psychic development, and thence on lifelong mental health, has become much better understood, too. The gene-centric biological determinism that had initially characterized the decade, and that could be used to justify conservative social and educational policies opposing investment in public education, not to mention outright bigotry, thus ended up being undermined by some of the very projects that the Bush administration had underwritten.

In other words, neurocentrism is no longer the calling card of the mind sciences. It had come along with public enthusiasm for all things "neuro," which for a few years became a ubiquitous, homunculus-like predicate in the media and publishing worlds. It then waned by necessity, along with public enthusiasm and neuro-fatigue. Public interest in the neurosciences and psychology does continue to simmer today, especially when they address general issues of psychology and well-being, psychiatric disorders and neurodegenerative diseases, but the reductionist enthusiasm has ebbed — much for the better.

Now we have a different problem. The recoil went too far. Related to the change of mood is the less welcome growth of skepticism with regard to scientific research generally. Broadly unaware that scientific results and interpretations are provisional, the public tends at once to overvalue and to undervalue the scientific enterprise — attributing to it a capacity to deliver certainty, as it seemed to do at the height of the neurocentric decade, and dismissing it when this desired certainty is not at hand. This misconception of science is precisely what feeds into pseudosciences like the phrenology of yore and the dangerous myths of today, from anti-vax theories to the denial of climate change. An awareness of what scientific research is and what scientists do is necessary for the proper calibration of trust in the value of their expertise. This holds true for the mind sciences as well. These need to be, and in fact increasingly are, informed by philosophical argument and humanist concerns, since by its very nature, the study of the human mind at work upon itself remains a minefield of confusions.

These confusions regarding the scientific study of mind are far from new. The study of the brain as it has been practiced since the late nineteenth century, when the neuroscientist Santiago Ramón y Cajal ushered in modern neuroscience with his discovery of the neuron, is not the study of the mind and the psyche. The study of the brain zooms in on the organ and its microscopic components. The study of the mind, by contrast, starts from observations of human behavior. Studying the brain does indeed provide clues about the mind, but the obverse does not necessarily hold, especially given how complex the brain is. The territory has been mapped, the places named, the sulci and gyri identified, some functions recognized and some mechanisms understood, to some extent — yet so much of it is still unknown. In 2004, the neuroscientist Gerald Edelman entitled a book on consciousness *Wider than the Sky: The Phenomenal Gift of Consciousness*, a title drawn from the poem by Emily Dickinson — "The Brain —

is Wider than the Sky" — that is unavoidable for those who want to conjoin humanist musings about meaning with the hard-edged world of scientific experiments. Edelman offered an attempt, one of many at the time, to show how the brain gives rise to the mind.

But this does not mean that the brain and the mind are identical. And along with the ebb, since the Decade of the Brain, of reductionist enthusiasm and phrenological equivalence, there have emerged over the past two or three decades increasingly rich theoretical constructs and empirical data bolstering arguments *against* the identity of mind with brain, arguments that until recently were purely the remit of philosophy. The philosophers may enjoy contemplating the mind at work upon its own processes, as they always have. But today the empiricists — neuroscientists and psychologists — are in a better position to provide answers to some of these philosophical questions. They look at ourselves from without, while trying to build an image of the thinking, subjective entity that we each are.

It does seem obvious that without the brain there would be no mind — and no advanced animal life at all. The Hippocratic doctors of ancient Greece were craniocentric, as was Plato — though not Aristotle, who believed that the heart was the seat of it all. But brain and mind are, by definition, different entities. We know what the brain looks like. In contrast, no one has ever seen a mind. Nothing visually contains the mind — not even the brain. The assumption that brain produces mind, at least to some degree, arose at some point in the history of self-conscious humans out of correlations between accidents and behavioral changes, and of course well before the advent of brain imaging. Human psychology, however, concerns persons, not the gooey organ within their skulls. Brains, in sum, are necessary for minds, but minds are not reducible to brains.

In fact, out of the ancient recognition of how strange it really is that intangible mind should arise out of tangible matter, there was born the renowned "mind-body problem," which posits the irreducibly mysterious nature of higher mental life and consciousness. The apogee of this problem in the West was the dualism famously perfected in the seventeenth century by Descartes — famously mocked by Gilbert Ryle three centuries later as "the ghost in the machine" — which split apart immaterial mental experience from the material body in which mental life took place. Dualism is a powerful and seductive theory, because thoughts and feelings do not have the concreteness of matter, at least in everyday experience. It also informs religious beliefs about life after death in many societies besides Western ones: the awareness of the self-aware mind goes hand in hand, metaphysically and anthropologically, with the awareness of death. The West was marked by the Cartesian version of dualism, not least because it was compatible, including for Descartes himself, with Christian dogma. Thought and feelings pertained to the immaterial (and therefore immortal) dimension of humans, which was called soul, and non-human animals were considered soulless, mortal mechanisms.

Within the framework of secular modernity, there was no longer any political need to please the Church with a metaphysical doctrine of human exceptionalism. With Darwinian evolution, and the accompanying reconception of humans as evolved animals, human cognition and emotion could be studied in scientific rather than metaphysical terms.

From the late nineteenth century, scientific psychology, as established most notably by William James in America, Wilhelm Wundt in Germany, and Théodule Ribot in France, began to parse our corporeal beings, and did away with any immaterial soul. (In this regard James' view of spiritual life was an exception within scientific materialism.) The psychology that emerged then took as a given that subjectivity could be studied through a combination of observation, introspection, measurement, clinical evidence, and philosophical acumen.

But scientific psychology did not put the mind-body problem to rest. The anxiety bred by the conception of ourselves as mortal animals has never gone away. Religious feeling persists in all corners of the world. And the metaphysics of mind are not reducible to the science of mind: the mind-body problem has remained in the philosophical conversation of the last and current centuries, in particular with the so-called "hard problem" of consciousness, in the formula of the philosopher David Chalmers. As he contended in 1996, however successful we may become at parsing the mechanisms involved in "the cognitive and behavioral functions in the vicinity of experience," missing from the picture are the *qualia* of experience — that is, what it is *like* to have any experience at all, in the oft-quoted words of Thomas Nagel, whose essay "What Is It Like to Be a Bat?," published in 1974 remains a reference point for the anti-materialist argument. The problem as Chalmers states it delimits conceptually the bounds within which an empirical account can have explanatory power, and beyond which it acts somewhat like snow that will not stick to a persistently slippery terrain. On this view, experience and biology partake of two different orders, and so consciousness necessarily escapes the physiological mechanisms that make it up.

Not everyone agrees that there is a "hard problem," however: the snow, so to say, could eventually stick. The neuroscientists who study the nature of felt experience take for granted that it is a biological phenomenon through and through, and on a continuum between lower-order and higher-order mechanisms. Their concerns are not philosophical: the existence or not of the problem of consciousness is not relevant to their empirical research. And it is noteworthy that the notion of a "hard problem" arose as such — as a problem — precisely at the height of the neurocentrist Decade of the Brain, when, with materialist reductionism at its apogee, the old mind-body dualism was replaced with a brain-body dualism that split the brain apart from the rest of the body. This split ensured that cognition was studied apart from the embodied brain, irrespective of the biology involved in cerebral activity, of cell physiology, of genetics, and also of the environment in which the living organism develops and lives. It fed into the development of computational neuroscience, and of its conception of cognition as disembodied and affectless, out of the cybernetics of earlier decades. It also sundered the continuum between lower-level mechanisms that Chalmers, like his early modern predecessors, had deemed available for empirical study, and the higher-order ones that he deemed indeed impregnable to empirical accounts. Now the human animal was as if split into three parts: machine-like brains, machine-like bodies, and disembodied minds.

This brain-body dualism has begun to diminish only recently, over the past two or three decades. But this is the case mostly within some circles of psychologists, for everyday language tends to remain dualistic — "it's all in the mind" means that it is not real; emotions are conceived to float in an abstract realm; your body "belongs" to you; and so on. (Early in his memoirs Bertrand Russell recalled a philosophically amusing old adage: "What mind? No matter. What matter? Never mind.") Some areas of philosophical speculation are still conducted as if biology were entirely incidental, in an enactment of the dualist stance, in part because the conceptual structure is missing for a proper integration of scientific theories into philosophy. Yet from its earliest beginnings philosophical contemplation overlapped with empirical observation. When Thales asserted that all is water, he offered an empirical description as well as a metaphysics. Etymologically, metaphysics is what comes "after the study of nature," sequentially after Aristotle's *Physics*, later denoting what transcends empirical study. And until the modern era philosophers were also "natural philosophers" — scientists, in other words — who conducted empirical enquiry.

Today we do have the tools to construct empirical answers to philosophical questions about the nature of self and mind: what we need to develop now are the tools to understand *philosophically* these empirical answers, to develop a proper "science humanism." Yet owing to the divisions between disciplines, few humanists pay attention to science — just as few scientists are in a position to "humanize" their research. In recent decades, there even have been attempts in the humanities and social sciences to dissolve matter and deny the empirical character of science entirely, by making it into just another human expression — social constructionist models that envision biology entirely as a phenomenon that cannot be known apart from the context in which it is theorized, of import only as a cultural occurrence. Computational neuroscience, meanwhile, yields increasingly complex models of a disincarnate "mind," while what the world knows as "artificial intelligence" is surpassing some aspects of human cognitive competence at increasing speed.

Despite these admittedly powerful and often concealed redoubts of dualism, a growing number of researchers in neuroscience and psychology are now taking on board how the brain is in fact interconnected with the body —and that, as the neuroscientist Antonio Damasio has put it, the brain serves the body, rather than the other way round. This is so because, like all else on earth, the brain has evolved into its present shape out of primitive life. As Damasio described it in 2018 in his *The Strange Order of Things: Life, Feeling, and the Making of Cultures,* from the brainless single-cell organism, such as bacteria, endowed with the capacity to perceive and act upon its perceptions, grew increasingly complex multi-cellular organisms that eventually developed nervous systems to coordinate their multiple parts. Bodies evolutionarily precede the brains that serve them, and consciousness, as indeed all higher mental function, is an upshot of processes internal to the evolution of life. Mental experience encapsulates felt experience, and without the body there would be no feeling — nor any brain, either.

This is also why it is no longer possible to hold on to the old story according to which the faculty to reason and to contemplate cosmos, life, and self is a function of a disembodied thinking thing — Descartes' *res cogitans*, posited in opposition to the extended bodily thing, *res extensa*. With his epochal *Descartes' Error*, which appeared in 1994, at the height of the neurocentric moment — and based on imaging research conducted with his wife Hanna Damasio —Damasio first explained how, without emotional activity and input, deliberations that seemed to partake of rational evaluation were disabled. From then on, and via their subsequent research and his writings, Damasio was at the forefront of neuroscientists who showed how central emotion is to our highest faculties, and how the notion of a disembodied brain, let alone a disembodied mind, is a fantasy that has nothing to do with our biological reality. The so-called "affective turn" in neurosciences and psychology was launched. Research on emotions accelerated, not only in the sciences but also in philosophy and, more recently, the social sciences: the rationalist and cognitivist canon remains, but emotions are finally being considered centrally. Unlike a thought, a feeling is much less easily mistaken for an abstraction untethered from experience. Whether or not a thought is incorporeally determined, as Descartes believed, having a feeling entails experiencing a physical sensation. And so the "affective turn" was conducive to the notion of the person as a psycho-somatic unity.

In the 1990s philosophers also insisted that the mind must be understood not only as embodied, but also as embedded, enactive, and extended within the environment with which it interacts dynamically — that our experience is the upshot of this dynamic interaction of brain and body in relation to the world, and that our minds are a dimension of this interactivity. In fact, this conception of the body's relation to thought and experience had already been central to phenomenology in the late writings of Edmund Husserl and, monumentally, in Maurice Merleau-Ponty's *Phenomenology of Perception*, which appeared in 1945. On this approach, known as "4E cognition," our tools are also aspects of minds that extend beyond individual skulls. It is misleading, in this account, to contemplate minds in isolation, since we have evolved as social beings. The subject is primarily "intersubjective," as the philosophers Emmanuel Lévinas and Paul Ricoeur argued, following Merleau-Ponty. The first-person, interactive, felt experience that phenomenology embraces as necessary to our self-understanding has re-entered the realm of science, which is filling in the philosophical picture. A number of philosophers and scientists have joined this phenomenological approach with some aspects of Buddhism, most notably Francisco Varela, whose *The Embodied Mind: Cognitive Science and Human Experience*, written with Eleanor Rosch and Evan Thompson and published in 1992, marked a turn for students of cognitive science who believed that scientific investigation of the mind must begin with subjectivity.

Since then, our understanding of corporeal subjectivity, from the bottom up rather than from cognitive heights, as it were, has grown tremendously. It depicts the central nervous system — brain and spinal cord — as crucially interconnected with the peripheral nervous system, which includes the somatic and autonomic nervous systems. Feelings from skin, muscles, skeleton, and viscera are processed in the brain which monitors their functioning, yielding what is known as interoception. In turn, interoception meshes with and acts upon exteroception, the perception of external stimuli via the five sense modalities. Together these sense-perceptions constitute our very sense of self.

The study of interoception has intensified among psychologists over the past decade or so, yielding insights into the somatic basis of the self, the centrality of emotions to its constitution and of bodily states to awareness, well-being and illness. In the words of the neuroanatomist Arthur D. Craig, whose research on the topic has been foundational for the many studies that have multiplied since, interoception is "the sense of the physiological condition of the body," whether conscious or not. Interoceptive signals travel along specific neural pathways from all bodily systems from skin to gut — vasomotor, cardiac, digestive, sexual, respiratory — and include the sensing of pleasure, pain, hunger, thirst, temperature. They are processed in particular in an area within the cerebral cortex called the insula. Increasingly targeted and sophisticated studies are showing how our sense of self is indexed on these dynamic perceptions and on the brain's constantly predicting internal bodily states. In turn, these processes reflect the homeostatic regulation of the organism within an always changing world, without which it would not be viable. These constant feedback processes "provide the basis for the subjective image of the material self as a feeling (sentient) entity, that is, emotional awareness," as Craig puts it. Consciousness, according to this analysis, is the upshot of the neurally encoded capacity to represent these processes as feelings. And in turn, these feelings are indications of our fluctuating bodily states within the world of non-selves, which shapes who we become from infancy on. As many researchers are showing, including developmental psychologists, or the neuroscientist Vittorio Gallese with his notion of "embodied simulation," we are intersubjective from birth: without others, we do not develop stable selves. And because this multi-pronged and conceptually rich body of ongoing research begins with the subject, it avoids the conundrum that was faced by the disincarnate sciences of the mind that were developed in the age of reductionism, and which resulted in the "hard problem" of consciousness. No, we are not "just" our brains, and this current science is showing how that is the case.

With this intense focus on the biological underpinnings of the self as a dynamic entity that is embodied, interactive, and intersubjective, as opposed to disembodied, fixed, and isolated, experimental sciences are meshing with philosophical speculations. They had been conjoined in antiquity — Aristotle, remember, was a metaphysician *and* an empiricist — and to some degree in early modernity, when Descartes, too, practiced empirical research. They met again in the late nineteenth century. Now, armed with insights from phenomenology, daring at last to use the first-person as a starting point for scientific inquiry, we are digging deep into our flesh, extracting from its infinitely complex layers the very consciousness that, for so long, seemed always to escape us. In so doing, we are also building the scientific picture underlying what millions look for and experience in practicing yoga and other somatic disciplines. The insights from yoga comport nicely with the discoveries of phenomenology.

As we can see from this brief history biological reality is never a neutral given: scientists start from preconceptions about the nature of their object of study. The names on the maps are not inherent to the maps. They must be coined, and they are not fixed, either. Scientific research always takes place within a cultural context that informs its priorities. While it is not reducible to its context, bias is always present. And over the last few decades, cultural context has been partially responsible for this increased attention to the body, which, not surprisingly, has also become central within literature and the arts, humanities, and social sciences. Popular culture, certainly, is body-obsessed in complex ways. But more positively, outside the dualist redoubts that persist in some academic circles, some religious communities, and generally in folk psychology, it is acceptable and even necessary to say today that humans are embodied creatures among other embodied creatures, in the sense that our feeling and sensing body is centrally constitutive of what we are. Cognitive sciences now ally also with anthropology to study embodied and extended cognition — how *homo sapiens* is the begetter and user not only of symbolic languages but of tools and artifacts. We adapt to our environments, while extending our selves, and building cultures of and with *things*: humans live within artifactual rather than natural settings.

This re-centering of the study of humans onto the body — and of the human body onto the natural world — is an aspect also of the ecological emergency. It is now painfully clear that the old notion of our supposed superiority over other animals, and our lording it over the whole of nature, has been arrogant and destructive. (The pandemic was a reminder of this: viruses can stop us if we invade wild territories — such as bat havens — that are not ours to enter.) The very consciousness that seemed to be our privilege — for long in the guise of the old rational soul — is in fact organically based, an outgrowth of a natural process, and indeed we can best understand it in relation to the consciousness of other animals, which is increasingly studied as well. This is a return not only to the late nineteenth-century roots of scientific psychology, but even earlier, to Lucretius, who wrote in *On the Nature of Things* that "mind and spirit are both composed of matter," and to the seventeenth-century "libertines" who adopted Lucretian materialism.

It is always tempting to balk at this materialist picture and to reify our self-consciousness into an abstract Cartesian entity. But in doing so we forget that our very capacity for self-consciousness, material as it really must be (what goes on in the mind or between minds by definition goes on in the body or between bodies), allows precisely for the capacity to do so, and for us to be taken in by our very capacity. Daniel Dennett suggests something that seems similar, with his notion of consciousness as illusory, but he believes that consciousness is "just" an illusion — and that is emphatically not the point that I am making here. Rather, consciousness as we experience and understand it is a materially and ontologically real capacity, but we are unable to understand how it arises precisely because that is its all-too-human limit in humans. There is only so much that our brains can do. Animal consciousness is also real, but it probably does not extend to this multiplication *ad infinitum* bred by our self-reflection in a hall of mirrors.

And so we cannot leave our self-definition there. We are animals, and knowing that we are helps us to understand ourselves. But in virtue of our highly complex brains, we also differ from the other animals in ways that we need to comprehend in order to understand ourselves. Only humans *study* consciousness: our metacognition, that is, our self-reflexive awareness, does seem to define us and constitute our apartness. That very thought, in turn, is another instance of our self-reflective metacognition, which is the root and stuff of history, philosophy, art, science — of culture, in short, which in its variegated manifestations remains our human prerogative. Other animals can be acculturated, birds may learn specific songs, chimps can learn tool use and mating behaviors — such processes exist throughout the natural realm. But our very nature is defined by the cultural dimension, and the variety of human cultures is potentially infinite: the sciences of the mind are therefore bound by their inevitably cultural structure and mission.

No other creature is interested in its brain or has an idea of a mind — in fact, the very concepts of "mind" and "culture" are themselves cultural artifacts, developed within anthropology and related disciplines. And so, the notion that all species may have a kind of consciousness is asymmetrical: we may attribute it to our dog, say, but the dog does not know this in the way that we do, nor will it be aware that, like us, it may in turn be attributing consciousness to us. At any rate, whatever awareness it has is not elaborated further than its experiencing it. It may share with us mechanisms of attention and volition, it may experience anger and joy, but it does not study how, or ask why, these mechanisms and emotions occur. Neither dogs nor dolphins, neither elephants nor octopuses, study anthropology or philosophy — or write diaries or poems or books. What characterizes our species, besides our elaborate tools, is our propensity for introspection and abstraction, for projecting ourselves into the future on the basis of the remembered past, for imagining what is not present — using elaborate symbolic forms to embody the non-present, as Suzanne Langer emphasized — and, finally, for constructing cultures out of our awareness of death. We also make stories, theories, and trouble out of our perceptions and predictions.

This human prerogative, which in some instances we may call tragic, is also what defines us in relation to the increasingly sophisticated artificial agents that we are creating — the ultimate artifacts, which may seem to act and look more and more like us. There is no turning back: as technology gains in power, we face the need to re-assert the bounds of our humanity, in contrast to the kinds of faculties that are displayed by these artificial agents. There will be similarities, of course, but the differences are what will define us. Certainly these machines are farther away from us than are the non-human animals to whom we may attribute consciousness. They are neither born nor mortal. They are not biological, they have not evolved over millions of years as bodies that flexibly adapt to a fluctuating environment, they are not constituted of billions of proteins, molecules, cells, an immune system, hormones, enzymes, and neurotransmitters, and they are not conceived within the body of another mortal. In short, they are not "wet," as Siri Hustvedt put it in her important essay "The Delusions of Certainty."

Yet we are increasingly merging large aspects of our identities and activities with the electronic circuits that we have created. Gmail retains traces of our lives better than we do — though that does not mean that it "remembers," because memory is made of dynamic processes that pertain to a self, a self that forgets as much as it remembers, and therefore differs entirely from the storage system of AI. Memory is emotionally valenced, and AI entities do not have emotions, so far. Granted, robots are multipart systems, and though they are now able to learn how to navigate within changing environments, they begin their "lives" as circuits stored within the artificial body, in contrast to our nervous system, which is the upshot of dynamic embodied processes. Our minds are not incidentally "housed within" a body: as is becoming clearer in our post-dualist age, it is precisely because there are bodies — complex biological systems — that there are minds. What is bewildering today is that we have developed the capability to reverse these age-old bottom-up processes and engineer mind-like mechanisms out of algorithms. We are able to build these machines, though, thanks in part to our understanding of the brain and the embodied mind, and it is no secret that one motivation for the public support of neuroscience over the past decades has been its utility to the AI that increasingly, and with perplexing speed, undergirds all aspects of our private, social, economic, cultural, and political lives.

Something else is missing from AI besides emotions — simple ones like fear or complex ones like shame, ambivalence, nostalgia, melancholy. It is the need for *meaning*, which is inscribed within the narrative patterning of the human mind from birth onward. The sense of both individual and collective history and belonging. And the sense of beauty, the poignancy of finality, physical desire, the pleasure of food; and the sense AI agents do not somatize illnesses, feel pain, suffer from exhaustion, have anxiety attacks or depressive episodes; they do not have eating disorders or develop dementia; they do not enjoy the garden in the spring, have sex, fall in love. They do not feel claustrophobic if stuck too long in one place, or travel for pleasure, or make war or murder or take drugs. They can also lie; perhaps one day they will know how to lie willingly, instead of just proliferating false information. They "know" a great number of things, but nothing about the meaningful narrative that makes up a mortal life.

It is legitimate — and an obligation of our moment — to be concerned about the growing power of these artificial agents. But to worry that they could replace us is to forget what humans are. The misplaced worry is itself worrisome. It stems from the same faulty intuition that for so long led humans to ignore their potentially ailing bodies, or to suppose that a brain could just as well grow in a vat. We tend to mistake models for reality and brain maps for minds, to scant or entirely neglect how phenomenologically complex and sensorially rich each experienced moment really is. We project onto machines our all-too-human fears and hopes. Yet it is only by understanding ourselves better that we will be able to develop the culture of care that we need to confront the crises of our time. Care was not a priority in the heady days of 1990s optimism, when knowledge of the brain was touted as the route to enlightenment. But it is so today, all the more that the forces of reaction are ascendant. Against these, and in order to advance self-understanding, we should build an alliance of the psychologists, neuroscientists, and engineers with the philosophers, artists and historians. Such an alliance would enable us never to lose sight of our humanity, whose redefinition only humans can forge.

CARLOS FRAENKEL

What the Night Sky Teaches

Is astronomy the key to our wellbeing? If we "learn the harmonies and revolutions of the universe," Plato wrote in the *Timaeus*, we will attain "the most excellent life offered to humankind by the gods." The pre-Socratic philosopher Anaxagoras was even more dramatic:

> And they say that when someone asked Anaxagoras for what reason anyone might choose to come to be born and to live, he replied to the question by saying that it was "to be an observer of the sky and the stars around it, as well as moon and sun," since everything else at any rate is worth nothing.

For Anaxagoras, stargazing is the only thing worth doing. Without it, we would be better off not existing at all. These days, I'm sure, lots of people would be thrilled to gaze at the stars if the spectacle could offer them respite from what's going on down here, let alone lead to "the most excellent life." But can it?

In 2020, the Nobel Prize in physics went to three astrophysicists — modern-day stargazers, if you like — for their work on black holes: Roger Penrose for showing that black holes, strange though they are, fit squarely with our theory of the universe; Reinhard Genzel and Andrea Ghez for discovering the black hole at the center of our own galaxy. The year before, the first-ever photograph of a black hole was published to great fanfare. Every newspaper showed the dark circle, surrounded by a ring of fire, on the front page. Eight interlinked observatories, from the South Pole to Hawaii to the Chilean desert, turned the earth into a gigantic telescope to capture the supermassive object five hundred million billion kilometres away.

Invariably such events are accompanied by a certain rhetoric celebrating mankind's curiosity and how it pushes the frontiers of knowledge. But imagine how puzzled we would have been if the laureates had announced from the podium in Stockholm that life is worthless unless we study astronomy. Wouldn't we have dismissed them as mad?

In my own family, the enthusiasm for astronomy runs low. It took my son and me a couple of hours to screw together the telescope that he was given for his sixth birthday. After dinner we aimed it at the sky. We saw mostly darkness with a few fuzzy flashes. Finally we found the moon. On the pale, stained surface we made out craters. It held his attention for about a minute.

"Did you see the man on the moon?" I asked.

"That's a fairy tale, dad!" he replied. But if I could get him on a rocket ship, he would have loved to jump around there, like the astronauts in a documentary he had seen. Then came his older sister's turn. "Cool," she said. "It really does look like cheese." That was the end of our space exploration. Since then, the telescope has been collecting dust in a corner of the living room. Clearly we have not been heeding Anaxagoras' and Plato's counsel.

The only constellation I can identify is Orion, thanks to the belt. I wouldn't make a Thracian maid or anyone else laugh the way Thales did. He was the first Greek philosopher, and Plato tells this story about him in the *Theaetetus*:

> Thales was studying the stars, and gazing aloft, when he fell into a well; and a witty and amusing Thracian maid made fun of him because, she said, he was so eager to know what was up in the sky, but failed to see what was in front of him and under his feet.

"The same joke," Plato says, "applies to all who spend their lives in philosophy." Plato is keenly aware that ordinary people see philosophers as ridiculous stargazers. He, of course, thinks that the joke is on ordinary people. They don't comprehend that stargazing is of much greater value than the things they desire: money, fame, pleasure, or, to take it down a notch, ice cream with friends or a night on the town.

I have spent my life in philosophy: borrowing philosophy books from the local library as a teenager, writing a doctoral thesis in the discipline, and teaching it at a university for two decades. My parents were not enthusiastic. My mother would have preferred to see me become a doctor, a lawyer, or an engineer, like my cousins. My father proposed carpentry: doing something with my hands, he hoped, would ground me in the real world. "Philosophers," he once explained to my daughter, echoing Plato, "always have their heads in the clouds." "So are birds philosophers?" my daughter wisely replied. (She was three at the time.)

More troubling, however, is that after all these years I am still in the camp of the Thracian maid. My head may be in the clouds on occasion, but I have no interest in dusting off the telescope to look at the stars. Does that mean that I'm doing it all wrong? Or is my world just so different from Plato's world that we cannot conceive philosophy in the same way? The stakes are high: if stargazing is what makes life worth living, I'm living a life that is not worthwhile.

A few years ago we took my daughter and her friends to a planetarium on her birthday. They were happily nibbling on their popcorn while the moderator explained the size, the age, and the composition of the universe, including, of course, the mysterious black holes. Then he said something about a "sense of wonder." This provoked me. Whatever wonder this picture of the universe arouses, I thought, it is certainly not what philosophers felt in the past. Had they come across black holes, they would have been terrified.

Now imagine a planetarium show moderated by Plato. We would learn about an altogether different universe: a geocentric one with a system of nestled concentric spheres carrying the stars, planets, sun, and moon around the earth. Plato would point out the amazing mathematical precision with which ancient astronomers described the orbits of stars and planets. They turn with flawless regularity, like wheels of a celestial clock: "the moving image of eternity"! On earth things are messier, he would acknowledge, but they are still very predictable: the offspring of oak trees are always oak trees, of horses, horses, of men, men. The seasons follow each other every year. And everything is perfectly coordinated: the intricate order that allows the eye to see; the organs working together to enable all kinds of living beings to thrive; earth, water, air, and fire that furnish sustaining environments for them.

Consider a random pile of driftwood, swept up on the beach. Then consider the complex mechanism of a clock. Both have causes, but the former's causes are blind and the latter's are intelligent. For Plato, the evidence was overwhelming that the universe is like a clock, not like a pile of driftwood. In fact, it is the most breathtaking piece of craftsmanship. He never even entertains the possibility that it could be the effect of blind causes. As a clock requires a clockmaker, Plato reasons, the universe requires a Maker. That Maker, he contends, is a Divine Mind, called *Nous* in Greek. "All the wise agree," Plato writes in the *Philebus*, "that *Nous* is king of heaven and earth." In short: for Plato the universe displays an intelligent designer's intelligent design. And the first to figure that out, Plato claims, was Anaxagoras.

Aristotle likewise posits *Nous*, a Divine Mind, as the cause of the universe's rational order. In his *De philosophia,* he proposes a thought experiment: imagine people who spend their lives in comfortable caves under the earth. They have never seen the natural world. One day "the jaws of the earth open," they emerge from their caves, and they are astounded by the spectacle of nature. They first see the earth, the seas, the clouds, and the winds. Then they behold the sun, the moon, the planets, and the stars — "their courses settled and immutable to all eternity." What does this spectacle teach the cave dwellers? From the universe's rationality and beauty, they immediately infer that "there are gods and these great works are the works of the gods."

The Divine Mind, according to Aristotle, does not have a body. So how does it move the heavens, he ponders in the *Metaphysics*, with no arms to push or pull? It moves them "as a beloved" (*hos eroton*), he suggests in the most poetic passage of all of his writings. Love makes the world go round. The Divine Mind is the "Unmoved Mover." Eternal circular motion is how the heavens — living, ensouled, and perfectly wise beings, for Aristotle — express their love for God and imitate his eternal and immutable existence.

We can now see why astronomy was the intellectual summit: it is a gateway to God. By studying the stars, in the ancient account, we connect to the Divine Mind, just as we connect to the mind of the clockmaker by studying the mechanics of the clock. Moreover, the heavens are moral models: they live perfectly rational lives. The more our lives resemble theirs — unerringly loving and contemplating God — the better off we are.

As we left the planetarium, I reflected on how physicists today would frown at Aristotle's claim that the desire to imitate God determines the structure of the universe. Most black holes arise from the death of stars. Love of God must be the last thing that these star tombs experience. "Holes," moreover, is an utter misnomer: they are the largest and most compact masses of matter in the universe. (The one in the 2019 photograph packs more than six billion suns.) Their gravitational pull turns them into the stuff of nightmares. They are often called "monsters" because nothing can escape them, not even light (hence their blackness). Nobody knows where things end up that pass the so-called "point of no return." Physicists call it "singularity" because at the center of black holes the known laws of physics do not apply.

If black holes cross my mind at all in day-to-day life, where the sun still rises and sets as if the Copernican revolution never happened, I chase them away with a shudder. Mostly I hope that they will not swallow the earth. They surely do not point to a Divine Architect—as the wheels in a clock point to the design in the mind of a clockmaker.

I didn't want to disturb my daughter's birthday party, so I did my best to hide the gloom that I felt in the planetarium. Her birthday cake was decorated with the solar system. The icing on my piece included fragments of Saturn's rings. "Isn't it interesting," I said to one of the parents in attendance, "that philosophers in the past saw the heavens as the most sublime expression of divine rationality?" She smiled politely but didn't reply. I'm sure that she thought I was weird. Then she turned away to chat with another parent. The heavens may have fallen silent, but in our busy everyday lives we don't care.

Plato knew that his picture of the universe was not undisputed. In the *Laws* he mentions philosophers who argue that "nature and chance," rather than "intelligent planning," explain the structure of the universe. He has in mind, among others, Leucippus and Democritus, the ancient atomists. But the strongest case for the pile-of-driftwood-view was made by the Epicureans. The Epicureans did not deny that gods exist. But why, they asked, would the gods get their hands dirty and craft a universe if they are blessedly happy, as everyone agrees they are? Instead the Epicureans posit blind causes, both mechanical and random: the weight and the natural motion of atoms moving through infinite void, and the notorious "swerve" that makes atoms deviate from their natural downward trajectory. As Lucretius explains in *On the Nature of Things*: without the "swerve," atoms "would all fall straight down through the depths of the void, like drops of rain, and no collision would occur… In that case, nature would never have produced anything." The "swerve," then, determines the universe's structure. It takes on the role that Anaxagoras, Plato, and Aristotle assigned to the Divine Mind.

Yes, we can grasp the natural order, the Epicureans reassure us. But gazing at the stars no longer connects us to God. So why bother? Because science for the Epicureans is valuable as a means: it dispels false beliefs about the gods, and about death, desire, and pleasure. After studying nature we will not be terrorized by superstitions about vindictive gods, or by wrong ideas about dying and the afterlife. Nor will we be in the grip of baseless, culturally induced desires and the disruptive passions to which they give rise: greed, envy, frustration, anger. Science, then, is still key to a happy and unperturbed life.

But if we held no false beliefs, the Epicureans insist, we would have no reason to investigate the universe: "If our suspicions about heavenly phenomena and about death did not trouble us at all … and, moreover, if not knowing the limits of pains and desires did not trouble us, then we would have no need of natural science." In line with this insouciant attitude to science, the Epicureans offer a range of different explanations to natural events — eclipses, rainbows, clouds — without trying to settle between them. Any mechanical explanation will do, as long as it does not refer to divine agency and is consistent with sense perception.

The Platonic sage gazes at the stars to get from the intelligent design to the intelligent designer. Knowledge, in this view, has *intrinsic* value. As *Nous*, God is the sum-total of knowledge. Every truth that we grasp — the nature of horses, Jupiter's orbit, the essence of justice — strengthens our bond with the divine and increases our share in the best life. The Epicurean sage gazes at the stars, by contrast, to remove the superstitions that disturb our peace of mind. Knowledge only has *instrumental* value. The link to the divine has been severed. Indeed, the Epicurean gods, whose bliss does not require dispelling falsehoods, do not possess knowledge! What joy could they get out of contemplating the random configurations of swerving atoms which make up the Epicurean universe?

The Epicureans didn't stand a chance in antiquity. The core intuition underlying the Platonic view was too powerful to be seriously challenged. The universe was like clockwork, not like driftwood. And the heavens remained the chief proof for that. Here is how the Stoics, the arch-rivals of the Epicureans, put it (in the words of Balbus, Cicero's spokesman for Stoicism in *On the Nature of the Gods*): "What can be so obvious and clear, as we gaze up at the sky and observe the heavenly bodies, as that there is some divine power of surpassing intelligence by which they are ordered?" Consider again how absurd it would be if the Nobel laureates in 2020 had made such a statement. So, then, what changed?

Max Weber described the reversal in a lecture in 1917. Stressing the "immense contrast" between science in Plato's sense and modern science, he declared:

> Who still believes that the insights of astronomy, biology, physics or chemistry can teach us something about the meaning (Sinn) of the world? ... If anything, the sciences are suited to completely eradicate the belief

> that the world is a meaningful place. And science as a path to God? Given its distinctly atheistic nature? That this is its nature nobody today will call into doubt. Deliverance from the rationalism [...] of science is the basic condition for living in community with the divine.

But how, exactly, did the reversal come about? One popular narrative pins the blame on Copernicus. The French philosopher of science Alexandre Koyré offered a classical formulation. The Copernican revolution, he explained in 1957 in *From the Closed World to the Infinite Universe,* led to

> the destruction of the Cosmos, that is, the disappearance, from philosophically and scientifically valid concepts, of the conception of the world as a finite, closed, and hierarchically ordered whole (a whole in which the hierarchy of value determined the hierarchy and structure of being, rising from the dark, heavy and imperfect earth to the higher and higher perfection of the star and heavenly spheres), and its replacement by an indefinite and even infinite universe which is bound together by the identity of its fundamental components and laws, and in which all these components are placed on the same level of being. This, in turn, implies the discarding by scientific hought of all considerations based upon value-concepts, such as perfection, harmony, meaning and aim, and finally the utter devalorization of being, the divorce of the world of value and the world of facts.

The thesis was neat and influential, but it was wrong. Yes, the clockwork-view of the universe was shaken. The heavens, as Koyré noted, ceased to be special: before Copernicus, their perfect circles around the earth were the paradigm of God's craftsmanship. After Newton, gravity ruled everything from planets to apples. The universe also got a lot more unwieldy; whatever wisdom was manifest in its structure became harder to discern. What, for example, did the Divine Mind need so much empty space for? Yet the clockwork-view wasn't anywhere close to collapsing. Newton, for one, had no doubt that God set up the laws of the new physics. And Kant, in the *Critique of Practical Reason*, still extols "the starry heavens above me" as one of two things that "fill the mind with always new and ever-growing admiration and awe, the more often and more intensely we reflect on it." (The passage was inscribed on Kant's tombstone when he died in 1804.)

But even if astronomy after Copernicus was no longer as reliable a route to the intelligent designer, biology still was. In his *Parts of the Animals*, Aristotle already noted that while plants and animals may not be as exalted as celestial bodies, they are much easier to study because "we live among them." They, too, bear witness to purposeful design — to "what is not random but for the sake of something." The "nature that crafted them provides extraordinary pleasures to philosophers who are able to know their causes." As he dissected cats and squids, Aristotle quoted Heraclitus: "for there are gods here, too."

When Hegel equated "the rational" and "the real," in his *Elements of the Philosophy of Right* in 1820, he continued to maintain the ancient belief that reality is a manifestation of the Divine Mind. He called the Divine Mind *Geist*, and, in the *Encyclopedia of the Philosophical Sciences*, he explicitly connected it to *Nous*, the deity of Plato and Aristotle. In the early nineteenth century, in other words, we were still watching God think when we grasped the universe's rational order.

The clockwork-view also persuaded the young Charles Darwin. In his *Autobiography,* he writes how much the "old argument of design in nature … charmed and convinced" him when he was a student in Cambridge. He had encountered the "watchmaker analogy" in William Paley's *Natural Theology, or Evidences of the Existence and Attributes of the Deity Collected from the Appearances of Nature*, from 1802, which was required reading for Cambridge undergraduates at the time. Even Richard Dawkins — today's noisiest atheist — admits that he would have accepted the proof from design if Darwin had not come up with the theory of evolution. But Darwin did come up with it. And once he found "the law of natural selection," Darwin writes in the *Autobiography*, the "old argument of design in nature" went down the drain: "We can no longer argue that, for instance, the beautiful hinge of a bivalve shell must have been made by an intelligent being, like the hinge of a door by man. There seems to be no more design in the variability of organic beings and in the action of natural selection, than in the course in which the wind blows."

Random causes — the mutations driving natural selection — play a key role in generating what appears like design in living beings: plants, animals, humans. If Copernicus removed divine craftsmanship from the heavens, Darwin did the same for the earth. *That* was when the pile-of-driftwood-view really came into its own. The nineteenth century, then, marks the great rupture, not the Copernican revolution and its consequences, as Koyré believed, or the new philosophies of the seventeenth century — Descartes, Spinoza, Locke — or the eighteenth-century Enlightenment.

Between Hegel and Nietzsche, God dropped out of the

philosophical picture. From a universe chiseled by a Divine Mind we move into one without metaphysical meaning. Nietzsche, in *The Gay Science*, captures the shift:

> The total character of the world is [...] in all eternity chaos — in the sense not of a lack of necessity but of a lack of order, arrangement, form, beauty, wisdom, and whatever other names there are for our aesthetic anthropomorphisms. [...] Let us beware of saying that there are laws in nature. There are only necessities: there is nobody who commands, nobody who obeys, nobody who trespasses.

Note that Nietzsche's universe remains governed by causal necessity that scientists can grasp. (Consider again the pile of driftwood: if you know the laws of physics and the particular causes at work, you can explain exactly how it came about.) What Nietzsche denied is that the universe displays the intelligent design of an intelligent designer: "order, arrangement, form, beauty, wisdom." Instead it is random — in the sense of "purposeless," not in the sense of "undetermined." The downfall of the Divine Mind, moreover, knocks down the human mind as well. Knowledge no longer forms the bond between God and man. This is what Nietzsche means when he writes "how miserable, how shadowy and transient, how aimless and arbitrary the human intellect looks within nature."

At the end of the nineteenth century, the idea gained traction that science and religion are at war with each other. Two books in particular popularized it: John William Draper's *History of the Conflict between Religion and Science*, in 1874, and Andrew Dickson White's *A History of the Warfare of Science with*

Theology in Christendom, in 1896. Galileo's trial and Christian condemnations of the theory of evolution were routinely adduced as evidence for the alleged war. This is not the place to discuss the flaws of the conflict model, which are considerable. Here I am describing something completely different: a rupture *within science* — reason turning against itself. "All the wise agree," Plato wrote, "that *Nous* is the king of heaven and earth." Following the lead of Anaxagoras, Plato, and Aristotle, biologists, physicists, and astronomers studied the structure of animals, the laws of motion, and the trajectories of the stars as the gateway to the Divine Mind. That framework was still in place in the nineteenth century. And then it fell apart. Darwin's scientific career is emblematic of the shift: it was sparked by the Platonic framework and ended up sounding the death knell for it. Today "all the wise agree" that intelligent design is outside the boundaries of science. The idea is kept alive mostly by the anti-modern resentment of the fundamentalist Christian fringe.

Did we bury the Divine Mind prematurely? After all, the greatest scientist of the twentieth century seems to agree with Plato that *Nous* governs heaven and earth. Einstein called his view of the universe "cosmic religion." To sign up, he thought, we need to accept only necessity and intelligibility: that universal laws determine everything and that the human mind can comprehend them. But that much even Nietzsche was willing to concede. Did he, unwittingly, leave a door open to bring the God of the philosophers back from the dead? Einstein speaks unforgettably of the "mysterious comprehensibility of the world," and claims to find God in "the sublimity and marvelous order which reveals itself both in nature and in the world of thought." Echoing the ancient astronomy fan club, he even celebrates the human mind's ability to "grasp the mysterious force that moves the constellations."

I am not convinced. For one thing, there is the empirical objection against Einstein's determinism: the randomness at the heart of quantum mechanics. If God doesn't play dice, quantum mechanics — which Einstein opposed to no avail throughout his life—suggests that God does not exist after all. But even if we can defend necessity and intelligibility, I don't see how, on their own, they can ground a cosmic religion. Let us grant that the pile of driftwood is completely determined and completely intelligible. That hardly implies that it is God's work. Einstein insists time and again that his God is not the personal God of traditional faith "who concerns himself with the fate and actions of human beings." Fine, but that was also true about the Divine Mind of Anaxagoras, Plato, and Aristotle. Even if God has more important things on his agenda than caring about petty human worries, there still must be an agenda that we can discern if we are to give the name "religion" to such a theism.

In his *Exhortation to Philosophy*, Aristotle proposes a thought-experiment: what would we do if we were on the "Isles of the Blessed," a place where all our material needs — hunger, thirst, shelter, health — are taken care of, so that we would not have to worry about a thing? Would the freedom that we would enjoy in such circumstances be a blessing or a curse? How would we spend all the time on our hands? Hang out idly on the beach until we die? Isn't a life without purpose a nightmare, even if it comes with every comfort?

For Aristotle, the answer is plain: if we pay money to watch sports and theater, he argues, all the more should we be keen to contemplate the rational order of the universe. It is the best show on offer, and it's free. On the Isles of the Blessed we would devote our life to *theoria*, or contemplation. That is Aristotle's idea of paradise. It is easy to see the attraction of such a paradise if the universe is like a clock. But what if it is like a pile of driftwood? Even if it is in principle intelligible, why make the effort? What sublimity would we be contemplating? The obvious answer is the one the Epicureans give: knowledge may not have intrinsic value, but it has great instrumental benefits. It is good as a means to other things that we value: controlling nature, finding medical treatments, developing technologies, grounding good social policies, resisting ideologies, fake news, and the lies of demagogues.

Unfortunately, things aren't quite so simple. We may cheer science for making our lives safer, more comfortable, and less vulnerable to decay and manipulation. In this sense, modern science is arguably a stunning success. But there is an existential price to pay. Let me explain.

After my children were born, my wife and I started to compile photo albums. I have no illusions about them. They are kitsch, as the four of us cry "cheese" for the camera. But they are dear to me anyway, because they are documents of what has become the emotional center of my life. The meaning of photo albums is a paradox: they are treasured by the people whose happy memories they hold, but utterly meaningless to the rest of the world. Would you ever display your neighbor's photo album on the coffee table? The paradox tells us something: that the meaning our children have for us is distorted, or rather created, by love.

If I were to take such an explanation to an evolutionary psychologist, he would thoroughly disenchant its emphasis on love. He would explain that what I call "love" is actually an attachment that evolution has selected for, because it increases the chances of my offspring's survival and thereby of the perpetuation of my genes. Do I want to know this? I feel conflicted. I have no doubt that there is a basis in biological reality for the evolutionist's disenchanting account. And in general I am all for scientific progress. But in my personal life? There, I feel, I must protect the magic from the truth. Is it anti-intellectual or irrational to draw boundaries around the explanatory power of science in our understanding of our inner lives? Or can we, whatever the impact of our genes upon our inner lives, carve out a space for a different — yet likewise legitimate — way to understand love?

The same wish for protection from the idea that science should have the last word grows exponentially when I consider the universe at large. In this instance I seek protection not from biology but from astronomy and astrophysics. I cannot detect evidence in the cosmos of divine craftsmanship. I see a vast, mute, dark, mostly empty space that burst into existence fourteen billion years ago, where I spend a short time on a small planet in one of countless galaxies, living a life of no cosmic consequence. That life, moreover, emerged from the primordial soup by means of amoebae, apes, and all the chance encounters of my ancestors.

Contemplating the universe in this way is a powerful antidote for vanity; and so, to keep myself honest, I look up to the heavens once in a while, briefly, from the corner of my eye. Yet its lesson of humility notwithstanding, what I see in the night sky or through a telescope cannot give my life value and purpose. On the contrary, it threatens to obliterate my mortal and terrestrial reasons for getting out of bed in the morning: family, friends, writing, teaching, a cup of coffee, a glass of wine, a concert, a noble cause. From the cosmic perspective, my goals and my projects seem trivial and pointless. If I want to hold on to what gives my life meaning, therefore, I must shield myself from the universe rather than contemplate it — the exact opposite of what for Plato yields "the most excellent life." The cosmos as we now understand it is no longer useful for my soul.

But is the universe not reasserting, at this very moment, its power to dazzle people around the globe, as the James Webb telescope reveals it to us in ways we had never seen it before? Who is not amazed by the spectacular pictures of galaxies dancing and cartwheeling, stars glimmering like jewels in the dark, or Jupiter and Neptune's enigmatic glow? There is beauty in the light, shapes, and colors. There is mystery as we look at cosmic landscapes such as the "Pillars of Creation" or cosmic cliffs such as the "Carina Nebula" — structures unimaginably far away in place and time. We have no clue what happens in them (or happened in times immemorial). Yes, the pictures may even inspire awe — a secular awe — if we let them pull us out of our human-all-too-human concerns and dare to lose ourselves for a moment in the universe's vast expanse.

But what are we to make of these emotions that quickly fade as we return to our daily lives and our (by cosmic standards) trifling worries, joys, and sorrows? If the Webb telescope does not point to an intelligent designer (or at least the possibility of one), does it point to something meaningful at all? The mystery that we experience is not religious, as when we recoil in the face of an inscrutable divine will, manifest in the universe's design. The mystery reflects, to put it bluntly, our ignorance. The more that ignorance is lifted — through even more powerful telescopes, new forms of space travel, and so on — the more intelligible the universe becomes. But intelligibility, as Nietzsche stressed, does not translate into meaningfulness. The universe we glimpse through the Webb telescope may be visually mesmerizing, but unlike Plato's universe it cannot provide us with a purpose in life.

Plato thought that studying the stars can replace the things that we commonly desire with something much better. If stargazing could lift us out of our mortal existence and put us in touch with something eternal and divine, there would be nothing ridiculous about it, no matter how much a Thracian maid may giggle. But if the stars are not a springboard to the divine, then staring at them for too long risks leaving us with nothing to care for at all. In a universe punctured by black holes, the Thracian maid may have the last laugh.

DAPHNE MERKIN

Frau Freud

In memory of Michael Porder

I

September 29, 1939, 20 Maresfeld Gardens, Hampstead, London: on the first Friday after Sigmund Freud's death, having accepted more than a half-century's imposed impiety at her husband's insistence, the seventy-eight year old Martha Freud started to light the Sabbath candles again. *Licht-bentshn,* as the ceremony is called. You light a pair of candles just as the sun goes down; circle your hands in a sweeping motion three times to gather the light and savor the candles' warmth — the spirit of restfulness that they are meant to convey — and then you cover your eyes with your hands while reciting the blessing in which God is thanked for sanctifying us with the commandment to light these candles.

Enter Shabbat the Queen, as the Sabbath is known in Jewish tradition, a presiding feminine presence in a patriarchal environment where most of the active, time-specific commandments, such as the wearing of *tefillin* or phylacteries (a pair of small black leather cubes, containing pieces of parchment inscribed with Biblical verses, one of which is strapped around the left arm, hand, and fingers and the other is strapped above the forehead) for the morning prayers, fall on men, since women are presumed to be busy with other priorities, such as housekeeping and childcare. And now here was the widow of one of the most formidable enemies of religion fulfilling one of the few obligations incumbent upon women under Jewish law. It was, surely, a form of poetic justice — or perhaps a testament to the hold of the past, however abjured it may be.

She was born Martha Bernays on July 26, 1881 in the German port city of Hamburg, into a highly regarded and intellectually advanced Jewish family to whom such recurrent observances meant a great deal. With her performance of the act of lighting candles at a prescribed moment on the Jewish calendar, one might argue that Martha Freud was being more than assertive: she was being defiant. In doing so, she was re-establishing her autonomy by renouncing a pattern of submission to her husband's wishes. She was taking a deliberate step backward, toward her family ethos and the traditionalism of her origins before she became the compliant, devoted caretaker that Freud desired her to be, the "adored sweetheart in youth" who became "the beloved wife in maturity." And she was also taking a step forward, towards the post-spousal woman she would become after the death of her husband, and reclaiming a small part of the ancient ritual-laden religious tradition that had been instilled in her while growing up.

It was a tradition that her fiercely anti-clerical husband, whom she always referred to as "Professor," as though she were his eternal student, ridiculed, forbidding her to light the Sabbath candles when they set up their own home. A cousin of Martha's once recalled "how not being allowed to light the Sabbath lights on the first Friday night after her marriage was one of the most upsetting experiences of her life." And Isaiah Berlin, who visited the couple at their house in exile in London, recalled that husband and wife were still arguing the issue of lighting candles, however playfully, as late as 1938: "Martha joked at Freud's monstrous stubbornness which prevented her from performing the ritual, while he firmly maintained the practice was foolish and superstitious."

The Freuds' fifty-three years of marriage are reputed to have been exceptionally harmonious — one of their few disputes was said to have been about the correct way to cook mushrooms — but the couple's divergent attitudes toward Judaism remained a source of underground conflict. On the face of it, they were wholly deracinated Jews in a golden age of Jewish deracination. They celebrated Christmas and Easter, and their son Martin, in his memoir *Sigmund Freud: Man and Father,* testified that none of the six children had ever entered a synagogue. Freud, a confirmed atheist whose work was dedicated in part to the debunking of the monotheistic worldview as a neurotic illusion, delighted in ribbing Martha about her religious attachment, pretending not to know the Hebrew name for "candelabrum," for example, in a note he wrote her in 1907 after visiting the Roman catacombs: "In the Jewish [catacombs] the inscriptions are Greek, the candelabrum — I think it's called Menorah — can be seen on many tablets."

As if he didn't know that it was called a menorah! He had learned the Bible as a child, after all, and it is doubtful that he lost his grasp of basic Hebrew or religious objects. Freud never denied his Jewishness, and went so far as to credit his religion for his own lack of prejudice and his uncowed single-mindedness. Yet he was always highly ambivalent about his Jewish identity. He demanded that Martha not fast on Yom Kippur, arguing that she was too thin to fast, and the only one of his books in which he referred overtly to his Jewish connection was *Moses and Monotheism*.

In this regard he maintained a firm distance between his public and private allegiance — insisting, for instance, that psychoanalysis was not in any way a "Jewish science," or *judische Wissenschaft*, which is how the Nazis and earlier anti-Semites had disparaged it. In a letter to Ferenczi, Freud wrote that "there should not be such a thing as an Aryan or Jewish science. Results in science must be identical, though the presentation of them may vary." His awareness of the danger in having a specifically Jewish quality attached to his work, which could lead to antisemitic resistance to the psychoanalytic movement and render it less universally applicable, led him to court the Swiss psychiatrist Carl Gustav Jung, despite Jung's very different ideas about psychoanalysis — and more curiously, despite Jung's own anti-Semitism and racial theories. Freud put all his hopes into Jung, whom he called his "son and heir," until they had a disagreement about the uses of mythology which led to a permanent estrangement.

Yet the story of Freud's Jewishness, the myth of his complete alienation from his patrimony, which is based largely on his non-observance of even the most fundamental of Jewish rituals, is more complicated than has been implied in most of the writing about him. (This misapprehension about Freud's complete ignorance of Judaism was recently invoked yet again in Adam Kirsch's essay "Freud as Talmudist" in the *Jewish Review of Books).* In contrast to the general image of Freud as an *am ha'aretz,* an ignoramus, severed from his Jewish roots, we have a letter that he wrote to the chief rabbi of Vienna in 1931, for example, in which he passionately declared: "I am a fanatical Jew. I am very much astonished to discover myself as such in spite of all the efforts to be unprejudiced and impartial." And more fully a few years earlier, in 1926, accepting an award from the Bnai Brith on his seventieth birthday, he told his audience in a letter that he had joined Bnai Brith because

> I myself was a Jew, and it always seemed to me to be not only shameful but downright senseless to deny it. That which bound me to Judaism—I am obliged to admit it—was not my faith, nor was it national pride; for I was always an unbeliever, raised without religion, although not without respect for the so-called "ethical" demands of human civilization. And I always tried to suppress nationalistic ardor, whenever I felt any inclination thereto, as something pernicious and unjust, frightened as I was by the warning example of the peoples among whom we Jews live. But there remained enough other things to make the attraction of Judaism and Jews irresistible—many dark emotional forces, all the more potent for being so hard to grasp in words, as well as the clear consciousness of an inner identity, the intimacy *(die Heimlichkeit)* that comes from the same psychic structure. And to that was soon added the insight that it was my Jewish nature alone that I had to thank for two characteristics that proved indispensable to me in my

> life's difficult course. Because I was a Jew I found myself free from many prejudices that hampered others in the use of their intellects; and as a Jew I was prepared to take my place on the side of the opposition and renounce being on good terms with the "compact majority."

"Raised without religion"? Hardly. A complicated case, clearly.

To better understand the Freuds' respective positions on Judaism, one need look no further than their individual backgrounds. "I was born on the 6th of May [18]56 in Freiberg/Moravia," Freud wrote in a letter to his colleague Paul Federn in 1912. "My father and mother came from Galicia. My mother, née Nathansohn, from Brody, of very distinguished ancestry (the Nathansohn-Kallir family), my father of the merchant class. According to tradition, as he once reported to me, the Freud family is said to sometime have left their hometown of Köln [Cologne] during a period of persecution of Jews and then to have migrated eastward."

Throughout his lifetime, Freud, who was born Sigismund Schlomo Freud, went to great lengths to portray himself as having grown up in a deeply assimilated Reform Jewish family, steeped in modernist values and Viennese culture. (His family moved to Vienna when he was four.) It was a family, or so he led his colleagues and relatives to believe, in which Jewish holidays were minimally observed, and his own religious education was scanty, leaving him with but the vaguest understanding of Hebrew or Yiddish. A large part of our idea of Freud as a "godless Jew" — the term coined by the historian

Peter Gay, himself an assimilated Jew who translated his last name from "Froelich" to "Gay" after becoming an American citizen and wrote extensively about Freud — derives from Gay's insistence that Enlightenment values had completely displaced religious and ethnic ones. (This was consistent with Gay's simplistic view of the Enlightenment itself.) Gay's description of Freud's father Jakob's position on Jewish matters shows how the notion of total secularization was absorbed unquestioningly by Freud scholars: "Jacob Freud had emancipated himself from the Hasidic practices of his ancestors; his marriage to Amalia Nathanson [his second wife and Freud's mother] was consecrated in a Reform ceremony. In time, he discarded virtually all religious observances...."

It is worth pointing out that ritual observance is hardly the only measure of Jewishness. The truth about Jakob Freud's relationship to his religious background is richer, as was his son's. The father, too, was a complicated case. The Freud family consisted of transplanted Eastern European Orthodox Jews — *Ostjuden*, or Eastern Jews, looked upon with disdain as primitive and uneducated by German and Austrian Jews — who were only slightly assimilated, if at all. According to Emanuel Rice, a psychiatrist who closely examined this subject in his book *Freud and Moses: The Long Journey Home,* Jakob had studied for years in a yeshiva in Tysmenitz, Galicia and was referred to in his youth as a "*yeshiva bocher,*" a yeshiva student. Rice also cites a granddaughter of Jakob's who lived with him toward the end of his life and remembered him "reading the Talmud (in the original) at home." If that is so, then Jacob possessed a considerable degree of Jewish literacy and cultivation.

Then there is the famous and much debated issue of the Phillippson family Bible — a German translation of the

Tanakh — that Jakob gave his son on his thirty-fifth birthday, with an inscription in Hebrew that included a skillful pastiche of ancient quotations composed in the traditional manner, drawn from various Jewish sources. The inscription — "To my dear son Shlomo" — is written in a hand that is clearly comfortable with writing Hebrew. Although this dedication has been parsed by *hoch* analysts who assumed that Freud could not read Hebrew (an impression fueled by Freud himself), scholars such as Rice and Yosef Hayim Yerushalmi, in his *Freud's Moses: Judaism Terminable and Interminable*, have shown that Freud had a considerable Jewish education and would have understood the inscription. (And indeed, one might ask, why would his father have inscribed such an important gift in a language that his son could not read?) Similarly, Freud's insistence that he could not understand Yiddish — the "jargon" of the Ostjuden — is dubious, because his mother Amalia regularly spoke Yiddish. In addition to which, Rice argues, based on the testimony of one of Freud's grandsons, Sigmund's mother remained religiously observant until her death in 1930. This would go some way to explaining why Freud arranged for his mother to have a strictly Orthodox funeral and burial — although it would not explain why he chose not to attend it, sending his daughter Anna in his stead.

Martha Bernays' background, on the other hand, was indubitably Orthodox (*"frum wie ein Stecken,"* or "religious as a stick," as my mother, an observant German Jew, used to say), one in which hidebound observances were scrupulously maintained. Her mother, Emmeline, wore a *sheitl,* or wig, which was required by the rabbinical tradition to preserve the modesty of married Jewish women, and kept a strictly kosher house. Hers was a tenacious and domineering personality, though outwardly she came across as mild and soft. These traits would antagonize her future son-law; he described her as "alien" and wrote his fiancée that "I seek for similarities with you, but find hardly any." (At the same time he conceded that Emmeline was "a person of great mental and moral power standing in our midst, capable of high accomplishments, without a trace of the absurd weaknesses of old women.")

Martha's family was renowned in the Jewish community for their scholarship and their leadership. Isaac Bernays, her grandfather, was the chief rabbi of Hamburg in the 1830s and 1840s, and was respected for his combination of secular and religious knowledge, expressed in his sophisticated philosophical views, his linguistic skills, and his superior grasp of Torah, Midrash, and Talmud. He was a distant relative of Heinrich Heine; he appears often in Heine's letters, and upon his death in 1849 he was acknowledged by Heine to have been an extraordinary personality. Bernays served in this important pulpit in the early years of the Reform movement and opposed it bitterly, formulating in response an approach in which it was possible to live, with certain limits, in both the religious and secular worlds. Bernays' conception greatly influenced his student Samson Raphael Hirsch, the rabbi and theologian who provided Modern Orthodoxy with its guiding principle of *Torah Im Derech Eretz,* or Torah and the way of the world. (Hirsch was my great-great-grandfather.)

Despite Bernays' strict commitment to Orthodoxy, he was also considered to be something of a religious modernizer, known for his innovative sermons given in German, and for bringing secular subjects — German, natural science, geography, and history — into the curriculum of the Talmud Torah charity school, which had formerly been limited to Hebrew and arithmetic. Hirsch and Bernays became acquainted when Bernays, after attending the University of Wurzberg and studying at the yeshiva of Rabbi Abraham Bing, the chief rabbi of Wurzburg and a well-known Talmudist, became a private tutor in the house of Hirsch's father. Hirsch followed Bernays' practice of fusing the Jewish and secular realms with the hope of keeping the tidal wave of Reform Judaism at bay. (Family lore has it that at the Hirsch school in Frankfurt boys did not wear yarmulkes during secular classes.)

Two of Bernays' sons were university professors. The eldest, Jacob, was a prominent philologist and classicist, a man of prodigious learning who was one of the pioneers of *Quellenforschungen,* or source criticism, according to which the primary method of classical studies was the intense study of the surviving texts of the ancient world for the purpose of coaxing from them knowledge of all that did not survive. He was famous for a controversial interpretation of Aristotle's concept of catharsis, which he read not in moral terms but in medical ones — thereby making himself a kind of precursor to Freud's own approach to the subject. His adherence to Jewish religious convictions prevented him from becoming a full professor at the University of Bonn, and so in 1853 he helped to found the Breslau Jewish Theological Seminary, which became one of the great institutions of modern Jewish scholarship. There he taught classics, history, German literature, and Jewish philosophy. In 1866 Jacob was finally appointed an assistant professor and chief librarian at Bonn, but he remained involved with the seminary at Breslau. His younger son, Michael, was a Goethe and Shakespeare specialist who was professor of German literature at the University of Munich. He converted to Christianity (as did Isaac Bernays' brother Adolphus) in 1856 and was baptized, which led his family to break with him at the same time as it furthered his career.

Isaac's other son, Berman Bernays — Martha's father — was a merchant, as were the parents of his wife; Berman later became secretary to the well-known economist and constitutional law expert Lorenz von Stein, a great liberal who may have been the earliest theorist of the welfare state. When Emmeline (née Philipp) married him in 1886, his profession was given as "journalist." One of four children (three older ones died in quick succession), Martha was born in 1881 and grew up in Hamburg in fairly modest circumstances. When she was six years old, her father served a stint in prison for bankruptcy; she is said never to have spoken of this incident. Freud's uncle, meanwhile, was imprisoned for trading in counterfeit rubles and rumor had it that his father was implicated in the scandal. The writer Jenny Diski suggested, in a review of a biography of Martha Freud by Katya Behling, that Martha and Sigmund were united by a shared legacy of public shame.

Martha's family moved to Vienna when she was eight, but she, as well as her mother and sister Minna, never lost their attachment to Hamburg. "Neither she nor Minna ever made the slightest concession to the spirit and lifestyle of Vienna," Behling observes in her biography, "and even after fifty years in Austria they still spoke perfect standard German." To refuse the spirit of Vienna was to live the life of a stubborn traditionalist. One of Martha's two elder brothers, Isaac, died at the age of sixteen, when she was eleven. (This was another loss that she shared with Freud, who also had a brother who died at a young age.) It is worth noting that these extraordinary lineages lasted more than one generation: Freud's sister Anna married Martha's brother Eli, and not long after they moved to the United States their son Edward Bernays was born, who, with his pioneering studies of public opinion and its manipulation, became the father of press relations, mass marketing, and psychological warfare — in other words, a formidable shaper of modern life.

II

Despite being portrayed in later years as intellectually indifferent (in particular to her husband's theories), the young Martha developed an interest in art and literature during her years at school. She had a keen appreciation of music and was an avid reader who knew the German classics (Goethe, Schiller, and so on); she had a special fondness for Stephan Zweig and Thomas Mann. Although the time she could allocate to reading was severely cut back during the busy years of her marriage, running a large household according to her high standards, she would return to her love of books after her husband's death. During their courtship, Martha frequently wrote Freud letters in verse, and he shared his thoughts on John Stuart Mill with her. His first present to her was a copy of *David Copperfield* — Dickens became of one Martha's favorite writers — although he warned her off the rude parts in *Don Quixote*, stating that they were "no reading matter for girls." By the time he met Martha in April 1882, her sharp mind, slim and attractive figure, and coquettish charms had attracted many suitors. She had already turned down one proposal of marriage.

The first time Sigmund Freud spotted the almost twenty-one-year-old Martha Bernays was at his family's dining table; she was visiting his sisters together with her sister Minna. Martha was peeling an apple during their conversation: a decorous feminine activity, suggestive of industriousness and nurturing. The twenty-six-year-old Freud was an anxious, somewhat self-important medical student with next to no experience of women, despite being the favored brother of five sisters and his mother's *goldener Sigi*, who was given a room of his own in his family's small apartment. One wonders whether things might have gone differently if he had glimpsed Martha in a different guise, less the domestic woman in a genre painting and more like her sister Minna, eager to compete intellectually and inclined by nature to take up more air. "Since I learned that the first sight of a little girl sitting at a well-known long table talking so cleverly while peeling an apple with her delicate fingers, could disconcert me so lastingly," Freud wrote to Martha in June, 1885, "I have actually become quite suspicious."

In any case, the young Martha presented a winsome picture, with her hair worn in a center part and pulled back in a chignon, elegantly clad in a high-necked dress with a lace collar and lace-up ankle boots. Soon, although rather awkward and shy, Freud was sure of his feelings for Martha and began calling her "Princess" and sending her a red rose every day accompanied by a poem in Latin or another foreign language. By the middle of June in 1882, a mere two months after they met, the couple was secretly engaged despite Emmeline's opposition to the match — she considered Freud's financial prospects to be dim. Freud began writing his "darling girl" and "darling Marty" long rhapsodic letters over the next four and a half years of their engagement — the famous *brautbriefe*, as their correspondence came to be called. It was only after Martha's eldest brother Eli became engaged to Freud's sister Anna on Christmas in 1882 that the couple felt comfortable in announcing their own engagement, although Freud never officially asked for Martha's hand in marriage. In Freud's first fervent letter to her, he wrote, "Dear Martha, how you have changed my life"; but he was also an incorrigibly jealous suitor, expressing absurdly patriarchal horror that his fiancée had travelled on holiday with only her younger sister for company: "Fancy, Lubeck! Should that be allowed? Two single girls travelling alone in North Germany! This is a revolt against the male prerogative!"

Sigmund would later tell Martha that theirs was an instance of *leibe am ersten blick*, love at first sight, although it is unclear whether this was wholly mutual; Martha appears to have warmed up a bit more gradually. He would go on to observe to her in one of the nine hundred and forty letters that he wrote to her during the four-and-a-half years of their courtship and engagement (they also collaborated on a secret journal, a *Geheime Chronik*) that she was not "in the strict painterly sense" a beauty, but that she had qualities he considered more important, such as generosity, wisdom, and tenderness. One wonders what his fiancée, a young woman just coming into a sense of her attractiveness to the opposite sex, made of this faint praise. (Freud's own mother had been considered a great beauty in her day and the appeal of female comeliness was never lost on him.)

During the period in which he experimented with cocaine, Freud, worried about her pallor, sent Martha a small dose to put color in her cheeks, and referred jauntily to the disinhibiting effect that cocaine had on him. "Woe to you, my princess, when I come," he wrote to her on June 2, 1884. "I will kiss you quite red and feed you till you are plump. And if you are forward you shall see who is the stronger, a gentle little girl who doesn't eat enough or a big wild man who has cocaine in his body." On February 2, 1886, toward the end of another letter, he wrote: "Here I am, making silly confessions to you, my sweet darling, and really without any reason whatever unless it is the cocaine that makes me talk so much."

"I was told," writes Sophie Freud, Martha's daughter-in-law, in her *memoir Living in the Shadow of the Freud Family,* "that her greatest attraction for the young Sigmund Freud had not been her slender grace or charming features but her inner peace and serenity. She radiated calmness; and he sensed instinctively how wonderful it would be to have her near him after a day of hard work." As for the scrutinizing suitor himself, Freud had good features, a thick beard and a penetrating gaze, but it seems that Martha initially found him too short and a bit intimidating.

It is difficult to cobble together an image of the pre-Freud Martha Bernays because we have few accounts of her before he enters the picture (and not many more after). From the few impressions that have been documented, she seems to have been both self-contained and curious, a dutiful daughter who retained some independence of mind. She loved to read whenever she found the time, went to plays, and was a demon for needlework of all kinds. Most of all, Martha was marked by the North German sense of discipline, by a horror of shoddiness and leaving things half-done. Her daughter Anna would later observe to her own biographer, Elizabeth Young-Breuhl, that "my mother observed no rules, she made her own rules."

Although there were those, such as his brilliant Hungarian disciple Sandor Ferenczi (whom Freud eventually broke with as he did with so many of his followers), who contended that Freud's unresolved connection to his narcissistically controlling mother Amalia left him with a fear of intimacy and of sexually passionate women in particular, it seems that, at least at the beginning of their involvement, Freud couldn't get enough of his "deeply beloved, most ardently worshipped Martha," as he described her in 1882. As long, that is, as she lived up to the very particular image that he had of a desirable mate. During the course of their epic engagement, undoubtedly fed by Freud's anxiety as to whether Martha loved him with the same ardor that he loved her (Martha was by nature more reticent) and by his fiercely suspicious nature, Freud bullied her into becoming more of the docile and governable woman he was seeking. Despite maintaining that he did not want her to be a malleable toy doll, he sneered at her efforts to put her foot down and openly disliked what he called her "tartness."

Somewhere along the way it seems that Martha lost some of her moxie — her unfettered and even feisty spirit. One can see a glimpse of that spirit still peeking through late in their engagement, when she wrote Freud in irritation: "You now always only write once about each thing, and then nothing more however much I ask. I'm not used to this, my good man, it is certainly high time I brought you to heel, otherwise I'm quite sure to go completely thin and green for sheer annoyance and exasperation." But by this time Martha could not have been left in any doubt as to precisely what it was that her husband-to-be expected in his partner: a certain docility, and clear and separate spheres of influence. "I will let you rule [the household] as much as you wish," he decreed, "and you will reward me with your intimate love and by rising above all those weaknesses that make for a contemptuous judgment of women." Perhaps in keeping with Martha's understanding that her fiancée wanted to remake her into a more subservient personality, some of her letters show her posing as an intellectual innocent in need of Freud's assistance: "I finally have read your postcard with Max's help because it was difficult to read.

Yes, that's how stupid your dear girl is."

The critic Frederick Crews, a disenchanted Freudian and ardent enemy of psychoanalysis, all the same wrote perceptively about the Svengali-like attitude toward Martha that hovered right beneath Freud's almost fulsome expressions of adoration. "When he wasn't complaining about his present aliments and future neglect," Crews observed in *Freud: The Making of an Illusion,*

> the unhappy fiancé was instructing his beloved in how to become a properly deferential mate. He made it clear that she would have to change some of her ways, and the sooner the better. It was precisely Martha's most admirable qualities — unself-conscious candor and spontaneity, a trusting nature, freedom from class prejudice, loyalty to her family and its values — that struck him as in need of revision. Thus he rebuked her for having pulled up a stocking in public; forbade her to go ice skating if another man were along; demanded that she sever relations with a good friend who had gotten pregnant before marriage; and vowed to crush every vestige of her Orthodox faith and to turn her into a fellow infidel.

Although Crews is focusing here exclusively on the dictatorial aspect of Freud's attitude toward his future wife, it is nonetheless a fairly accurate and unattractive picture — conventionally masculine for its time, perhaps, but especially disappointing in one of the great free-thinking apostles of modernity.

III

How did the Freuds' marriage negotiate the age-old problem of combining sexual passion with enduring love? Is there evidence in Freud's writings of his view of the institution of marriage, and of the possibility of lasting erotic attraction? And how confidently can we infer from his "scientific" remarks on conjugal life to the character of his own marriage?

There is not much to go on. Curiously enough, the index of the *Standard Edition of the Complete Psychological Works of Sigmund Freud*, the Strachey edition, has no entry for "wife" and only a smattering of references under "marriage." Still, he famously wrote about the disjunction between romantic affection and carnal desire in 1912, in a paper titled "The Most Prevalent Form of Degradation in Erotic Life," a psychoanalytic exploration of what we call the Madonna-Whore Complex, in which he observed that "where such men love, they do not desire, and where they desire, they cannot love."

Freud attempted to explain this phenomenon by looking to the restrictive cultural mores of his time and the inhibition on both men and women to delay sexual engagement well beyond the age of maturational readiness — "the long period of delay between sexual maturity and sexual activity which is demanded by education for social reasons," which resulted in a "lack of union between tenderness and sensuality." He went on:

> In very few people are the two strains of tenderness and sensuality duly fused into one; the man almost always feels his sexual activity hampered by his respect for the woman and only develops full sexual potency when he finds himself in the presence of od a lower type of sexual object; and this again is partly conditioned by

> the circumstance that his sexual aims include those of perverse sexual components, which he does not like to gratify with a woman he respects. Full sexual satisfaction only comes when he can give himself up wholeheartedly to enjoyment, which with his well-brought-up wife, for instance, he does not venture to do. Hence comes his need for a less exalted sexual object, a woman ethically inferior, to whom he need ascribe no aesthetic misgivings, and who does not know the rest of his life and cannot criticize him.

Freud's own marriage was conspicuously de-romanticized and then rather quickly desexualized after its emotionally impassioned beginning; the letters, which include overt references to erotic longings on both sides, seem to confirm the fatalistic analysis of conjugal love and desire in his paper. Although Ernest Jones, Freud's British colleague and hagiographic biographer, deemed this vast collection of correspondence "a not unworthy contribution to the great love literature of the world," the analyst Martin Bergmann once quipped: "We have wonderful courting letters before marriage. After marriage we only get laundry letters. It's all practical. We don't have a single love letter after marriage."

In an earlier paper, from 1908, called "'Civilized' Sexual Morality and Modern Nervous Illness," Freud provided a larger framework, a civilizational framework, for his dour view of marital life, in which he presented a somewhat disheartening view of the damage to intimate relations that is inflicted by the process of socialization that humans must go through in order to co-exist peacefully with others. "Experience teaches us," he observed, "that for most people there is a limit beyond which their constitution cannot comply with the demands of civilization. All who wish to be more noble-minded than their constitution allows fall victim to neurosis; they would have been more healthy if it could have been possible for them to be less good." And so he asks "whether sexual intercourse in legal marriage can offer full compensation for the restrictions imposed before marriage." And he answers:

> There is such an abundance of material supporting a reply in the negative that we can give only the briefest summary of it. It must above all be borne in mind that our cultural sexual morality restricts sexual intercourse even in marriage itself, since it imposes on married couples the necessity of contenting themselves, as a rule, with a very few procreative acts. As a consequence of this consideration, satisfying sexual intercourse in marriage takes place only for a few years; and we must subtract from this, of course, the intervals of abstention necessitated by regard for the wife's health. After three, four, or five years the marriage becomes a failure insofar as it has promised the satisfaction of sexual needs....The spiritual disillusionment and bodily deprivation to which most marriages are thus doomed puts both partners back in the state they were in before their marriage, except for being the poorer by the loss of an illusion, and they must once more have recourse to their fortitude in mastering and deflecting their sexual instinct....Women, when they are subjected to the disillusionments of marriage, fall ill of severe neuroses which permanently darken their lives....A girl must be very healthy to tolerate it, and we urgently advise our male patients not to marry any girl who has had nervous trouble before marriage.

Many critical points could be made about the dark conjectures that Freud offers in this paper, which seem to be based more on personal experience than on scientific findings or cultural observations. Why, for instance, must married couples content themselves "with a very few procreative acts," unless one believes that the sole purpose of sexual intercourse is procreation? What about sexual pleasure, a subject about which Freud extensively theorized? And his hypotheses about women's fragility when faced with "the disillusionments of marriage" seem both ill-conceived and misogynistic — a blinkered attempt to understand female sexuality, which he regarded as murky and mysterious, in keeping with his idea of women as the "dark continent."

In any event, Martha and Sigmund were married on September 13, 1886 in Hamburg. Frau Bernays became Frau Freud; she was twenty-five and he was thirty. Since a civil wedding on its own was not officially recognized at that time in Austria, the couple had to marry a second time under a *chuppah* with full Jewish ritual, despite Freud's annoyance. The ceremony included the groom giving the bride a ring as well as crushing a glass underfoot in remembrance of the destruction of the Temple in Jerusalem — a memory of sadness in the midst of happiness, which in other contexts was a dissonance that Freud often studied.

Freud seemed to have felt abandoned within minutes of casting in his lot with Martha. "Once one is married," he opined, "one no longer — in most cases — lives for each other as one used to. One lives rather with each other for some third thing, and for the husband dangerous rivals soon appear: household and nursery." He added that, "despite all love and unity, the help each person had found in the other ceases. The husband looks again for friends, frequents an inn, finds general outside interests." Hardly a chipper forecast for what lay ahead, but then Freud, despite his inner reserves of strength, was often the one who expressed anxiety. The task of reassurance fell to the unflappable Martha, who learned how to soothe him.

The union produced six children in nine years, by which point Martha was thirty-four. After three children had been born, the family moved to Berggasse 19, near the university quarter in Vienna, where their apartment occupied an entire floor but was rather small and dark. Martha, who was in charge of their finances, set about looking after her new husband with the utmost attention and care for both his appearance and his comfort. She laid out and brushed his clothes for him — which were, as Martin, Freud's eldest son, reported in his reminiscences, "cut from the best material and tailored to perfection." It was said that such was the diligent nature of her caretaking that she put the toothpaste on his toothbrush.

While her husband worked up to sixteen and even eighteen hours a day, Martha, carried around an enormous bunch of keys, the better to oversee a household that included, despite the family's relative lack of money, a cook, a governess, two nannies, and a chambermaid. She ran the large family's schedule like a well-oiled machine. Lunch was served promptly at one o'clock every day, a formal meal often featuring *tafelsptiz* or *Rindfleisch,* boiled beef and vegetables, with a horseradish sauce, a favorite of Freud's. Sophie Freud, Martin's daughter, recalled in a memoir that Martha maintained impeccable standards: "At each meal Mrs. Freud has a pitcher of hot water and a special napkin at her place, so that if anybody made a spot on the tablecloth she could hurry to remove it. Only her husband was permitted to make as many spots as he wished." Dinner was at seven, after which Freud usually worked until midnight.

The children, who were Martha's domain when young although of keen interest to their father as they grew older, seem to have been suitably well-behaved, their parents having instilled in them the importance of their father's work. As Martin recalled, "There was never any waiting for meals: at the stroke of one everybody in the household was seated at the long dining-room table and the same moment one door opened to let the maid enter with the soup while another door opened to allow my father to walk from his study to take his place at the head of the table at the other end."

Jenny Diski, in her review of Behling's biography, observed that the exemplary bourgeois surface that Martha helped to provide — "the rigid table manners, ordered nursery, and bustling regularity" — enabled her husband to organize his "deeper, hardly thinkable thoughts" into "something that looked like a scientific theory." By polishing that surface and keeping the clocks ticking in unison, Diski grandly concluded, "Martha was as essential to the development of Freudian thought as Dora or the Rat Man." This may have a grain of truth to it, in the logistical sense that an orderly environment allowed Freud to concentrate on his work, but it strikes me all the same as something of an exaggeration — as though Mrs. Einstein were to be credited with facilitating her husband's ideas about energy and mass.

The simple truth is that Freud never had any plans for Martha to be an intellectual partner or to participate in his intellectual life in any way. He was happy for her to take care of his every need and to view him as the genius of his age, the equal of Newton or Darwin, just as she was happy to call herself Frau Professor after Freud was given his title in 1902. Although he seems to have initially been drawn to Martha's cultural sophistication, Freud quickly felt the need to downplay her braininess, a demotion in which she willingly acquiesced. Early in their engagement he referred condescendingly to "the charming confusion in your dear sentences." In his memoir Martin Freud recalls that when his parents had distinguished visitors over for dinner and a learned guest began to recite from *The Iliad,* Martha had already departed the premises. "My mother," Martin writes, "who knew no Greek and, in consequence, was without any admiration for Homer's immortal epic, had quietly withdrawn earlier."

Then, too, there was the slight puzzlement that she expressed at her husband's choice of profession, as though his high-flying speculations were beyond her ken. "I must admit," she said, "that if I did not realize how seriously my husband takes his treatments, I should think that psychoanalysis is a form of pornography." The Viennese analyst Theodor Reik reported that, based on conversations with Martha during walks that they took together, "I got the decided impression that she not only had no idea of the significance and importance of psychoanalysis, but had intensive emotional resistances against the character of analytic work. On such a walk she once said, 'Women have always had such troubles, but they needed no psychoanalysis to conquer them. After the menopause they become quieter and resigned.'" That sentence, so dismissive of the real problems faced by herself and other members of her sex, is painful to read.

IV

After the birth of their sixth child, the Freuds — or more precisely, Freud — decided to practice abstinence as a means of contraception. While he believed that pregnancy "is a normal state in a young woman," he also held that *coitus interruptus* led to neurosis, a view that was based on some misbegotten Darwinian notion about the right and wrong "discharge" of semen. In some ways, of course, Freud was very much a man of his time and place, fascinated by the notion of "perverse" desires but also cautious and somewhat sexually inhibited. Freud professed to dislike Vienna, the hothouse capital of the Hapsburg empire, writing to his colleague Wilhelm Fliess that "I hate Vienna with a positively personal hatred." But Vienna was all the same the center of intellectual life in Europe — a bubbling cauldron of ideas about literature, music, art, architecture, science, and philosophy — and therefore a stimulant to his thinking. It was also a city whose culture was intensely preoccupied with sex. While modernist painters and writers dug deeply into erotic life, the bourgeoisie had a more prurient and censorious attitude toward sexuality, especially as it applied to women and children. Women were expected to be chaste before marriage, and the youthful exploration of sexuality through activities like masturbation was vehemently discouraged. (Freud's fine sense of humor did not desert him on even on salacious subjects such as these. The problem with masturbating, he once observed, is knowing how to do it well.)

In his research and his theory, Freud indicted these Victorian mores as a source of neurotic conflict, and his views on infantile sexuality ("one of the sources of Freud's enduring appeal, I believe," observed Paul Roazen in his book *Meeting Freud's Family*, "is that he so often took the side of the suffering child"), were remarkably forward-looking — and yet those same Victorian mores were reflected in some of his own constricted views on the subject of carnal pleasure. "I stand for an infinitely freer sexual life," he wrote in a letter, "although I myself have made very little use of such freedom. Only so far as I considered myself entitled to." Having proposed that the sexual drive was necessarily self-divided (as he believed all the drives were), he took the view that sex could never be completely gratifying.

His ability to sublimate erotic desire in his work was remarkable, and in a small book about Leonardo da Vinci he observed that Leonardo's apparent asexuality set him "above the common animal need of mankind." In a letter written to Fliess in 1897, when he was forty-one, Freud made a reference to ceasing connubial relations entirely. "Sexual excitation is of no more use to a person like me," he wrote, although he attested to some incidents of sexual intercourse with Martha later on, recording in his diary at the age of sixty that he had "successful coitus Wednesday morning." He also wrote to Fleiss that he often suffered from impotence. (Some scholars have argued that Freud's decision to abstain from sex, although ostensibly to avoid having more children, may have stemmed in part from an unconscious desire to get back at Martha for her sexual reticence during their prolonged engagement.) According to Oliver Freud, who was born fourteen months after Martin, neither parent thought to talk their sons about the birds and the bees. A family doctor was enlisted to teach the boys about sex.

Freud's own sexual behavior reminds us that he was not only the champion of psychological and sexual enlightenment in his work, but also the champion of the rewards — and demands — of sublimation and repression. In 1936 he characterized his married life with a startling degree of restraint in a conversation with Princess Marie Bonaparte, one in a bevy of his female friends that included Minna Bernays, Princess Bonaparte, Lou Andreas-Salome, Hilda Doolitle, and Helene Deutsch, with whom he shared his thoughts. "It was really not a bad solution of the marriage problem," he said, "and she is still today tender, healthy, and active." When one compares this wan statement to his impassioned declaration to Hilda Doolittle, the poet H.D., who spent several years in analysis with him, that "I am an old man and you don't think it worth your while to love me," they almost seem to come from two different men.

To his son-in-law Max Halberstadt, he conveyed his relief that his children had turned out well and that Martha "has neither been very abnormal nor often ill." (Recall the patronizing passage in the paper of 1908 about "regard for the wife's health.") This was a far cry from the sentiments that he felt during their engagement, when he clashed with Martha's mother about who had the greater claim to her daughter: "Marty, you cannot fight against it; no matter how much they love you I will not leave you to anyone, and no one deserves you; no one else's love compares with mine." Martha, by contrast, sounded more enthusiastic when describing her marriage to her granddaughter Sophie: "I wish for you to be as fortunate in your marriage as I have been in mine. For during the fifty-three years I was married to your grandfather, these was never an unfriendly look or a hard word between us." With accommodation and compromise on her part came harmony in their conjugal relationship, whatever it may have lacked in the way of higher communion.

This brings us to the sensational theory, originated by Jung and fanned over the decades by Peter Swales (also known as "the guerilla historian of psychoanalysis"), that after ceasing to sleep with his wife Freud embarked on an affair with Minna Bernays, Martha's smart, witty, and acerbic younger sister. The two had corresponded while Freud was pursuing Martha, and clearly they had a companionable relationship. Among other things, they were both avid card-players. They lived together in the same household for forty years — first on Berggasse 19 in Vienna, where Minna moved in in 1896, and then at 20 Maresfeld Gardens in London. Indeed, the sleeping arrangements in Vienna were weirdly intimate, as I saw for myself when I visited Berggasse 19. Minna's small sleeping quarters were right next to Sigmund's and Martha's bedroom, and the only way Minna could get to her room was to go through the bedroom that the Freuds shared.

The two also took trips together, and the rumors of their illicit liaison were fueled in 2006 by a German sociologist who found a yellowing hotel ledger entry written in Freud's distinctive scrawl at an inn in the Swiss alps where the psychoanalyst, then forty-two, and Minna, then thirty-three, stayed for two weeks in 1898. The couple had registered as *"Dr Sigm Freud u frau"* — as husband and wife. They took the largest room at the inn, which had the equivalent of a double bed. This last detail persuaded some Freud loyalists, such as Peter Gay, of the veracity of the rumors, although I myself remain dubious. For one thing, they might have checked into a single room because of Freud's frugality; they were anyway used to being in close quarters and it is unlikely, given the Victorian ethos of the era, that they could have rented the room if their actual unmarried relationship had been made clear. For another, despite his heretical approach to religious strictures and his theoretical advocacy of greater sexual freedom, Freud strikes me as a man fairly haunted by guilt, and he would have been disinclined to cheat on his devoted wife. There was also the fact that Minna was not particularly attractive and female appearance was important to Freud. In one of his early courtship letters he told Martha that her nose and her mouth were shaped "more characteristically than beautifully, with an almost masculine expression, so unmaidenly in its decisiveness." Such a microscopic analysis of his future bride's less than ideal features suggests that he was a critical observer of female appearances. Then too, he himself had once noted to his future wife that "similar people like Minna and myself don't suit each other specially."

Who, then, was Martha Freud? Why is she so hard to find amid the obsessive interest and research that swirls around her husband? Was she really just a contented *Hausfrau*, an efficient manager of a busy household, a firm, undemonstrative, but affectionate mother, and a devoted wife who "tried as much as possible," as she wrote in response to a condolence letter after her husband's death "to remove the *misère* of everyday life from his path"? Assuming that Freud's ideas about everything from female psychology to wayward sexuality to neurotic conflict were drawn even slightly from his own experience, what influence did Martha's personality and her interactions with him have on psychoanalytic theory? It is hard to imagine her living with him for more than half a century and not having had some impact on him beyond making sure that his boiled beef was served on time. In addition to which, as Sophie Freud points out in her book, "some of Freud's most fundamental discoveries were made by observing his own children. Mrs. Freud was his assistant in helping to transform the nursery into a psychological laboratory. But the children were not to know they were being used as guinea pigs. 'Above all, the family must be normal,' she said."

It is all the more surprising, then, that Martha has been of so little interest or consequence to the many biographers of her husband. In recent years there has been Katya Behling's biography of her in German, as well as a novel called *Mrs. Freud* by the French writer Nicolle Rosen. There is also a short memoir by the Freuds' long-standing housekeeper, Paula Fichtl, but it does not add much to the overall picture except for the author's own adulation for Herr Doktor and her unstinting admiration for Martha's capabilities and resilience. As Behling recounts in her biography, Martha was astonishingly courageous. When, shortly after the Anschluss, a group of armed SA men showed up at Berggasse 19, sending Paula into a tizzy, Martha is said to have maintained her composure, suggesting that "the gentlemen" might wish to deposit their rifles in the umbrella stand for the duration of their visit. And when another phalanx of Nazis stormed into their apartment a few days later, Paula's upset was met with an ironic comment: "Surely, Paula, you did not expect the Nazis to come with flowers."

Is Martha's featureless, sphinx-like presence an odd gap in the story, a glitch in the hermetic, all-consuming narrative of male genius? Or does it point to some deeper absence, some way in which Martha willingly went along with being sidelined from her husband's larger concerns the better to ensure a peaceful home from which Freud could venture out with his unconventional, often alarming ideas? One might argue that in a certain fashion she was her husband's muse — not a particularly glamorous or inflaming one, but a steadfast, earth-bound figure who helped him roam freely in his head.

It was perhaps Martha's very ordinariness — her "fully developed and well-integrated" personality, as Ernest Jones put it — that cast into relief the neuroses and the pathologies that Freud found everywhere he looked.

Freud's attitude to Martha, which verged on the fondly dismissive, is not irrelevant to the sense that psychoanalysis missed out on some of the big questions, particularly about women, and fell short of its liberating aspirations. Yet it is too easy to dismiss her as a martyr, unless one adds that she was a willing and seemingly contented one. Indeed, who is to say that she wouldn't have played the role of helpmeet to a lesser figure as well, to a man who was not a genius? Or that despite her intelligence and sensibility, that she, like many people, was simply not driven to live up to what might have been her potential? Not every wife, no matter how intelligent or talented, wishes to compete with her husband. The competitive impulse, which looks to us invariably like a strength, can also derive from weakness and an infirm sense of self. Martha clearly knew who she was. Her dignity is undeniable. Her power derived from being the ultimate caretaker and *ur*-wife, presiding over the circumstances that facilitated Freud's work. One might even see Martha's abnegation of self — if abnegation it was — as an adult example of "altruistic surrender," which was the term that her daughter Anna Freud coined for the children she worked with at the Tavistock Clinic who sacrificed their own well-being in the service of another child.

In any case, Martha seems to have gone through something of a sea-change in the wake of her husband's death at the age of eighty-three in September 1939, after years of excruciating jaw cancer. Aside from returning to lighting the Shabbos candles, she took to reading again, often sitting on the stairs or on a chair on the half-landing between the ground floor and the first floor at Maresfield Gardens, and even developed a curiosity about Anna's patients, marveling at how expensive child analysis was. Although she remarked that life had "lost its sense and meaning" without her husband, she carried on in exile with her energetic and orderly existence, and appears to have relished being at the center of a crowd of doting and often celebrated visitors who came to see her. She might be said to have embodied the spirit of Goethe's *das Ewig-Weibliche,* or Eternal Feminine, a concept that is profoundly alien to us but was a pillar of Martha's culture. As a frail but vivid old woman who had been the lifelong companion of an undeniable visionary, she must have aroused curiosity of her own accord. Frau Freud died in London on November 2, 1951 at the age of ninety, and was cremated and her ashes joined with her husband's ashes in an ancient Greek vase in something called the Freud corner in the Golder's Green crematorium, taking her mystery — her hopes, her disappointments, and her regrets — with her.

JAMES R. RUSSELL

The Poet Misak Medzarents, and Two Poems

He was born in 1886 in Armenia, in a remote mountain village called Pingyan above the Aradzani River. It was not the typical Armenian village of the Ottoman Empire, subjugated by Turkish authorities and terrorized by marauding Kurdish tribes in the guise of tax collectors. Pingyan was an unusual place: it was secure and very nearly free, a place where life could be happy. After the Moslem conquest of Anatolia began in the seventh century, Armenians struggled to preserve their liberty in princely states that juggled alliances with larger powers and tried to hold their heads above the flood of invasion by Turkish and Kurdish nomadic groups. After the fall of the Armenian

Bagratid capital Ani in the east, the extinction of the Armenian Cilician kingdom in the south in 1375, and with that, the end of national sovereignty, little strongholds of freedom endured to which men might make their way — the mountain fastness of Sasun above Lake Van, Artsakh (today's Nagorno-Karabagh) in the east, Zeitun in the southwest, and, in the northwest of historical Armenia, the village of Pingyan. (The name derives from the diminutive, Benik, of its founder, a prince named Benjamin.)

The houses, churches, schools, mills, and monasteries of the village clustered on the steep mountainside, below a well-defended pass; the villagers went to their fields on the other side of the river across a bridge with a great iron gate that was locked at night. The name of Misak's family, the large Medzadourian clan — the young poet was to shorten the name to Medzarents — suggests they were descendants of a noble "great house" (*medz dun*) who had heard of the fortress village and made their way there across Armenia, centuries earlier, from Ani or even farther east. The villagers spoke Armenian, not the Armeno-Turkish of much of the Armenian community in Anatolia. They used metal tokens inscribed in the Armenian alphabet for trade, and maintained a school in which the Modern and Classical forms of Armenian were taught. They were horsemen and marksmen, and in their homes books shared the walls with guns. Some families owned businesses in the distant Ottoman capital, Constantinople, and were prosperous; workingmen sent remittances home.

It made for a happy boyhood, for a time. Misak learned Armenian classics and foreign languages at school, read poetry, rode horseback to the fields, heard work songs, dozed and dreamed under trees, listened to his mother's prayers and to legends about water spirits, and played with his friends. The Armenian massacres that began in 1894 and were to culminate in the Genocide of 1915 affected even Pingyan, and the family moved for safety first to the city of Sepastia (Sivas), then in 1902 to the capital, where Misak's father had a business. In Sivas, a Moslem butcher's son stole up from behind and stabbed Misak in the street. He survived the attack, but it traumatized and weakened him. The family chose the comparative safety of Constantinople, with its large Armenian community: Misak went to school, made friends, frequented the offices of literary journals, read widely, and was a prolific writer. When he was twenty-one he published two small volumes. But it was the year before his death, in 1908, of consumption: his life, like that of his precursor Bedros Tourian, was destined to be short.

Tourian had invented modern Western Armenian poetry almost singlehandedly, in the short years before his death in early 1872. Armenians closely followed European literary trends, and in the period between the lifetimes of the two poets Symbolism had become the dominant trend in poetry, music, and the arts. Through the use of dream imagery, indistinct allusions, exotic colors, and magical patterns of sound, Symbolists sought to open the doors of perception to an emotional and aesthetic sensibility towards a supernatural reality that, they believed, lay just beyond the everyday. The French poet Stephane Mallarmé and the composer Claude Debussy most famously exemplify the movement; but it can be argued that its beginnings were much earlier, and that William Blake and Edgar Allan Poe were proto-Symbolists. I will have more to say about Poe presently, in the discussion of what I consider to be Medzarents' greatest poem, which I will give in translation.

Medzarents was described by his contemporaries, and sometimes derided, as a Symbolist, and he retorted defensively, in versified satire. The characterization is fair for some of his lyrics, but it is not complete — his work is not confined by narrow categories and definitions. There is evidence, in the form of a few fragments of poems, that Medzarents was developing a new style, sharper, harsher, more vivid, that reflected political events and a revolutionary consciousness. An analogous evolution from early Symbolist verses to a raw and jagged, sharply strident, revolutionary kind of verse typifies the work of the greatest Eastern Armenian poet, Yeghishe Charents, eleven years Misak's junior, one of the great early non-Russian poets of the Soviet Union. Charents lived longer, but not by much: he was killed in November 1937 in the Stalinist purges. He wrote homoerotic verses that were unpublished in his lifetime and that still arouse controversy among the ultra-nationalist establishment in post-Soviet Armenia. We cannot know with any certainty what Medzarents would have written had he lived on in the turbulent twentieth century: he died on the eve of the Ottoman revolution and just a few years before the Armenian genocide. It is almost certain that he would have been murdered with the other two-hundred-and-fifty-or-so Armenian luminaries of the capital at the start of the Genocide in April 1915. The life was far too short; the future, far too dark.

Let us consider one poem in detail, with its far-reaching ramifications. It is called *Gaydzer*, or "Sparks," and was published September 10, 1905 in the journal *Masis* with another verse and the heading *Yergu sirerk*, "Two Love Songs"; and it was reprinted in the poet's first volume of verses, *Dziadzan*, "Rainbow," two years later. The political activist, publisher, and literary scholar Aram Andonian wrote the preface to the book. The poem consists of four quatrains; each line is seven syllables in length. (Armenian stress is regular: the accent falls on the final syllable of a word except for enclitics — short unstressed words, of one syllable, following a longer one.) The rhyme pattern of the poem in the original is a conventional one: ABCB BCCD BCBA ADDD. Here is my translation.

> The drumbeat of my soul and its tambourine's
> Trill this night descend in laughter.
> Like cymbals clashing, they delight:
> My memories clap their hands together.
>
> Accompanying the castanets' song
> Your falcon's eyes' flame,
> Purple-born and fire,
> Burn within my soul again.
>
> Drunken on that intangible ambrosia
> With kisses redolent of flowers
> Sway there in mad dances
> The regal lady's undulations.
>
> The dark night gently wears away!
> Oh, just once more, just once again!
> My soul intoxication craves
> In the rivulets of fire flowing from your gaze.

The poem is a reverie, an induced, dream-like act of imagination by the author at night within the four walls of his room. There are frequent images of fire, but the title, "Sparks," suggests that the fire could ignite but has not yet; and before dawn the passionate but insubstantial vision fades, even though the poet pleads for it to stay. The first three stanzas progress through the five senses, each more physically immediate than the one before it. The first stanza bursts on the reader with vividly percussive sound: drums, tambourines, cymbals, and hands clapping. The second stanza moves to the sense of sight: fire and flame evoke bright red and rich gold, and the poet also uses the epithet *dziranedzín* to describe the fire in his imaginary beloved's eyes. This word is a calque, that is, an exact translation of a foreign word according to its parts, of the Greek and Latin adjective *porphyrogenitus*, literally "born to the purple," meaning "noble." In Armenian it is, serendipitously, richly alliterative. It is a word that describes a quality while also making one think of a color, and part of the way it makes the connection is through the repetition of a sound. That is a game that certain special words can play in our minds, making us see and hear in a new and wider way.

The third stanza combines the remaining three senses of smell, taste, and touch: the poem overwhelms with voluptuous imagery of flowers, intoxication, and kisses. The poet is drunk on *nectar* — the Greek word, whose variant and equivalent is *ambrosia* — means, literally, "immortal," and is echoed by the compound word *dzaghg-anúysh. Dzaghíg* is "flower"; *anúysh* is a Classical Armenian loan word from pre-Islamic Persian meaning "immortal nectar" again. In Modern Armenian, with the diphthong reduced, *anúsh* also means "sweet." The Armenian for "kiss" is *hampúyr*, which means literally a sharing of fragrances, such as sweetness. Through Medzarents' choice of words, in sum, the senses all blend into one another.

In the final quatrain of the poem, the sensuous vision fades as morning dawns, though the poet begs it to linger and prolong his self-induced intoxication. The final word of the poem, a Classical Armenian compound most familiar from the Hymn of Vesting of the Divine Liturgy, is *hrahosán*, "flowing with fire"— used here of Misak's beloved's gaze. The word here recalls the poet's palette of crimson, purple, and gold; but in its liturgical context it alludes to the fire of the Holy Spirit that descended upon the Apostles in their upper room and conferred upon them the gift of tongues. Linguistic inspiration is precisely what this poem is about in the first place; but the final stanza also reminds one plaintively that the sumptuous scene conjured so richly by the poet's imagination is insubstantial as a dream. The reader of English will be reminded here of Prospero's words in *The Tempest:*

> Our revels now are ended. These our actors,
> As I foretold you, were all spirits and
> Are melted into air, into thin air:
> And, like the baseless fabric of this vision,
> The cloud-capp'd towers, the gorgeous palaces,
> The solemn temples, the great globe itself,
> Yea, all which it inherit, shall dissolve
> And, like this insubstantial pageant faded,
> Leave not a rack behind. We are such stuff
> As dreams are made on, and our little life
> Is rounded with a sleep.

As I was writing the first lines of this essay, the sun was beating down and the branches on the pomegranate tree in our California garden were bent to the ground with fruit. They reminded me of the words in poetry that are heavy, dense with many meanings; we have already seen how Medzarents chooses ripe words bursting with juicy seeds. There are yet others in this poem that harken back to antiquity, to the archaic pleasures of noble hunters, to regal feasts. *Shahení*, "falcon-like"; *pampish(n)*, "queen"— Armenian is an ancient language with roots in the Thraco-Phyrgian akin to proto-Greek, layered with the vocabulary of many centuries, and these words are redolent of the Parthian age, the heroic epoch of the fourth century chronicled in the *Epic Histories* of P'awstos Buzand. My teacher and friend Nina Georgievna Garsoïan, who passed away last year at the age of ninety-nine, published the definitive translation and study of that work, in which it is related that the Sasanian Persian Shah of that time, Shapur II, captured his perennial rival and enemy, the Armenian Arsacid Arshak II.

The story is taught in every Armenian school: Shapur had his servants sprinkle Armenian earth on the ground of his banqueting tent. When Arshak trod upon alien Iranian soil, he meekly professed fealty and submission; but when he stepped on the earth brought from his native land, he angrily promised rebellion. At the royal feast later that fateful day, he derided Shapur as the usurper of the throne of his own clan, the Parthian Arsacids, and audaciously demanded his rightful place at the head of the table. Arshak was clapped in irons and imprisoned in a place called the Fortress of Oblivion, from whose dark confines no inmate ever emerged. The prisoners' very names and memories were expunged from official records and forbidden by law to be spoken. But the Armenian king's faithful eunuch Drastamat (a Parthian word meaning "welcome") secured permission to entertain his liege lord one last time, with royal viands and dancing maidens. At the end of the revel, Arshak seized a fruit knife and plunged it into his own heart, lest he live past the end of the entertainment and return to the dim existence of a captive. Thus did the voluptuous vision end; and from his choice of words and images it is all but certain that Medzarents had the famous episode from P'awstos' history in mind.

Epameron — ti de tis, ti de ou tis? Skias onar anthropos, declared the poet Pindar in a celebratory ode to the victory of an ancient Hellenic athlete. "Thing of a day. What is somebody? What is he not? Man is the dream of a shadow." Yet when glory rests upon a man, the moment in his life's span is sweet as honey, he adds. But when the laurels wilt, the dream fades, the revel ends, the vision flies away, we have the poem, the play, the historical saga, the ode. What is it that gives these written and spoken words power over millennia? What is it they immortally capture? What can they do that the reality of an ordinary day cannot?

Let us take Medzarents' word, *dziranedzín*, in the second stanza of the poem discussed above. It means "born to the purple," and thus combines a color with the idea of nobility. It has a particular sound-signature, a musical quality, in the poem, too, for it resonates very strongly with other words the poet has already used in the first stanza: *dzidzágh*, "laughter," *dzĕndzghá*, "cymbal," and *dzap'*, "clap". Armenian *dziraní* means "purple," but it is also the color of Homer's wine-dark sea, for thus we find it as *dziraní dzóv* (the latter word meaning "sea") in the earliest Armenian poem, the Song of the Birth of Vahagn recorded by the historian Movses Khorenats'i. The word *dzirán* means also "apricot," a fruit originally from China that the ancient Romans called the Armenian plum. Apricots, the fruit a medieval writer in Asia praised as "the golden peaches of Samarkand," were an expensive commodity, even as cloth dyed in the royal purple was precious. The Russian linguist Pyotr Kocharov has convincingly argued that the Armenian word is a very early loan from Old Iranian *zaranya-*, meaning "golden."

That origin goes far to explain the semantics of the word in its development through time, its wide array of meanings and associations. As a thing, a *dzirán* is a choice fruit of fiery, red, and purple hues. As a color, *dziraní* evokes a range of hues over the spectrum; and as a quality, it confers nobility. (The Biblical and later Hebrew word for purple, *argaman*, is likewise freighted with the implication of nobility and great value. It is derived from Akkadian *argamannu*, which has the dual meaning of "purple" and "tribute." An ancient Anatolian derivation is possible, but I would suggest again a very early Iranian origin, comparing for instance the Iranian-in-Armenian name Argawan, "precious." In Hebrew magical texts, *argaman* serves as an acronym for the names of the angels Uriel, Raphael, Gabriel, Michael, and Nuriel, its meaning as a word on its own doubtless conferring additional nobility upon its celestial reference.)

Now, one can call a word — say, *dzirán* — a signifier. That is, it signifies, refers to, names an object, a thing in the physical universe. The thing that the signifier refers to — in this case, an apricot — is the signified. In general, the signifier is arbitrary: there are different words in different languages for an apricot, and none of them has a provable relationship to the object it denotes. (I say generally, because most languages also have onomatopoeic words that echo the perceptible sound or quality of the thing or action that they describe.) It is also the case that the signifier is inadequate fully to express the reality of the signified. I can say "apricot," but the colors of the fruit in the sun, its silky feel, the juice, the pit within — obviously one word cannot carry all these features, and even a page-long description would not be the same as an immediate experience. A long shadow thus falls between signifier and signified, over the centuries of human speculation about language: we feel instinctively that there must be a relationship, but there is not. To compensate, our ancestors crafted the myth of an

Adamic language, the primordial, perfect speech in which the first man gave each of the animals its true name.

But look what Medzarents has done! As we have seen in the analysis of his chosen term, *dziranedzín*, his signifier is more, not less, as a word sparking various mental and aesthetic associations. It is a signifier that has more to it than the signified. I think that this can serve as one good definition of a poem (not to the exclusion of other definitions, of which there are many): a literary form in whose lexicon a signifier is to be encountered that is greater than the signified.

That definition has implications worth further thought, but I don't want to say farewell just yet to Medzarents' magical word *dziranedzín*, which means literally "to the purple born" but also much more. We encounter the English form of its Greek parent, *porphyrogenitos*, in 1839 in the poem "The Haunted Palace" by Edgar Allan Poe:

> In the greenest of our valleys
> By good angels tenanted,
> Once a fair and stately palace —
> Radiant palace — reared its head.
> In the monarch Thought's dominion,
> It stood there!
> Never seraph spread a pinion
> Over fabric half so fair!
>
> Banners yellow, glorious, golden,
> On its roof did float and flow
> (This — all this — was in the olden

Time long ago)
And every gentle air that dallied,
In that sweet day,
Along the ramparts plumed and pallid,
A wingèd odor went away.

Wanderers in that happy valley,
Through two luminous windows, saw
Spirits moving musically
To a lute's well-tunèd law,
Round about a throne where, sitting,
Porphyrogene!
In state his glory well befitting,
The ruler of the realm was seen.

And all with pearl and ruby glowing
Was the fair palace door,
Through which came flowing, flowing, flowing
And sparkling evermore,
A troop of Echoes, whose sweet duty
Was but to sing,
In voices of surpassing beauty,
The wit and wisdom of their king.

But evil things, in robes of sorrow,
Assailed the monarch's high estate;
(Ah, let us mourn! — for never morrow
Shall dawn upon him, desolate!)
And round about his home the glory
That blushed and bloomed
Is but a dim-remembered story
Of the old time entombed.

And travellers, now, within that valley,
Through the red-litten windows see
Vast forms that move fantastically
To a discordant melody;
While, like a ghastly rapid river,
Through the pale door
A hideous throng rush out forever,
And laugh — but smile no more.

The poem is an allegory: the palace is the poet's head; the two luminous windows, his eyes. Long ago the king of Thought reigned there in serenity; but madness invaded the fortress of the mind and now all is chaos within: the windows that were once bright are now "red-litten" (or, as a variant of the text has it, "encrimsoned"). Jerome McGann, in a study of Poe's poetry, asserts that the key word of "The Haunted Palace" is "porphyrogene," which he considers both noun and adjective, and "fundamentally, a synaesthetic figure, both chromatic and phonetic," part of Poe's "musical architecture." That is, the word "porphyrogene" has manifold functions in the poem. It is both a word describing the king who sits in the palace, and his title. It evokes a color, royal purple, while also serving as a central chord of the poem's music — and most of all, it sounds just right.

Poe stressed the sound-structure, the musicality of poetry, some have said, even more than its overt verbal meaning, and built his great and final poem, "The Bells," around the single tantalizing word "tintinnabulation." It was a poem in a chrysalis, ready to open its wings and fly as music: the Russian translation of the poem by the Symbolist Konstantin Dmitrievich Bal'mont became Rachmaninoff's Third Symphony; and Phil Ochs, the great American protest singer-songwriter of the 1960s, took its tintinnabulation to the guitar. Medzarents would have loved it. McGann, who studied "The Haunted Palace," is mistaken, I believe, in thinking that Poe coined the word "porphyrogene": we have reviewed its long and noble pedigree. But he is right to stress the centrality of the term: the word brings together, like its Armenian cousin but perhaps not as variegatedly, different concepts and different kinds of realities and perceptions. It is one of those poetic signifiers that are more than the signified. The word leads the reader, as Poe wrote in his essay "The Poetic Principle," "to perceive a harmony where none was apparent before."

Valerii Bryusov, a Russian Symbolist poet of the turn of the twentieth century, was enamored of Armenian culture and in 1916 he edited a volume of translations by various hands including his own, called *The Poetry of Armenia from the most ancient times down to our own days*. The book, whose proceeds went to the relief of Armenian refugees from the Genocide, includes several of Medzarents' poems, though not "Sparks." (The poem was translated into Russian, badly and not by Bryusov, in an anthology published in Erevan in 1987.) But in 1924 Bryusov did translate Poe's "The Haunted Palace" into Russian. The translation is of interest here for two reasons: first, the poem has an affinity to Medzarents' "Sparks," and it is worth knowing how a poet so strongly attracted to Armenian verse approached it. The other reason is perhaps less intuitively obvious and requires some explanation.

Why are Medzarents' poems so chromatic? If color was so important to him, wouldn't it have been more sensible for him just to paint a picture? It is not an unreasonable question: in the years before reproducible media such as photography and cinema attained prominence in the arts, painters were a much more visible presence than they are today. This was no less the case for Armenian Constantinople or Tiflis than for Paris or St. Petersburg. Martiros Saryan's palette blazes with the gorgeous colors of the Armenian landscape; Hagop Kojoyan's delicate hues evoke Symbolist reveries. I think Medzarents intended for us to read his poems and then make the mental effort to see his colors, which are also sounds and emotions, within our own minds. Every viewer of a painting sees it differently because his mind is taking in the picture and organizing it in a way that is particular to him. In a sense he is participating in the creative process of the artist, supplying colors. Even more so, the reader of a poem with a rich chromatic lexicon is making a multi-faceted creative effort, provided that he is attentive, perceptive, and engaged. The neuroscientist Eric Kandel has argued, following the pioneering art historians of twentieth-century Vienna who employed the findings of psychology in their research, that an important part of what makes a work of art great is that it is ambiguous: it forces the viewer to consider and select various possible meanings.

As we have seen, the factor of ambiguity as a component of artistic mastery is eminently applicable to literature, as well as to painting. In the former case, the act of translation reveals the beholder's share explicitly. It is a window into the laboratory of his mind. A great translator is himself an artist, and the choices he makes when rendering a particular term from one language into another enhance our perception of the poem. Bryusov in his translation of "The Haunted Palace" devotes particular attention to Poe's palette: he chooses *izumrúdnaya*, "emerald," to lend extra scintillation to Poe's superlative, "greenest," in line one. Poe's "yellow, glorious, golden" of becomes *púrpur, zláto* "purple, gold": two words have replaced three, with purple in its metaphorical sense of regal rendering "glorious" and adding chromatic variation to the scene. For "gold," Bryusov has selected the archaic *zláto*, with its aura of storied antiquity, over modern Russian *zóloto*. Poe's "Pearl and ruby" are reversed to *lal, zhémchug*, with a marked Arabo-Persian loan-word for the ruby, *lāl*, standing in for the more common *rubín*. The color red is of unique significance in Russian art and symbolism — the common word for it, *krásnyi*, originally meant "beautiful." As for Poe's "Porphyrogene," all Bryusov has to do is to reach into Russia's own Byzantine heritage and retrieve the well-known Slavonic calque upon the Greek original: *Porfiroródnaya*. (It is a queen, not a king, because thought is a word of feminine gender in Russian.) And so the original, with all its fertile ambiguities, is there in its perfection, with only an alteration in dress.

This discussion of a poem of Misak Medzarents has treated the complexity and depth of his vision and language; and these subjects have prompted further considerations in brief about the definition of poetry itself and even the nature of the perception of literary art. After a brief sketch of the historical setting we turned from the dark prospects that lay beyond the short life of the poet to that which endures unshadowed, the work. That work draws upon the millennial resources of the Armenian language to express intricate visions; and sometimes the verses of Misak Medzarents are suffused with a pantheistic joy. Here, in my translation, is his greatest poem, his *ars poetica*, an invitation to the reader to travel farther into the realm of delight.

With what intoxication...

To my friend Kegham Parseghian

With what intoxication! The trees, in the light,
Trees in the wind and the rain,
Shaggy-tressed trees, trees that to the heavens strain,
And saplings green, as sea waves
Collapsing to the bosom of the corn strewn,
Dazed, all drink of the swelling sunburst of life.
With what intoxication! The grass above the soil rising
Opens to the light, amazed,
For the moment of its life the dewdrops that are its eyes.
With what intoxication! Flowers in the dew,
Flowers in the light, accustomed to the hand,
Swoon in their expectation.
With what intoxication!
Every field and hill upon green brow
Bind the flowers' multicolored wedding band.
With what intoxication! From the lovely plains
And his bride, the dale, the red foot stork
Returning home imbibes his longing's satiation.
With what intoxication! Blackbirds
Drink the light and whisper it, alert,
In orchards' leafy fastnesses.
With what intoxication! Snow-white jays afloat
On high seem to swim as they perambulate upon the sky,
Taking wing, gilded on the glowing firmament.
With what intoxication! The turtledove her nuptial

Bed arranges in the shady cover of a tree
And waits for her husband in expectant passion.
With what intoxication! The butterfly unfolds upon
The tiny sparkling lakelet of its leaf
And with its milky wings constructs its canopy.
With what intoxication! On the purple plain
To scarlet flowers hies the bee,
To suck upon the little female nipples, luxuriating.
With what intoxication! The seas are blue;
River waters, abundant; springs, brimming;
The rill, swiftly purling; lakes, azure —
The rill, his locks green-fronded, tossing,
Passes intimate among the willows, blue as the moon.
With what intoxication! Clouds shake their heads,
The wondrous liquid massing in their breasts;
Which like a snaking thread descends
To slake the hot gold thirst of earth.
With that intoxication drink their fill
Upon the parched soil's universal burn
All creatures born, all flowers grown:
Drunk, the wave laps in embrace the perfumed tree;
Thyme and mint and basil growing wild
And storax, frankincense, aromas teeming
Are embracing, drunken, every thing,
All shapes and forms, all colors gleaming,
All essences and elements: He
Whose rainbow every thing reflects, returning,
God! Who from God knows where has come to them.

ROBERT ALTER

What Flaubert Taught Agnon

Agnon and Flaubert: the conjunction is, at first blush, altogether unlikely. Their background and the kind of language in which each wrote could scarcely have been more different.

Agnon, the commanding figure in Hebrew fiction in the twentieth century and the recipient of the Nobel Prize in Literature in 1966, grew up in an Orthodox Jewish home in Buczacz, Galicia, in the eastern end of the Hapsburg Empire. Yiddish was his first language, and he wrote a few stories and some poems in Yiddish when he was in his teens. He had no formal general education, but his mother read the classics of German literature with him, for German was the language of cultural prestige under the Hapsburgs, even where, as in Galicia, it was not the vernacular. In any case, the focus of his early education was on traditional Hebrew and Aramaic texts — the Bible, the Mishnah, the Talmud, Midrash, and the plethora of commentaries on all four of those hallowed works. He decisively turned from Yiddish to Hebrew because Hebrew was for him, as he wrote in one of his stories, "the language of all the generations that had gone before us and all the generations to come." In keeping with this idea of the eternality of the language, the Hebrew that he wrote was essentially the Hebrew of the early rabbis in idiom, lexicon, and grammar, though it exhibited some elements of later strata of the language — but very few from modern Hebrew. To invoke a counter-factual analogue, it would strain the imagination to think of Flaubert writing in the French of the medieval *fabliaux.*

One must add that Agnon, with scant exceptions, was repeatedly coy and evasive about his relation to European writers. He like to present himself as a traditional Hebrew teller of tales, which sometimes he was. The often proposed link with Kafka — especially after Agnon began writing dreamlike or surrealist stories in the 1930s — is a case in point. When he was asked, in an interview at the Schocken Library in Jerusalem after he received the Nobel Prize, whether he was influenced by Kafka, he was clearly nettled. "Kafka? Kafka?" he replied. "I have barely read one book by him." (But how many books, after all, did Kafka write?) Then he added, archly, "Of course, my wife has the complete writings of Kafka on her shelf."

Agnon came to Palestine toward the end of his teens, in 1908, and stayed in the port city of Jaffa. During this time, adapting to the secular Zionist milieu there, he abandoned religious observance. In 1913 he went to Germany, evidently with the intention of immersing himself in European culture as an autodidact — reading through all the books in a large library, as he extravagantly claimed to Gershom Scholem, who became his friend during his German sojourn. At some point in this period, he returned to Orthodox practice, which he would maintain until the end of his life. Scholem shrewdly observed in an interview on Israeli television after the writer's death that art was paramount for Agnon and that he was attached to religion because it served his purposes as an artist, his outward devotion to ritual and Jewish law confirming, among other things, the finely crafted rabbinic prose in which he wrote.

Early during his decade in Germany that ended with a return to Palestine, Agnon discovered Flaubert. On December 17, 1916, in a letter to Zalman Schocken, the department store magnate who had become his patron, he wrote: "Flaubert and everything about him touch me deeply. He is a poet who mortified himself in the tent of poetry.... It is fitting for every writer to read about him before he writes and after he writes. Then no book would be blighted." (All the translations from the Hebrew and the French are mine.) Note that he speaks of reading *about* Flaubert, not of reading him. The phrase, "mortified himself in the tent of poetry," plays on the rabbinic "mortified himself in the tent of Torah," suggesting a certain equivalence between the two, that is, between the devotion to the sacred text and the devotion to art. In calling the French writer a "poet," Agnon is thinking of the German *Dichter*, which can refer to anyone using language creatively.

The allusion to the French writer's biography reflects one important way in which Flaubert was important for him. The stories that he had written in Jaffa certainly evinced a prodigious talent, but the lyric prose used for them was often excessively florid. Flaubert, with the many hundreds of draft pages that he honed down to the compact masterpiece that was *Madame Bovary,* showed Agnon what a serious writer needed to do. In fact, during his German years, Agnon took many of the stories that he had written during the first six years of his career and extensively pruned them — with a Flaubertian discipline, one might say. In a few instances he reduced an effusive paragraph to a single telling sentence of six or seven words. The result was beautifully concise fiction of the first order of originality.

Yet it is inconceivable that Agnon would not have read *Madame Bovary* and in all likelihood *Trois contes,* or *Three Tales,* though perhaps not *The Sentimental Education,* arguably Flaubert's most original book. His closest connection with Flaubert is his novel *A Simple Story,* published in 1935. Four years earlier, the first Hebrew translation of *Madame Bovary,* by the short-story writer Devorah Baron, had appeared, and after his early acquaintance with the German version Agnon surely would have at least leafed through it and probably read it all the way through. Thus, as he began work on *A Simple Story,* Flaubert's novel would have been relatively fresh in his mind. The connection between the two books has been duly noticed in Hebrew criticism, which for the most part emphasizes themes and social setting. What may be more instructive in regard to the cross-fertilization between literatures is to consider what Agnon may have picked up from Flaubert about the novelistic representation of experience.

A Simple Story, set in the first decade of the twentieth century in a town much like Buczacz, is pre-eminently a novel of bourgeois life. It is Agnon's most perfectly wrought novel, though in regard to breadth of concerns and to formal innovation not necessarily his greatest. Although the protagonist, Hirshel Hurvitz, and his parents, Baruch Meir and Tsirl, are Orthodox Jews (we see him, for example, attending daily worship), this is no more than an external expression of their culture, for their lives are through-and-through bourgeois. The Hurvitzes are the owners of a general store, and the accumulation of wealth is their main preoccupation.

At the beginning of the book, a relative named Bluma Nacht ("Night Flower") shows up in their home to throw herself on their mercies after losing both her parents. The mercies prove to be far from tender as the domineering Tsirl, a habitual driver of hard bargains, agrees to allow Bluma to stay as a household servant without salary, only room and board provided. Tsirl immediately casts doubt on Bluma's competence for the job, but it quickly emerges that, having maintained her parents' home while her mother was failing, she is a skilled cook and baker and adept at keeping a household clean and orderly. At the time Hirshl is just sixteen, and Bluma is presumably about the same age. The two are drawn to each other in an attraction that is powerfully erotic, however discreetly it is intimated by Agnon. When it becomes clear to Tsirl that a serious relationship between them threatens to emerge, she banishes Bluma from the house, for she will not countenance her son, an only child, marrying a penniless relative.

Instead Tsirl arranges a marriage for him with the daughter of a wealthy Jewish farmer. The passive Hirshl submits, but he continues to be obsessed with Bluma. After the wedding he is desperately unhappy with his wife, recoiling from the smell of her perfume, feeling the words that she speaks to him as sharp nails being driven into his flesh. The birth of a son — as it turns out, the baby is sickly — does not improve matters. Hirshl begins to pay nightly visits to the house in which Bluma is now living. He stands outside in all weathers, dolefully looking up at the window where he imagines the woman he loves is standing. All this compulsive behavior culminates in a severe psychotic breakdown, and his father takes him to the city of Lemberg (Lviv today) for a cure in a residential facility with an eccentric psychiatrist who patiently edges him back to sanity by telling him stories. At the end Hirshl is reconciled with his wife — on the surface, happily, though Agnon hints in the way the conclusion is framed that this is not really a happy ending.

The plot, of course, is quite different from the plot of *Madame Bovary*, but it shares with the French novel a sense of the pervasive oppressiveness of bourgeois materialism joined with an unhappy marriage and the allure of a romantic connection — for Hirshl, manifestly impossible to realize — outside of marriage. The great nineteenth-century novels are often about lives that end in trainwrecks, and *A Simple Story* conforms to this pattern of the genre in its realist phase, using an oblique, understated version of the concluding disaster.

Agnon obviously did not need Flaubert to fashion a story
of this sort. The real-life counterparts to the Hurvitz family and other characters in the book were observed by him when he was growing up in Buczacz, and they would have been sufficient to fuel his imagination. What he could have picked up from Flaubert was certain clues for how to articulate the novelistic representation of such a world.

To begin with, Flaubert exhibited a sure sense of how to pull together the disparate elements of a long narrative through the deployment of recurring motifs. The color blue, for example, is an important thread running through his novel. When Charles first sees Emma on a sunny summer day, she is holding a blue parasol that casts a blueish (*bleuâtre*) shade on her face. She has blue dresses; her extravagant romantic fantasies unfold against imagined blue horizons. Agnon is quite likely to have noticed the recurring motifs in Flaubert, though he also could have seen them in Thomas Mann. It is a device he employed in most of his novels and in many of his stories. He makes ample use of it in *A Simple Story* through recurrences of food, coins, cigarettes, and many other motifs.

One of the most significant of these is the blind singing beggar. That figure may be directly taken from *Madame Bovary:* Emma, we recall, repeatedly hears the singing of a blind beggar on her departures for her assignations with Léon, her second lover. The moment before she dies, she again hears his song coming from outside her house. Details in literature sometimes draw on multiple sources, and as the Israeli critic Nitza Ben-Dov has persuasively proposed, there is a blind singing beggar in one of the tales of the early nineteenth-century Hasidic master Rabbi Nahman of Bratslav that Agnon surely would have remembered. In *A Simple Story* the blind beggar is associated with the world of song and romantic love that is the antithesis of all the mercantile values that Tsirl promotes, and when Hirshl encounters the singer in rags at the end of the novel, he gets rid of him by tossing to him an unusually large coin — clearly, the coin of his mother's realm. Emma's tragedy is underscored when she perishes from the arsenic that she has swallowed listening in anguish to the beggar's song that has marked her departures for the love affair ending in disaster; Hirshl's more hidden tragedy is to banish with a coin the singer and the dream of love evoked by the song, subsiding into a materialist bourgeois life devoid of melody.

Flaubert is often identified as the writer who perfected the technique of *le style indirect libre,* uninformatively referred to in English as free indirect style. This simply means the narrator's conveying to us the unspoken speech of the character in the third person, with tenses switched from present (which the character would use to herself) to past. Dorit Cohen, in her luminous book *Transparent Minds,* had a better term for it; she calls it narrated monologue, but since academics prefer rebarbative language, her apt designation never caught on. Agnon made abundant use of free indirect style in *The Hill of Sand,* a brilliant novella that he created through extensive revisions of an earlier story after he came to Germany. The young protagonist is an aspiring poet constantly pulling back from engagement in eros, and Agnon gives a Freudian spin to free indirect style by exposing through the character's unspoken words sexual desires that his conscious mind represses. *Madame Bovary* in fact employs *le style indirect libre* only from time to time, but always with striking effectiveness, and the same is true of *A Simple Story.* Instead Flaubert utilizes a range of different procedures for representing consciousness, and in this, too, Agnon follows suit.

Let us look at a few brief examples of free indirect style from both novels. After her first experience of adulterous love with the libertine aristocrat Rodolphe, Emma returns to her home, and "seeing herself in the mirror, she was amazed by her face. Never had she had eyes so big, so black, nor of such depth. Something subtle spread through her whole being and transfigured it." Everything here about the bigness and blackness and depth of the eyes, her transfiguration, is of course Emma talking to herself, and these sentences are a study in self-deception. What Emma sees in the mirror is not her actual image, but her image as she imagines it transfigured by her experience of romantic love. Flaubert than moves from narrated monologue to monologue proper as Emma calls out, "I have a lover! I have a lover!" To this the narrator adds his own analytic comment about Emma's train of thought, which is devasting through the force of the simile it uses (Agnon, as we shall see, does this, too): "relishing the idea as if at another puberty that had befallen her."

Now consider two instances of this technique in *A Simple Story,* one involving Tsirl and the other her son. Early in the novel, Tsirl explains to herself why it is legitimate for her to employ Bluma without salary.

> Seemingly, a denial of payment was entailed in this, but whoever looks into the heart of the matter sees that Tsirl was right, for when Bluma comes to marry, will Tsirl run around to charities and say, "Provide a dowry my relative"? No, she herself will give according to the years she has served. Besides, what payment could Bluma expect? Why, she had never been a servant to others, and so she has been learning about housework from Tsirl.

From beginning to end, the passage is an exercise in self-justification. The expression "whoever looks into the heart of the matter" translates as whoever would follow Tsirl's self-serving train of thought. Tsirl casts herself here as a heroine of generosity in the prospect of eventually paying Bluma the amount that she would have earned through years of labor. The remark, moreover, about her learning housework from Tsirel is a blatant lie to herself. She is in no way involved in housework and knows precious little about how to do it, whereas Bluma arrives at her home thoroughly experienced and skilled in managing a home.

There is a linguistic complication in this and related passages. Tsirl, of course, is thinking in Yiddish, which Agnon conveys in Hebrew, at most occasionally giving a Yiddish turn to the phrasing, and Tsirl would scarcely have known any Hebrew. The phrase "according to the years she has served" approximately recalls the formulation of the law in the Torah pertaining to the so-called Hebrew slave, actually an indentured servant for a period of seven years. Tsirl is unlikely to have been familiar with the Hebrew of this verse, and so we have a kind of surreptitious intervention of the narrator who is mediating Tsirl's unspoken speech in Hebrew, an intervention that suggests Tsirl is disposed to regard Bluma as a virtual slave. This biblical echo is a small illustration of how Agnon Hebraizes the Flaubertian technique as he adopts it.

And here is a fairly straightforward deployment of free indirect discourse for Hirshl. The baby boy he has begotten, as I have noted, is sickly. Hirshl, contemplating the ailing newborn, expresses his concern in the following manner: "If Bluma were caring for him, he would regain his strength. And so Hirshl would imagine himself standing on one side of his son and Bluma on the other and his son recovering. God in heaven knows that Hirshl's sole intention was for the sake of his son."

The first sentence is free indirect discourse. The second sentence is the narrator's report of Hirshl's imagining. Such switches back and forth in modes of representing thought are a common feature of the technique, as we saw in Flaubert's move from narrated monologue to actual monologue ("I have a lover!") to the narrator's summarizing judgment of what the character feels. Both these sentences here reflect the lovestruck protagonist's perception, or fantasy, of Bluma as a healer, a comforter, an all-around bestower of blessings. The third sentence slides back into free indirect discourse. "God in heaven knows" is a virtual refrain in this novel, a formula invoked by characters who are actually not paying much attention to God in heaven — who are, one might say, taking His name in vain. Hirshl has to insist that God would confirm the purity of his motives because he guiltily senses that they are really not about concern for the child.

Free indirect discourse is a technique that is particularly effective for exposing self-deception, as it follows the characters talking to themselves while we as readers can see that what they are saying to themselves patently lacks credibility. In the passages I have reviewed, this is clear in Emma's telling herself she has been visibly transfigured through adulterous sex, in Tsirl's congratulating herself on her magnaminity toward her poor relative, and in Hirshl's avowing to himself that his sole concern was to imagine his son getting better while we understand that his imagining is all about Bluma, not about his son. In all these instances, it is evident that free indirect discourse is a beautifully efficient and effective instrument of characterization. We all sometimes tell lies to ourselves for the sake of our own self-regard or to avoid discomfiting thoughts. The novel, with its commitment as a genre to exploring the complexities and contradictions of character, often takes advantage of this technique that deftly achieves precisely the end of representing the ambiguities and the little hypocrisies with which people live. In this regard, free indirect discourse works especially well for characters lacking self-knowledge, which is obviously the case for Emma, for Tsirl, and for Hirshl.

Another way of representing consciousness, in which Flaubert may have been a pioneer, is the visual rather than the verbal evocation of what is going on in the character's head. Here is Emma, running through a stand of trees, utterly distraught because she has just been abruptly cast aside by Rodolphe: "It seemed to her suddenly that fire-colored globes were bursting in the air like incandescent balls, flattening out and turning, turning, to melt into the snow, among the branches of the trees. In the center of each of them, Rodolphe's face appeared." By now, I suppose that passages like this have come to seem familiar in serious novels, but in the middle of the nineteenth century, when this was written, it was innovative. There is something going on here inside the character's head that is not words, neither the narrator's summary of what someone is thinking or words that the character is saying to herself, but rather a visual sequence of images spinning through that highly distraught head, the evocation of a hallucination.

There is little in the evolution of literature that is entirely new. The technique, for example, of unifying extended stretches of narrative through recurring motifs that we observed in both writers was vividly evident in the Hebrew Bible long before Flaubert invented Emma's blue horizons and Agnon the blind beggar and his song. Think of the significant recurrence of garments, especially ones used for deception, in the Joseph story, or of the reiterated presence of cloaks in the Samuel narrative, from the "little cloak" that his mother would make him every year when he was a priest's acolyte as a young boy to his cloak torn by Saul and turned into a dire symbol by Samuel in his wrathful maturity. Even *le style indirect libre,* so often associated with Flaubert, can be found as far back as in Madame de Lafayette's *La Princesse de Clèves,* written in the seventeenth century.

What we see, then, in Flaubert's visual rendering of hallucinatory experience is not an absolute first but a technique with precursors — there are also occasional anticipations of it in Dickens, for example, when a character is drunk or otherwise mentally confused. Flaubert works up this narrative procedure to a fine burnish — those fire-colored globules that seem like incandescent balls, each showing Rodolphe's face to Emma, which is thus the perfect visual representation of a woman's mind maddened by disappointment in love. A recurring motif, moreover, sneaks its way in here: the "turning, turning" is a precise echo of the "turning, turning" of the ball at the La Vaubyssard château that intoxicates and dizzies Emma as we move here from a turning that is a high to a turning that is a low. It also points to the constant turning of the carpenter's lathe in the village where Emma feels trapped. In regard to the visual representation of consciousness, then, it is not that the thing has never been done, but rather that it has never been done so well.

As a consummate literary craftsman in his own right, Agnon would very likely have noticed such moments as he read *Madame Bovary,* first in German and probably, much later, in Hebrew. His early fiction does not show instances of this sort of visual representation of the movement of the mind. Let me offer two examples of it in *A Simple Story.* After Hirshl's engagement to Minna, the rich farmer's daughter, has been announced, he attends a Hanukkah party, secular in character, where people are playing cards. As he sits at a table holding his hand of cards while looking at the players around him, this is what runs through his head: "The cards leaped from the hands of the card-players with a strange rapidity, until the hands could not be seen among them. Finally, the cards, too, disappeared, and black and red faces could be seen in the room, dancing before him and mocking."

This is not an extreme experience of derangement, like that of Emma running through the woods, distraught, desperate, panicked, after her love affair has suddenly collapsed. In fact, it is the sort of thing many of us are likely to have experienced at one time or another. Say you are persuaded by a friend to attend a political debate on a topic that is not of compelling interest to you, or perhaps you don't like such debates in general because you feel they generate more heat than illumination. As the voices of the debaters drone on, you mind begins to drift away from deciphering the meaning of the words, and everything around you dissolves into a cacophony of sounds that might suggest to you a flock of crows emitting their raucous cries. Something of this sort happens to Hirshl in this scene. He does not really want to be at this party. He has not been comfortable with the announcement of his engagement. In fact, he does not really want to marry Minna, but he sees it as a fate imposed on him by his parents that he cannot escape. And so at the card table his mind drifts off from the game, begins to see the cards dealt assuming a phantasmagoric velocity and then detaching themselves from the hands of the players.

Finally the red and black faces on the cards take on a hallucinatory autonomy, staring at him in mockery — in a way, every card is now a joker. Perhaps their mocking gaze reflects Hirshl's sense that he has done something embarrassing, even shameful, in agreeing to marry Minna. At this point in the novel Hirshl still retains his sanity, but the transformation of the cards into ominously derisive faces is a striking adumbration of the moment in which he will flip into insanity, running through the forest making the croaking sounds of a frog.

The way-station to that moment is his nightly vigils outside the house where Bluma is staying. Here, too, a visual evocation of consciousness is brought into play: "A veil had fallen over all the world and you can't even see yourself. But the image of Bluma broke through and rose before you as on the day she caressed your head when you came into her room and she fled and came back." The veil that has fallen over the world would seem to be both a result of night and fog and the anguished Hirshl's mental confusion. Through this murky haze, Bluma's image bursts forth and rises like a sun. That image of rising triggers a memory of the moment that he most cherishes in their unconsummated love, when she caressed his head as he sat on her bed, the only time she actually caressed him. Agnon uses the second person singular in order to bring us more directly into Hirshel's mind because this is him addressing himself, a variant form of narrated monologue.

The final sentence of this brief passage, "Hirshl rested his head on the handles of the lock," is a striking instance of how Agnon introduces a Hebraizing element in whatever he may have learned from Flaubert. This is the narrator's report, so we are no longer inside Hirshl's head. The lock is the door-lock, indicating that Hirshl is right up against the entry to the house, not looking up at it from a certain distance. The phrase "on the handles of the lock" is a direct quotation of the Song of Songs 5:5. It is one of the most poignant moments in that Biblical book and is beautifully apt for Hirshl's plight. The beloved in that chapter has teasingly put off her lover's plea to unlock the door. When she then goes to open it, her hands dripping liquid myrrh onto the lock, for she has perfumed herself for love, she finds that he has gone, and in desperation she runs out into the dark night streets to try to find him. The resonance between this lover's despair and the anguish of Agnon's protagonist is clear — the night, the tears, the seemingly lost lover (though for Hirshl the loss will be unending). As has often been observed, literary Hebrew is a constant echo-chamber, and at strategic junctures Agnon deftly call up a resonant echo. However Flaubertian he may sometimes seem, this is not a resource that Flaubert could have deployed in his French.

Neither novel restricts its treatment of character and theme to the representation of consciousness. Flaubert is particularly good at introducing concise and arresting judgments of his characters, usually through the vehicle of a striking simile. Early in the marriage of Emma and Charles, he is blissfully happy, sexually happy (though she probably is not), and happy in his illusions about the splendid woman he now has as his wife. This is how Flaubert summarizes the tenor of his contentment: "he went out, chewing on his happiness, like those who still masticate, after dinner, the truffles they are digesting." And here is Emma's experience during this same period: "As for her, her life was as cold as an attic with a skylight facing north, and boredom, silent spider, wove its web in the shadows into the corners of her heart."

A more complicated simile is occasioned by Rodolphe contemplating his mistress' protestations of love: "human speech is like a cracked cauldron on which we bang melodies to make bears dance when one would want to reach the stars." In this instance, Flaubert segues from Rodolphe's cynical disbelief in any woman's vows of love to a general reflection, of which Rodolphe would scarcely have been capable, of the painful inadequacy of all human speech. This simile of banging on a cracked cauldron while wanting to reach the stars has been justly celebrated.

Two instances of the narrator's incisive judgment of character through simile, both from Hirshl's desperate nights outside the house were Bluma is staying, show the connection with the Flaubertian procedure. "As soon as he reached that place, he hid so that no one would see him, like a drunk who pours himself a drink and fears they will come and take it away from him." The aptness of the simile is evident: it suggests that Hirshl's attachment to Bluma is a hopeless and damaging addiction. My second example is another case of Hebraizing a technique, for the simile is drawn from traditional Jewish practice: "Like a man standing on the night of Tisha B'Av when the heavens open and he raises his eyes upward to plea for mercy, so Hirshl stood looking up at Bluma's window. What did Hirshl want? Hirshl wanted Bluma to open her window and see him." Tisha B'Av, the day of fasting in commemoration of the destruction of the two ancient temples and other calamities of Jewish history, occurs in midsummer. The folk belief is that in the middle of the night on Tisha B'Av the heavens open, and at that moment pleas for mercy may rise unimpeded to God. The point of the simile is precisely its inappropriateness. Bluma up above in her servant's bedroom has displaced "God in his heaven." That displacement can cut two ways: either Hirshl's desperate longing for even a glance from Bluma is a kind of idolatry, or the overwhelming intensity of his longing for the woman he loves can be conveyed only by comparing it to a wretched person's plea for mercy from God.

What does this comparative scrutiny of two writers from utterly different literary traditions tell us about the broader issue of literary influence? In recent decades, scholars have justly tended to avoid the term "influence" as too crude and misleading a representation of what happens when one writer interacts with another. The term is not inappropriate, I think, when a workmanlike writer reads an original one: the stylistic effect of Hemingway's innovative prose on American hardboiled writers can properly be characterized as an influence. But something different happens when a great writer encounters on the page a great writer who came before him: it is a kind of alchemy. The earlier writer strikes a spark in the later one, gives him certain ideas about how things might be done, which he will then proceed to do in his own way. Agnon read Flaubert at a relatively early stage in his career — "before writing and after writing," as he worded it in his letter to Zalman Schocken. Then, I imagine, he would have said to himself something like this: "That is really good. I could in some way use that. But how would I handle it? How could I make it work in the style and the invented world in which I have been forging my own literary way?"

When a writer of the first order of originality discovers another writer of manifest mastery, something more deeply interesting than influence occurs. Agnon would have been Agnon in most respects if he had never read a word of Flaubert, but it seems safe to say that as he was gaining artistic maturity, Flaubert helped him, if even modestly, to become the writer whom he aspired to be.

In *A Simple Story,* Agnon was writing, a little anachronistically, a nineteenth-century realist novel, for which *Madame Bovary* could serve as a useful model. Yet he was too restless an artist to remain content with this mode of fiction. During this same period in the 1930s, as I have noted, he had begun to produce radically experimental short stories. In the 1940s and 1950s, he would explore new and anti-realist directions. In

Only Yesterday, in 1945, he devoted numerous chapters to the interior monologue of a dog named Balak, who proves to be the book's most philosophically reflective character, and its most engaging one.

Toward the end of the 1940s and into the 1950s, Agnon would fashion two remarkable dreamlike novellas replete with symbolism that were unlike anything he had written before. His last, uncompleted novel, *Shira,* which he was still working on at the time of his death in 1970, is a fascinating fusion of the symbolism of the novellas — leprosy is the most prominent symbol — with tormented sexuality and resonant reflections on art and truth. So Flaubert cannot be regarded as the dominant or decisive force in Agnon's career. But still the French master made a difference. He had spoken profoundly to the Hebrew writer, and played a role in his evolution as an original artist at a moment when he was just coming into his own.

RACHEL CONNOLLY

What's So Funny?

If you read this essay you will not become a better person. I will not delineate the most progressive stance that you could take on a recent development in politics or culture, taking into account the various relevant social justice considerations and concluding on a rallying cry. And neither will you be presented with a set of arguments advancing the liberal positions that you already support, but which a less well-informed, or perhaps simply more selfish, person theoretically would not. I will not invite you to feel a sense of personal satisfaction, maybe laced with anguish, about your own right-mindedness compared to that theoretical other person.

At the same time I will not hash out a supposedly controversial, but in fact well-trodden, stance on an element of progressive culture. Likewise I will not lament the overreaches of political correctness through a series of exaggerated or otherwise dubious examples. You will not be made to feel risqué and rebellious for holding a garden-variety regressive view which, particularly considering the influence of both demographic factors and self-interest, it is perfectly predictable that you would hold.

This will not be an essay in which the likes of Foucault and Kant are quoted liberally, to remind you of my steely academic credentials, because in such writing that is where my authority, and hence your interest in continuing to read, derives from. The fact is I don't have steely academic credentials. No PhD or Ivy League anything or Oxford or Cambridge. Actually I don't even have an undergraduate degree in this essay's subject. This is not a piece of writing in which I will use credentialism to flatter your sense of yourself as a highbrow intellectual type. If that is the kind of thing you're into.

There will be no disclosure of personal trauma, or of my dramatic emotional response to an occurrence which, to a less emotionally wrought observer, may not seem really so bad. I will not describe myself as being wracked with sobs or petrified or likewise in order to make you feel either titillated, or gratified as the kind of person who tends to present themselves similarly, or mildly heroic, or as the kind of stoical person who does not, but tends to sympathize greatly with people who do. There will not be the sense that by reading this and buying into my narrative you are a Good Person, siding with a Good Person who had something bad done to them by a Bad Person. I am not a good person. Well, I am sometimes. But I am more than happy to admit that sometimes (often) I am not.

I do have one thing to offer you if you keep reading, though: I am pretty confident I will make you laugh. This is not a big promise, maybe. But look around, there's not much of it on offer elsewhere lately.

The offbeat, weird humor in the novels of Percy Everett, Gwendoline Riley, Nicole Flattery, Monica Heisey, Sally Rooney (particularly in her dialogue) and Joshua Cohen is an antidote to what Parul Seghal identified last year as the dominance of the trauma plot in fiction, and its accompanying dour tone. But elsewhere, solemn accounts of distressing events have come to be seen as the quick ticket to producing novels which possess gravity and emotional heft, even now that this mode feels rote. As Seghal put it: "The invocation of trauma promises access to some well-guarded bloody chamber; increasingly, though, we feel as if we have entered a rather generic motel room, with all the signs of heavy turnover."

In the comment pages the same endlessly reiterated positions on culture war topics dominate. Dark clouds creep closer on every front (the pace of technological development, gender relations, race relations, the books taught in schools, mental health, attention spans, standardized testing and so on) as the storm of an impending apocalypse rages. AI is one topic getting the "four horsemen of the apocalypse" treatment a lot of late. Although actually it also had a moment in the spotlight not too long ago, in 2019, when columnists were saying that if GPT-2 (a text generator prone to writing chaotic, nonsense sentences with a bent towards the discussion topics popular on Reddit in 2017) was released, we would be "hurtling towards the cheering apocalypse," but it didn't happen that year either. The world of "personal essay" writing may no longer be orientated solely around courting mindless clicks with lurid and hyper-salacious tales of incest or embarrassing trips to the ER. But now it's all dramatic retellings of lackluster boyfriends, and models complaining about the rampant excesses of capitalism that they witnessed among the rich people they observed on all-expenses-paid holidays. Self-aware self-mockery, humor as a means to deflate tricky subject matter or give a sense of perspective, and dry asides, are all scant.

Twitter and TikTok are forums which ostensibly traffic in the exchange of jokes. But I would venture that the nature of content on both platforms, and the enjoyment of it, is more related to the comfort found in the repetition and recognition of certain tropes than in genuinely engendering laughter. Besides, part of what makes Twitter funny is how poe-faced and resolutely determined not to get the joke many who use it are — the fact that you can earnestly be called a fascist for saying you prefer not to use a dishwasher (that happened to me) and so on. Actually one of the funniest things about social media in general is the sense that you are frequently receiving solemn moral instruction from some of the absolute worst, most craven and cynical people in the world.

Technically there has been a glut of a certain kind of ostensibly funny big budget production on cinema and television screens lately. *Triangle of Sadness, The Menu, White Lotus, Succession,* and *Glass Onion* all use the grammar of satire (if not really the language, thanks to an often somewhat chaotic sense of message or target) in skits that purport to send up the habits and excesses of the obscenely wealthy. But even here, where humor is supposedly a selling point, it is devalued by the fact of it being teamed with an easy, popular, "fist pump"-style political message, as if to make an argument for the worthiness of the project. Because simply making something funny, with an interesting comment on, say, different types of character — that is apparently no longer enough by itself. The idea that mass market culture could be, on its surface at least, apolitical is deeply unfashionable presently — even if this could yield work with something more interesting to say about people or ideas, or a more sophisticated political message.

And it's no wonder these films argue for their existence by telegraphing an easily digestible (frankly often muddled, once you scratch the surface) political message. This is a response to how many people engage with cultural products now. Garth Greenwell wrote recently in *The Yale Review*, about his current cohort of fiction students: "When I work with students now, graduate or undergraduate, their primary mode of engagement with a text often seems to be a particular kind of moral judgment, as though before they can see anything else in stories or poems they have to sort them into piles of the righteous and the problematic." I would take this further and say that the frantic pace at which the adjudication must be made of whether something is righteous or problematic makes confusion over this judgment not only likely, but endemic. In this way a glib, digestible, superficial message which masks a darker underlying sensibility will see a work lauded for its progressive credentials, in a manner I find quite troubling.

In *Triangle of Sadness*, for example, a film about a luxury cruise ran aground, slapstick displays telegraphed a cozy, by this stage very familiar "Eat the Rich" message, which the film was celebrated for. Rich people were thrown wildly around the ship, vomiting and having diarrhea everywhere, when the boat hit turbulence; a rich elderly pair of arms manufacturers were blown up by one of their own bombs; rich people demanded that the beleaguered staff all queue up to go down a wet slide; and so on. (*Women Talking* is another example of a film in which a heavily signposted progressivism masks a borderline reactionary sensibility, but it is not trying to be funny.) But about halfway through, when the ship sank and an assortment of passengers were marooned on an island, the message gave way to a nihilistic parable about the inherent awfulness of human nature. One of the ship's maids, the only person with any practical skills left standing, was the most powerful among them and, of course, set about merrily abusing her new position. Anyone with power would behave badly, the message went. It was celebrated for its anti-capitalist sentiment, but it didn't exactly make an argument for redistribution.

This point about the obviousness versus the underlying political sentiment in popular art may seem unrelated to a wider thesis about the humorless state of our culture at present, but it relates to a general cultural calamity about subtlety, unexpectedness, and risk, which I think underpins this tendency. Humor, you realize when you start thinking about it in any depth, is a very mysterious thing. "No one knows why we laugh," John Carey wrote in an introduction to *The Joke and Its Relation to the Subconscious* by Freud. It also isn't clear why some people are funny and others are not. "The joke work is not at everyone's command," as Freud put it, in wording which demonstrates the immense comedic value to be found in the inherent fustiness of a book which tries to explain what jokes mean to us.

There is no formula which explains why a certain thing should be funny, or guarantees that it will be funny. Actually the lack of formula seems a definitional component of humor, since so much of what is funny depends on an element of surprise or unexpectedness. As it does on mysteriousness: the more you spell out a joke, or explain why something is funny, the less so it becomes. And this sits directly at odds with our risk-averse culture, where everything must be obvious, hyper-caveated, and over-explained. And the formula of any successful cultural product must be repeated until it feels tired and rote. If the first of the "funny rich people" films was funny, is the seventh? Or the eighth? There is a roteness to so many things now. A rote way to write about trauma, or romantic relationships, to deal with this or that uncomfortable interaction, to talk about progressive politics, to be unprogressive. But predictability and explanation are the mortal enemies of humor. I read recently something that seems to sum up so much of what feels missing from our culture currently: Jeff Bewkes, a former HBO boss, remembered himself telling the creator of *Sex and the City*: "I don't want ratings. I want a better show...stop explaining jokes." I sent it to a few friends who work as novelists and TV writers. The replies were all a version of: "Better times!"

Risk aversion and obviousness now dominate perceptions of what constitutes substance in art. We have become unsubtle in the way we understand emotional currency. Seriousness is considered the terrain of mawkish sentimentality, while humor is hokey and cozy. The two don't mix; one doesn't mask the other, as is often the case in life. This seems like a depressing thing to have to argue against. So I will share a poem by Rene Ricard instead, which, in a few unlyrical lines, renders an almost disquieting quantity and depth of emotional states, and an overall truthfulness that no amount of melodramatic adjectives about bad boyfriends could ever evoke:

I am young
And I am beautiful
And I will fuck you
Over just like everybody else

I have noticed this tendency towards risk aversion in interpersonal interactions, too. This is anecdotal and, depending on your circles, you may not have noticed the same. But I have become interested in the way in which people in their twenties and early thirties use the word "canceled" colloquially, among other related observations. I am aware that it has become hard to talk seriously about anything related to the idea of canceling because so much of the discourse around it is so shrill and, besides that, because the discourse is the equivalent of walking across a room with a floor coated entirely in mousetraps. But I think there is something important in what I have noticed so I want to try anyway.

The instances I am thinking of relate mostly to young men. Not because I think this is a trend among young men only, but because I am a young woman and recently I have been trying to speak to young men about their views on masculinity, which can be a tricky topic for men to discuss at present (and at other times too, for different reasons). And maybe especially tricky to discuss with a woman. I began instigating these conversations for a mixture of professional and personal reasons. I am often drawn to writing about contemporary male-female relations, the muddled state of communication between men and women at present, and certain flattening narratives concerning stereotypes of female personality traits, and thus the form that heterosexual relationships tend to take. The more I have written about these things, the more I have found myself seeking male perspectives to better inform my understanding of all this. In a personal capacity, too, I have detected a certain mood among many of the young men with whom I interact — a mood that I would define as a combination of listlessness, confusion, and despondency. I find this sad and a little unsettling so I am trying to understand it better. (I wouldn't say that life is so easy for young women either, but I don't really need to ask around to find out what that's like.)

Anyway, this has resulted in me instigating a lot of conversations that can be pretty uncomfortable. They tend to start out as fairly, even very, awkward. Also a lot of the men think that I am hitting on them (we tell ourselves stories in order to live), which then begets a whole other minefield of potential awkwardness and misunderstandings. The best response I have received so far was from a man who told me that, because he has a girlfriend, we would have to meet during the workday, by his office. I gathered that our meeting was to be clandestine. And my assumption was verified when we did meet. We were walking around and someone he knew happened to pass by and say hello. He sort of shrieked and elbowed me into a nearby alley.

When we get past all that, though, and we can talk, I learn a lot. I have noticed that the idea of being "canceled" comes up often, as a casual reference rather than an in-depth discussion of the phenomenon. A representative quotation: "It's nice to talk about this stuff. You can't really a lot of the time. People will think you're into Andrew Tate. You'd be canceled." (Andrew Tate is a misogynistic internet celebrity from Britain who has amassed a large international audience preaching hyper-masculinity, and has also been arrested for human trafficking.) I think you could use the fact that people are talking in this way to argue for or against the existence, the effectiveness, or the righteousness of cancellation as a "thing." Or actually, for or against any of the endless strands of argument that surround this topic. But I'm more interested in thinking about what exactly these men are using this word to mean. There is not a widely agreed definition of what being "canceled" consists of. But let's say that a functional definition is this: a social media (or otherwise public-facing) campaign to accuse a person of holding unacceptable views (rightly or wrongly) which has successfully stripped them of certain (but maybe not all) professional opportunities and seen them ostracized from certain (but, again, maybe not all) social circles.

Right now you are thinking about everything that is wrong and terrible about my definition and how you could write a better one instead. Never mind; my real point is that I don't think that this is what these men are using this word to mean. And I don't think they are using it to mean a less or more severe version of this either. For a start, because I'm not really sure how they could be canceled. These are broadly not people who must maintain a social media presence for work (with the exception of a few influencers among my sample, who tend to have a far more sophisticated understanding of how to manipulate these dynamics anyway). They mostly don't use social media much at all, other than as passive consumers. They don't inhabit particularly progressive social circles or professional worlds where their views are really anyone's concern. Besides, nothing we end up discussing is objectionable by a reasonable person's definition. I can't see that there would be even minor professional consequences for a carpenter who was known to have gentle disagreements with the tenets of liberal feminism, for example.

So what do they mean when they say "canceled"? Well, to go back to the earlier quote: "It's nice to talk about this stuff. You can't really a lot of the time. People will think you're into Andrew Tate. You'd be canceled." To me, the interesting thing is that the fear here is not that he would be discovered to secretly support Andrew Tate, but that he might accidentally say something which implied that he did. If I think about the possible bad consequences that could result from that, that whoever he is talking to might make an accusation, then he would probably try to explain what he meant and perhaps struggle to do so (some people are better at semantic precision than others). By this stage he would have lost control of the conversation. Then other people might be told and a misrepresentation of himself that he would find difficult to correct may spread. I'm not sure this would have professional consequences or the like. But maybe the idea of being misrepresented or misunderstood when trying to talk about something you feel deeply about is unpleasant enough by itself.

I may be wrong. But I can't see what else they would mean. And, if it is true that these men (and other people, I think) are scared to talk about how they really feel in case they are misunderstood or misrepresented, it may not matter. But I think it does. There are bigger problems in the world, of course. But I am a writer, not a social worker, a politician, or a doctor; and I insist that there is enormous value in trying to understand how other people really feel. As a person, too, I am starting to wonder if the mood of listlessness, confusion, and despondency that I have noticed is connected to this fear — to this jittery nervousness about the consequences of speaking honestly with other people.

This may seem like a digression from my point about humor, but I believe that it is a fundamental component of how we communicate with each other at present. Hence the blandness of the cultural products which are made and put in front of us. There is a base level of anxiety about misrepresentations and misunderstandings which might, at any point, send everything sliding down into a ravine. In such a climate nobody wants to take a risk.

No one knows why we laugh, but when I was thinking about how humor works in a social setting I kept coming back to the idea of trust. When you make a joke, you take the risk that the other people you are talking to may not get it. You would look stupid if they didn't get it, and everyone really hates to look stupid. So you need to feel there is at least a base level of good faith in the group. And when they laugh, their laughter demonstrates that you share an affinity of sorts, and there is a slightly strengthened bond between you, since you have all experienced something enjoyable together. The best outcome is that you trusted people and you were rewarded for doing so.

Something else I have noticed about humor, throughout my life, is that it can make hard things easier to talk about. I am from Belfast, born just before the Troubles ended, so I suppose I have close relationships with more people who experience untreated PTSD than maybe the average Western millennial does. Contrary to received wisdom about how trauma manifests, my observations have been that humor is a large part of the response. I notice it all the time. Just the other week, my mother told me that she had seen an interview in a magazine about a celebrity who talked about her memories of growing up, shopping for second-hand furniture in boutiques. "When I was growing up we'd have to do that every week because of the British army, but it was hardly boutiques," she said. "Actually no, that's not true," she went on, laughing. "It was closer to once a month." And actually it was very funny, although it loses something in the translation.

There is something about the nature of remarks such as these, which invite someone else to laugh along with you at what is essentially your hardship, that has long fascinated me. When someone frames their suffering through laughter, it seems to communicate a mysterious, hard to describe, quality of human nature. A resilience, a sense of lightness to be found in almost any circumstance, and a generosity too. A comment such as this one seems to say: I have seen it, the thing which you fear, and here I still am. It wasn't really all that bad.

The grittiness, the hardiness, the sort of blemished quality that I perceive, from my experiences, as fundamental to people can seem at odds with a view of human nature which is softer and more straightforwardly sentimental. But I sometimes wonder if my impression, in which we are all sort of down in the mud but together, wading haphazardly towards each other, is really the mushier of the two. I wonder too, if there is a deeper kind of sentimentality in the generosity inherent to communicating traumatic experiences this way. In a way that makes them easier to connect with, if not to fully understand.

The funniest person I know is my grandmother, who has lived a strange and hard life, by the standards of today. She tells the most entertaining, the most hilarious, stories about bleak situations and events that I find extremely hard to imagine. I don't know how we would have those conversations if they had to be told in grave terms. I don't know if she would want to have them, either. And she sort of sees everything in life this way too. Discussing a friend of hers who has had a lackluster thirty-year marriage, she said: "If she'd have killed him she'd have been out by now." On another man she does not consider to be handsome: "He could be coming up the road with the lottery under his arm and it would still be a no from me."

It is sad, and bad for our culture, that the weirdness and the energy and the vitality of remarks such as those feels so uncontemporary, so beyond us. We need to get better at taking risks again, and not only for the sake of humor. Did I make you laugh?

HELEN VENDLER

The Shaper

When I was young, I wondered what the essential ingredient in a successful lyric poem actually was. I had learned that a poem did not have to have meter and rhyme, that a poem could do without the first person, and that no topic was impossible to poetry. But when I was disappointed in a poem I could not say why it was lifeless. What, I wanted to know, gave satisfying poems their life-likeness and intensity?

At twelve I discovered that poems were not necessarily born as they appeared on the page, but often went through many drafts with seemingly unpredictable changes. I perceived, in astonishment, that poems grow and mutate like living things. But I could not determine the reasons behind the poet's revisions, and I spent a good part of my fifteenth year puzzling over drafts of poems by Dylan Thomas, sent to me in microfiche from the University of Buffalo, which held the originals in enthralling number and variety. Already, Hopkins and Thomas had convinced me of the indispensable value of sound, so what I was trying to deduce from the drafts was the reason for revisions in sound as well as in every other layer of a poem, from plot to commas. I found that by imagining myself into the sensibility of the poet holding the pen (and often copying out each successive draft myself), I could ask "myself" why "I" preferred this word to that, this length of line to that, this tone to that. I was unhappy when I could not "figure out" the motive behind a given change, but by the time I had investigated all the Buffalo holdings (there were, as I recall, about thirty drafts of "Fern Hill" alone), I could guess some plausible motives for alterations: "I" was hunting down a more striking metaphor or a more energetic rhythm or a better stanza-form or a firmer point of view. But I still did not see what was directing the whole suite of changes occurring in the multiple evolutionary episodes of the poet's accumulating pages.

I had already memorized (so as to carry them around with me) many standard anthology pieces, but even making them "mine" did not illuminate the sustaining underlying "law" which I was convinced must be governing all the poet's successive micro-revisions. I resorted to conventional ideas of how other verbal things (dialogues, fictions, arguments) were assembled: logic, listing, working toward and away from a climax, having symmetrical parts, but none of these seemed to offer the law for poems in general. Eventually, after some years, I realized that the deepest determining factor was what

Coleridge had referred to as his "shaping spirit of imagination." (I had glided carelessly over the adjective "shaping," registering only "spirit of imagination.") A mysterious human function, "shaping" lay hidden within every successful poem: it ruled not only the construction of the whole poem but also of its substructures, down to its multiple individual layers — stanzas, sentences, rhythms, tenses, sounds, articles, point of view, punctuation. My own mind lacked this indispensable ability to make magnetic matches across layers, and the lack explained why I was not a poet, in spite of the verses that I had composed between six and twenty-six (when, doing my thesis, I discovered that what I could write was prose).

What was that shaping function, I enviously wondered, and how did it operate? I had found no answer by introspection or by private composition: much as I was moved and delighted by the result of successful "shaping" (a poem that leapt off the page) and much as I was fascinated by its processes, I still could not understand the sureness of aim of a poem's intrinsic growth toward secure life (even life as a fragment). Hopkins, in his last poem, "To R.B.," compared the growth of a poem within the poet to a long pregnancy: the "sire" of the poem, its founding insight, has receded and seems lost but the mothering mind continues her patient work:

> The widow of an insight lost she lives, with aim
> Now known and hand at work now never wrong.

The composing poet knows when an arriving word matches the original insight and finds its aim: the hand at work is "now never wrong." "Never wrong" was what I had sensed in an achieved poem — that an invisible contour of mind and feeling had pre-existed the drafts, and to take on life the poem had to match that initiating (and ever-governing) contour. Every revision was another try at a match, an attempt to obey the glimpsed "law" which had to be fulfilled.

I say all this because when a strange new poet appears, it is not so much the "message" of the poetry that I hope to describe as the manner in which the message reaches us. How does the new voice create itself and what elements are implicitly being chosen or rejected as it speaks and we listen? Reviews of new poetry tend to dwell on the biography of the poet or the topical "message" of emotional concern (nowadays often political or ecological) put forward by the poetry. I always want, instead, an answer to my first question: is this poem one of those that will have the strength to survive? Milton hoped that he "might perhaps leave something so written to aftertimes, as they should not willingly let it die." Poems that can interest readers over centuries do not depend on topic or plot: they are more subtle, and more original, than that. In poems that outlast their own generation, the poet has found a voice and a way of thinking that does not sound or feel like anyone else's. Around the living poems lie the heaps of unoriginal verses of patriotism or love or death that have succumbed to the passage of time. (A few of those, erected into national anthems or religious rituals, remain fixed in cultural memory, whatever their lack of imaginative distinction.)

And so, thinking of our impulse to praise the strength of a new poet, I was impelled to write here about a young and "difficult" Vietnamese-American poet, Ocean Vuong. The glowing reception of his first two books (a "novel" and a volume of poems) did not quote enough for me to be able to judge them independently: public responses in blurbs and reviews alike understandably spent most of their space on Vuong's heartbreaking life after the Vietnam war. At two, as the war was ending, he left Vietnam with his mother and some relatives; at six, after a few postwar years in a Philippine refugee camp, he and his half-white mother (rejected in Vietnam) gain asylum in the States, but he is by then abandoned by his white American soldier-father, adding to the family's collective desolation. In Hartford, he forgets his first language while being schooled (and bullied) in English; at adolescence, feeling terror on discovering his own homosexuality and his ambiguity as a mixed-race person, he nonetheless conceals his sexual secret, falls in love, and finds embarrassed silent joy in his barren days. Then, as his beautiful and tender mother dies of breast cancer, he falls into suicidal depression and drug addiction, ending up hospitalized after an anguished nervous breakdown. Through these vicissitudes, he eventually makes his way to recovery, at Brooklyn College and New York University, through a rebirth of self in writing.

When Vuong's third book, a volume of poems called *Time is a Mother* which appeared last year, was given to me last Christmas, I could judge for myself. I was soon set back on my heels by poem after poem. Who would think an elegy could consist of nothing after its title except Amazon cash register receipts? These mute pieces of evidence reveal a history of Vuong's mother under the title "Amazon History of a Former Nail Salon Worker." The "poem" covers twenty-one months (two with no receipts at all). The items listed on the receipts vary, but there are recurrent categories: a painkiller, a gift for a child, some female-linked purchase, something aesthetic, something to eat, job materials. The first two "month-receipts" read:

Mar.

Advil (ibuprofen,) 4-pack
Sally Hansen Pink Nail Polish, 6 pack
Clorox Bleach, industrial size
Diane hair pins, 4 pack
Seafoam handheld mirror
"I Love New York" T-shirt, white, small

Apr.

Nongshim Ramen Noodle Bowl, 24 pack
Cotton Balls, 100 count
"Thank You For Your Loyalty" cards, 30 count
Toluene POR-15 40404 Solvent, 1 quart
UV LED Nail Lamp
Cuticle Oil, value pack
Clear Acrylic Nail Tips, 500 count

The reader begins, of necessity, to interpret the receipts: "I see, the woman has found a job — a chair in a nail salon — but she has to buy her own supplies. Whatever her pain is, she is buying Advil in multiples. She rarely leaves the Amazon site without ordering something to bring a smile to the face of her young child. They are poor, living on ramen, the cheapest meal to buy, the easiest to make. And she has bought a rust-preventing toxic paint."

The receipts get shorter and the pain gets worse: in December she is buying "Maximum Strength" Advil. And there is nothing at all under "*Jan.*" Has she been hospitalized? By February she needs a walker, and in March she buys a "Chemo-Glam cotton head scarf, sunrise pink." In April a receipt records "'Warrior Mom' Breast Cancer awareness T-shirt, pink and white," and in May a "Mueller 255 Lumbar Support Back Brace." Back in December, she had been preparing for spring, buying "Tru-Gro Tulip Bulbs, 24 pcs." But when June comes, there is only one item on the receipt:

Jun.

Birthday Card — "Son, We Will Always Be Together"
Snoopy design

In July, horrible to imagine, she orders from Amazon her own funeral urn and a large picture-frame (for a photo of her to be left to her son?). August: no receipt. By September, her aesthetic desires still alive, she orders "Easy-Grow Windowsill herb garden." The receipts for October and November anticipate her funeral, as she buys — knowing she will soon die — a new winter coat and warm socks for her son:

Oct.

YourStory Customized Memorial Plaque, 10 x 8 x 4 in
Winter coat, navy blue, x-small

Nov.

Wool socks, grey, 1 pair

As the apparently random purchases aggregate, they begin to tell a story, demanding to be pieced together by the perplexed reader. Each month's list creates a "stanza-with-variations" of this dual tragedy of a broken mother and her shattered son. At the end, the isolated son, wearing his new coat, stands next to his mother's grave, his only possessions a gaunt photo, an ash-filled urn, and a "Customized Memorial Plaque." This is a version of what Thomas Gray called "the short and simple annals of the poor," but instead of the somber stanzas of "Elegy in a Country Churchyard," this chronicle is articulated in the enforced clichés of Amazon Americana, from Snoopy to the "Eternity Urn," the "Perfect Memories" picture frame, and the "YourStory Customized Memorial Plaque."

Struck dumb by my compelled participation in this unprecedented format of grief, I thought, Who is this writer who can compose an elegy without using a single "poetic" word? Unconsciously, then consciously, the reader absorbs the bitter irony felt by the poet as he must copy these ignoble commercial words — wrenching for him, the reader, and the poem itself — that have become the stinted vehicle to convey his lovely mother's life and death. This starved funeral "poem" stations a single mourner silently creating a single ritual, the transcription of a symbolic Amazon liturgy. Yes, I would not willingly let this poem die, silenced as I was by Vuong's bold "shaping spirit" which invited me, holding discarded Amazon receipts, to intuit the pathos of his mother's story. This was a poem that bore out Stevens' insight that a convincing poem must, by its composed form, "resist the intelligence almost successfully."

What, I then wondered, would this poet do in a more traditional kind of lyric? I turned to a title bearing an immemorial Horatian allusion, "Ars Poetica as the Maker." It is Vuong's version of Genesis, exhibiting what is required in the twenty-first century if credible original creation is to occur: in it we hear the voice of a god as he creates a second Adam from the clay of the earth. This is material that has appeared for centuries in literature, in art, in music; what can the young artist's "shaping spirit of imagination" do to renew such worn and familiar material? Vuong will — shockingly — play god himself. Did Vuong know that the first vernacular play in medieval France dramatized Genesis, beginning with God's instructing Adam that he was formed from clay, and Adam's responding that he already knows that fact?

> "Adam."
> "Sire."
> "Formé je t'ai du limon de terre."
> "Je sais."

Like the medieval creator of *Le Jeu d'Adam,* Vuong removes the story from Genesis' distant third-person unfolding, "In the beginning, God created heaven and earth." Like any original artist building on an earlier text, Vuong creates in order to critique or repudiate the status quo of that text (therefore the eager and angry banning of books by church and state alike). As the presiding god, Vuong opens his Genesis obscurely in the first person, offering a series of truncated reasons for an action not yet revealed:

Ars Poetica as the Maker
    And God saw the light and it was good. — GENESIS 1:4

Because the butterfly's yellow wing
            flickering in black mud
was a word
    stranded by its language.
Because no one else
            was coming — & I ran

out of reasons.
So I gathered fistfuls
of ash, dark as ink,
hammered them
into marrow, into
a skull thick
enough to keep
the gentle curse
of dreams. Yes, I aimed
for mercy —
but came only close
as building a cage
around the heart. Shutters
over the eyes. Yes,
I gave it hands
despite knowing
that to stretch that clay slab
into five blades of light,
I would go
too far. Because I, too,
needed a place
to hold me.

So I dipped
my fingers back
into the fire, pried open
the lower face
until the wound widened
into a throat,
until every leaf shook silver
with that god-

awful scream
                & I was done,
      and it was human.

Allusions abound here, but Vuong makes sure that a missed allusion does not vitiate the poem: the words survive on their own and the poem remains coherent. His Ars Poetica is a correction of Genesis as well as an allusion to it, and it stems, surely, from Vuong's own formative truth — that without suffering, creation would not burst out of muteness into life. As Keats wrote to his brother George, "Do you not see how necessary a World of Pains and troubles is to school an Intelligence and make it a Soul?" The original Eden presented no pains and troubles; the God of Genesis did not create Adam with the intention of allowing him agony so that his "blank Intelligence" might acquire what Keats called "identity." Had the God of Genesis wanted to affirm that Keatsian truth, he would have made pains and troubles intrinsic to life in Eden, so that personal identity — and consequently individual art — could arise there.

Vuong's revision of Genesis is (to quote one of Pound's descriptions of poetry) a "dance of the intellect among words." It requires rehearsal here if the reader is to understand its choreography. In the beginning, according to Vuong's history, there was an apocalyptic fire destroying all of god's creatures, so that nothing now presents itself to "the Maker" as available material for creation except the ashes of aftermath (or so Vuong felt, one assumes, after the incineration of Vietnam by a fire invisible now but still boiling beneath the hostile halves of his country). The god of aftermath, seeing the depopulation of earth, tells us, in his own evasive speech, that he has decided to make a new creature more expressive than the beautiful, suffering, but inarticulate butterfly of his earlier effort. An unidentified questioner has asked this god why he decided, after the butterfly, to engage in further creation, and the god's reasons for recommencing — both cogent and idle — initiate the poem:

> Because the butterfly's wing" [had no language with which to express its pain];
>
> Because no one else was coming [to repopulate the earth];
>
> & [because] I ran out of reasons [not to].

Who is the questioner? The answer becomes evident if one recalls the first and second questions in the Christian catechism: "Who made you?" "God made me." "Why did God make you?" The second, tormented Adam needs an answer, but the god's reasons are slippery and inconsistent, exemplified in form by the changing lineation of his speech.

The narrative continues: the god of aftermath, troubled (like earlier, now extinct, mankind) by the paradoxical "gentle curse of dreams," creates a clay slab from the sooty ashes and creates five senses ("five blades of light") opening up the world to his experimental post-apocalyptic creature. He has thereby gone "too far," because it is the senses that enable his creature to sin and suffer. Blake's hammering god is the model for Vuong's own hammering "Maker": interrogating the Tiger, Blake asks what force created him: "What the hammer? what the chain? in what furnace was thy brain?" Yet the god invented by Vuong impedes the very senses he created. Because he cannot call them "good," he sets himself further tasks, "building a cage / around the heart" and putting "Shutters / over the eyes." Nonetheless, the god affords (for his own self-interested cultural survival) one form of agency to his nascent Adam (who is as yet an "it"): "Yes, / I gave it hands" so it could create, through art, a visible icon of its god: "I, too, / needed a place / to hold me." "So" — and then the purposeful phrases, one by one (advancing in quasi Anglo-Saxon two-step lines that pause halfway to take thought) reach the unforeseeable conclusion of the god's tripled opening "because."

Without language, his newly made Adam would, like the helpless butterfly's wing, be beautiful but stranded, and so the god must introduce violence in himself to complete (by self-mimesis) the violent creature who will erupt, because of its unbearable suffering, into articulation. Dipping his fingers back into the fiery magma of creation, the god "pries open" the lower face of the second Adam, wounding it hideously to compel the scalpel-slash to widen "into a throat." Vuong's poem ends in the incarnate scream of the wounded flesh. Vuong allows, however, before the end, an anticipatory and compensatory flash-forward into the silver light of poetic speech, when sibylline leaves (borrowed from Virgil, Hopkins, and Eliot) will flutter as the throat utters itself, with tortured sound, into human life. With the awakening of human language, the god ceases to act, and the parallel clauses ("I was done" "& it was human" declare the tragedy of divine metamorphosis as a god takes on human incarnation. (The Christian allusion works if you see it, and the poem works even if you don't.)

Vuong's volume, in its title *Time Is a Mother*, declares that he has experienced a new birth after the extinction-by-breakdown of his former existence: the poet's resurrection is accomplished through the discovery, with time and labor, of self-creation in words. The god of the poem, after allowing his sublime power to wax, humiliates it by gashing it into suffering flesh. Returning to the volcanic *ur*-fire to create his creature's face, he must savage it by widening a slash into a throat, enabling the new Adam, no longer an "it," to gain personal identity. The creator-god vanishes into the creature made in his image and likeness as it assumes its new being: "with that god-/awful scream." "I was done. / & it was human."

After reading these two poems – one located in the banality of Amazon receipts, the other located in the high drama of Vuong's resurrection into shaped articulation after his mute "death" in breakdown — I hardly expected the black humor and flashing street-life of other poems by Vuong:

This is the best day ever
I haven't killed a thing since 2006
("Snow Theory")

Scraped the last $8.48
from the glass jar.
Your day's worth of tips

at the nail salon. Enough
for one hit.
("Rise & Shine")

Hey.

I used to be a fag now I'm a checkbox.
("Not Even.")

Even the most contemporary of these poems pose some of Vuong's riddles: a single line in "Almost Human" offers not a choice among similar things but an "irrational" choice between dissimilar categories: "It was 2006 or 1865 or .327." This could be translated (with some help from Wikipedia on Wuong's birth date – 1988 — and the meaning of ".327") as:

> I was eighteen when I learned in a history class that the
> United States had had a Civil War that ended in 1865:
> I understood then that what we fled in Vietnam was a
> Civil War too. And when I turned eighteen, I read with
> fear that the .357 magnum revolver used by the police
> was being replaced by the more lethal .327.

In his "novel," *On Earth We're Briefly Gorgeous,* Vuong sometimes had to interrupt his largely autobiographical narrative in order to supply the factual origin and political dimensions of the war that doomed his family to American poverty (mayonnaise sandwiches), illiteracy (Vuong learned to read at eleven), and the harrowing screams of his grandmother's nightmares. He found in poetry a more accurate way than narrative to sustain his fragmented recollections: he could offer, screen by screen, individual shaped moments of memory. The reader remains alert, wondering what life-events could lie under his elliptical sentences:

> It's been a long time since my body.
> Unbearable, I put it down
> on the earth the way my old man
> rolled dice. It's been a long time since time.

The hooking of a "cool" syntax to unbearable sentiment is one of the many ways in which Vuong's language calls attention to itself, making itself visible by unsettling the common rules of narrative expression.

Or Vuong's language demands attention by a spectacular unsettling of time. One formidable twelve-page *tour de force* called "Künstlerroman" ("Story of the Artist's Life") tracks the poet's life backward, present to past, in ever-new variations. Opening in the full modernity of an electronic "now," the poet is unable to forget his traumatic past:

> After walking forever through it all, I make it to the end.
> The **REWIND** button flashes red__red__red.
> I sit down and push the button. The screen flicks on.

We learn later that the poet is recoiling from his approaching book-launch in an expensive hotel, and his reluctance to advance presses him backwards into and through galleries of visual memory, affixing montages of past over present, present over past, while including such contemporary extremes as repellent snatches from a gay sex chat-room accompanied by truncated "dick pics," and a reversal — by this survivor of napalm and family deaths — of the collapse of the Twin Towers and the explosion of bodies. It is a tableau of yearning, this reversal:

> Then the gypsum, calcite, plaster, and lead particles
> rise from the pavement in massive billowing clouds, and
> the North Tower reconstructs itself and September's
> clear and blue again, and the people float up, arms
> open, to stand looking out of windows in good suits,
> in good bones.

This impossible pageant of resurrection, as soon as it is envisaged, expunges any lingering belief in a heavenly afterlife.

On the page following the public death of the Towers, a private crisis, also reversed, transmits "the boy's" shock as he sees his mother knocked down by "his father's fist." The intimate violence creates a trauma as destructive as any public catastrophe:

> I see the boy walk backward into his house, ease his
> mother down on the kitchen tiles. His father's fist
> retracts from her nose, whose shape realigns like a fixed
> glitch. If I slowed it down here, I might mistake the
> man's knuckles for a caress.

As the auteur of his own film, the poet fancies himself able to carry out on the page the corrections of plot that life itself forbids. His will to reverse time extends in a playful moment to the cosmos itself, as "The Hubble telescope swoops the other way" and "Halley's comet shoots back behind the trees." Yet this astronomical innocence collides immediately, without even a comma's pause, with the sinister return of human experience "as the Humvees roll, again, into Iraq." The absence of any comma tells the reader that the auteur himself cannot retain cosmic "innocence" by a willed suspension of human aggression.

Vuong's long "Künstlerroman" exhibits, and argues for, a form of apparently "spontaneous" lyric composition which denies to the poem any of the usual geometric structures — linear, concentric, spiralling, vortical — that confer architectural coherence. Rather, it favors an "open" field of concern in which many futures offer themselves (a manner that underlies Whitman's expansive catalogues and far-flung geographical surveys). In Vuong's repeated reversals of sequence, the open field reaches us in a distorted way, as if perspective, grid, and climax are all inhibited when one has seen too much too young. It is a non-realistic realism, undeniable in its specific details but surreal in its irregular procedures, unloosing a successively crushing series of ungovernable effects.

Here and elsewhere in Vuong, the shaping spirit of imagination is the great mover. Routine sequential transcription — too often the fallback form for current American lyric — feels thin and lifeless next to Vuong's passionate lines of symbolic dislocation, where his images become incarnate in disturbingly disordered temporal or spatial form. How did this practice become native to the young poet? He reveals his ecstatic moment of liberation from narrative convention at Brooklyn College, when his teacher Ben Lerner tells him "You can do anything in poetry." At that permission, the young writer's driving confessional compulsion achieves its fusion with both the surrealism of his fragmented recollections and his corresponding linguistic distortions in grammar, syntax, and hierarchy. A painful linguistic choreography takes place as images confused by childhood perceptions and a frustratingly unwieldable school English coincide with the later confusions of addiction and breakdown provoking aroused despair, all to be enacted in an English betraying its alienated origins and beset by its compensatory furies. The idealistic Western art-fiction of a beautiful feminine Muse inspiring a dreamily reflective composer is put to rout in these poems, where the artist is buffeted by a psychic whirlwind of competing and irreconcilable facts, wishes, dreams, terrors, and regrets. It is a rich dynamic for an undeniable voice, fiercely directed by a shaping imagination as relentless as its raw material.

CELESTE MARCUS

A Liberal Zion?

In March of this year, the Jewish state was like a single organism whose arteries were straining to strangle one another. I visit the country regularly, but this spring I found it in the throes of a fever which has by now launched a new era of Israeli history. Liberal Zionists, freighted with the responsibility to cleanse and heal the country which Netanyahu and his brutish government every day besmirch, have taken to the streets of many cities and towns each Saturday evening since the seventh of January. Politics is the content of their struggle, but pain preceded politics. It was an intensely uneasy time. The country felt as if it had been violated from within. The mutual hostility and horror with which Israelis considered members of their own society, their own historical family, was staggering. A sort of primal shock seemed to permeate the country. And this time the state's wounds were entirely self-inflicted. One Saturday afternoon of that inflamed month, my father came home from synagogue and even before taking off his coat reported in a low, unfamiliar voice that the congregational leader whose responsibility it had been to offer the weekly prayer for the welfare of the state of Israel had broken into sobs mid-verse.

I was staying in Jerusalem; it is at once fortifying and discomfiting to run oneself over the grooves carved by history into the topography of that city. I waited for the Sabbath to set with the sun and then joined the protest which that evening, like the eleven preceding Saturday evenings (as I write the nineteenth weekly outpouring has just occurred), surged by hundreds and even thousands to the residential square in front of the President's House to protest the disgraceful fascistic devolution that Benjamin Netanyahu's new coalition government was perpetrating. When night fell and three stars appeared in the sky, I made the trek across the capital. As I climbed up Jabotinsky Street the sidewalks were clotting with people wrapped in or raising Israeli flags. I recognized some prominent Likudniks in the throng — Netanyahu had alienated some of his own. At the entry into the demonstration a group chanted slogans in support of the Palestinians and handed out stickers which read "there is no democracy with occupation," which a smattering of protestors stuck onto their flags; but deeper into the crush it was clear that this was a centrist, unmistakably liberal crowd. It represented the vast Israeli center-left, that silent, mysterious mass which at long last had made itself seen in response to an emergency. I was witnessing a rare phenomenon in politics: an enraged centrist throng of liberal patriots. These Israelis had come to reclaim their flag from the bigots and the thugs who were desecrating it. The import of that reclamation is immense.

I had been told by Americans again and again that these protests concerned only or mostly the "judicial overhaul" that Netanyahu was trying to force through the Knesset. Even before I arrived I knew that this was an incomplete analysis, that the controversy about the Supreme Court was only the beginning of a *Kulturkampf* that Netanyahu and his government had ignited. To keep himself in power, he and his allies are forcing Israel into the sordid ranks of post-liberal autocracies around the world. The crowd in which I stood that evening was in distinguished company: like dissident liberals in other countries, Israelis have joined the struggle for the resuscitation of liberal nationalism, which may be the most urgent political cause of our time.

I say resuscitation, because Israel — like the United States — was founded on liberal nationalism. The country's Declaration of Independence is a liberal document. The founders, despite being avowed socialists, enshrined individual rights and minority rights — classical liberal values. Indeed, the nationalism that flowered in the first half of the nineteenth century and which precipitated the establishment of many nation-states was largely conceived as an ally of liberalism (though there were, of course, notorious illiberal strains). Today, however, national movements almost everywhere are dominated by ethnonationalists, who cast themselves in opposition to globalists. The contemporary choice is increasingly between a vapid cosmopolitanism which has no respect for tradition or community and a blood-and-soil tribalism as grotesque as it is dangerous. But there is another option — a patriotism enriched by an abiding respect for individual liberty and minority rights. A liberal nationalism. That is the philosophy that guided Israel's founders. A woman in the crowd in Jerusalem that evening clutched a poster of David Ben-Gurion with tears pasted onto his cheeks. Right now the integrity of the project that he established is largely in the hands of the protestors. Will they make a new politics out of it?

Ben-Gurion was the founding prime minister of Israel and the patriarch who loomed over the two decades preceding the advent of the state and the first sixteen years of Mapai (the Labor party) rule after its establishment. He and his heroic comrades toiled to realize Theodore Herzl's dream: to found a state in which Jews could achieve what they called the normalization of the Jewish people, a Jewish homeland that was free and strong and open but also heterogeneous and multiethnic, and that therefore enshrined the rights of minorities — ethnic, racial, religious, and sexual — explicitly in its Declaration of Independence. A regime of perfect homogeneity is not only impossible, as an ideal it breeds bigotry. Liberalism, which is in the business of defending rights, must defend also the right to national self-determination; and if a nation-state is to be morally defensible, in terms of its treatment of its own citizens, then it must strive towards liberalism.

Yet the push towards a liberal nation-state is always aspirational, always asymptotic. It is an ideal that no state has perfectly realized. The integrity of the Zionist project is dependent not so much on the realization of that ideal as on the incessant dissatisfaction with the failure to realize it, and with the state's diligence in pursuit of it. The liberal is never satisfied, so a liberal nationalist is a dissatisfied nationalist. No country ever achieves complete liberalization, no matter how porous or flexible its national identity, but a nation-state is peculiarly tempted towards illiberalism owing to its entanglement of identity with power. For this reason, a Jew's nationalism should stoke her liberal zeal, her fervor for equality and justice — and her indignation at inequality and injustice — because the Jewish state's illiberalisms are committed in her name.

Israel's current crisis is the result of two distinct developments in Israeli history. The first is the dominance of the Israeli right, which in recent years has mainstreamed its radical fringe, and the second is the obliteration of the Israeli left. Netanyahu could not have won last year's election if there had been a viable left to oppose him, but there is no longer any substantive left in Israel. The tradition of the founders is no more. Yair Lapid and Benny Gantz are by no reasonable standard leftists. Ben-Gurion would have wept to know that Netanyahu would replace him as the longest running prime minister in Israel's history, but Israel must reckon with more than just the duration of Netanyahu's tenure: he has succeeded also in warping the Israeli political map so thoroughly that the term "Israeli leftist" is effectively meaningless. (He has had help from the Labor Zionists of our day, who have allowed their party to wither into obsolescence, and of course from the leadership of the Palestinians, whose lack of interest in a reasonable peace — and whose regular calls to violence — hold Israeli moderates hostage.)

There is a right in Israeli politics today but there is no meaningful left — the opposition seems lost; there is only a febrile, powerful illiberal nationalism and the fledgling formation of a liberal nationalist movement which will perhaps grow to accrue political power. The only robust liberal leadership in the Jewish State in recent decades has been these startling — and leaderless — protests. So dominant is the right-wing ethos in Israeli politics that it has become an unwritten rule never to bring up the Palestinians, at least if you do not wish to be marginalized. In order to advance anything like a liberal agenda, all partners in the fleeting Bennett-Lapid government, including Mansour Abbas, the heroic leader of the first Arab party to sit in a governing coalition in Israel, had to be tightlipped about their intentions. It is unsurprising that Netanyahu clawed his way back, though he was able to do so only by allying completely with the far-right — since no one in the center/center-right will any longer sit with him — thus opening the flood gates for Orban-style governance. (Posters and chants decrying the affinity between Netanyahu and Orban are a mainstay at the protests.)

The Israeli illiberalism that trouble critics of Israel most often concerns the treatment of the Palestinians and of Arab Israelis. Many of the criticisms are true. The treatment, or mistreatment, of Arab Israelis and of Palestinians in the West Bank and Gaza is of intense concern for liberal Zionists. But the Palestinian problem is not the only problem that Israel faces, nor is it the only toxin which infects Israeli society. The contrary view — espoused most obnoxiously among American Jews by Peter Beinart, who does not believe in a Jewish state anyway — the view that the occupation lies at the heart of all evils, is analytically false and politically useless. The occupation does not and cannot explain all, or most, of the struggle for the identity of the Jewish state now being fought in Israel's streets. The many poisons swirling within Israeli political culture do not flow from a single source. Like the Palestinians, the Israelis have their own internecine culture and politics, which are not completely reactive and exist prior to political and diplomatic occasions. Right now there are no heroes on either side of the Israeli-Palestinian conflict, but one day the conflict will come to an end, and not even that peace will determine the character of Israeli society. The Jewishness of the Jewish state and the decency of the Jewish state will not be legislated in Ramallah or in Washington. The monomania about the occupation simplifies Israel and obfuscates many other illiberal conditions which have afflicted citizens of the state since its founding. The left, everywhere, must learn to hold all the causes and factors and motives in its head at the same time.

One must know Israeli history to understand the current *Kulturkampf*. The Jewish state that Herzl conceived and that Ben-Gurion established was a secular state. This secularism had limits — it allowed the Orthodox (and later the ultra-Orthodox) rabbinate to hold sway over many spheres of public and private life; but it was a secular state. The Zionism that flourished in the *yishuv*, or the pre-state Jewish community in Mandate Palestine, was a Zionism nurtured chiefly by Russian socialism — specifically, by the *Narodnik* socialist movement which demanded that its adherents live by their values, and that if they believed in the right to a Jewish state they must build one. This socialism appealed to young, rebellious proletarian Jews who had been Jewishly educated but were eager to move beyond a religious tradition that they associated with political and physical infirmity. Their socialism conferred upon their nationalism a universal significance. It was the intention of these pioneers to create a socialist utopia in which an egalitarian society would be realized not least by Jews speaking a Jewish language. If it was possible in Russian, why not in

Hebrew? These idealists did not know that a socialist utopia is not realizable in any language.

The physical task was no less daunting than the intellectual and political ones: these pioneers consecrated their bodies to the bone-crushing work required to transform swamps and deserts into livable land. The ideal Zionist pioneer was tanned, muscled, disciplined, and indefatigable. Work itself was considered sacrosanct, it was treated as a kind of spiritual exercise, as if the sweat could cleanse one of one's origins. For the second time in history, then, a New Jew was born in that desert. But as is always the case with revolutionary endeavors, the Old Jew was not completely expunged; traces of him remained. Those who could not perform the work, or could not shed the past and convincingly recreate themselves, or could not speak Hebrew, or were not socialists and so refused to join the Histadrut (the General Federation of Jewish Workers), paid a heavy price. Social opprobrium has sharp teeth in a country built and run by family, and purists are always unforgiving.

The values and the prejudices of this New Jew dominated the leadership of the *yishuv* in which the Histadrut, founded in 1920, was among the most powerful institutions. (In Jerusalem recently I saw an old book that was presented to a family friend upon her graduation from high school in the 1950s and inscribed to her "upon her entry into the yoke of the commandments of the Histadrut," a startling and revealing use of the exact words that the ancient rabbis used to describe the commandments of the Torah. The usurpation could not be clearer.) When the state was established, the Histadrut and the government were so tightly wound around one another it was difficult to identify which limb belonged to which. But even in the pre-state period, when over ninety percent of the population was Eastern European and the secular socialists presided over nearly every realm of life, there were rumblings of right-wing or religious dissent. And within a few years of the state's existence there were two significant sectors of the Jewish population that did not conform to the reigning Zionist ideal and had no historical experience with the Enlightenment and its fruits. They were — and still are — the ultra-Orthodox and the ultra-ultra-Orthodox known as the haredim, which means "quakers," and the Mizrahim, which means "easterners." or the Jews from Arab countries. (Some of the "easterners" actually came from west of Israel, from north Africa.)

Ben-Gurion was thirty-five when he was appointed chairman of the Histadrut. He was sixty-two when he was awarded the premiership of the new state. After the early years of austerity, the socialist pioneers whose sweat had watered the seed of statehood were fattening into a burgeoning middle class. Over time the old socialist policies which secured the same salaries for field laborers as for professors and doctors lost their twinkle. Now that bourgeois life was possible, bourgeois life was appealing. And just as the leaders of the Labor movement had begun to outgrow their socialism, the demographics in the country shifted. The Ashkenazim, or Jews of European and Russian origin, remained the elite, but no longer the majority. In the 1950s and 1960s Arab countries purged their Jews and waves of Mizrahim, who had previously accounted for a small minority, surged into Israel. Four hundred thousand arrived between 1948 and 1956, and by the end of the 1950s Mizrahim accounted for over fifty percent of the Jewish population in the country. The weak and poor state opened its doors to them, in an extraordinary demonstration of national solidarity, despite lacking the resources and the infrastructure for absorption.

The appellation "Mizrahi" flattens distinct communities and traditions into a single Orientalist category. The Jews of Morocco, for example, were unlike the Jews of Iraq. Moroccans accounted for a small percentage of the Jewish immigrants arriving in the 1950s, but they were met with a persistent bigotry. Many of them were descendants of Moroccan Jews who had been permitted to study in French schools and assimilate into French culture until the Vichy laws went into effect in 1940. (Jews had been in Morocco since antiquity.) After 1948, as Arab hostility towards their Jewish neighbors increased, the wealthy Moroccan Jews could afford immigration to France. The poor went to Israel. There they were treated with contempt by a suspicious Ashkenazi elite whom they came to despise. It had been one thing to be discriminated against by the French or the Moroccan establishment, but quite another to be similarly mistreated by fellow Jews.

The affluent Jewish community in Iraq had enjoyed full citizenship and equal rights before the state of Israel was declared. Afterwards the Iraqi government passed a law allowing immigration to the newly declared Jewish state, assuming that only the rabble-rousing young Zionists would clear out, leaving the wealthy Jews behind. They estimated that about ten thousand Jews would leave. The Israeli government guessed that the number would be about four to five times that much. No one predicted that a hundred and twenty thousand Iraqi Jews would arrive between 1950 and 1952. The Iraqi authorities, shocked by these drastic numbers, put limits on the amount of money and valuables that Jews could take with them, and in 1951 they froze all Jewish assets.

These Jews, freshly penniless, arrived on the shores of a country that lacked the means to absorb them and the inclination to understand them. Levi Eshkol, the future prime minister who was then treasurer of the Jewish Agency, warned the Iraqi-born Shlomo Hillel, who organized the mass airlifts of Jews from Baghdad and later became a prominent Israeli politician, "Tell your good Jews that we shall be very pleased for them all to come, But they shouldn't hurry. At the moment we have no absorption possibilities. We don't even have tents. If they come, they'll have to live in the street." His warnings fell on deaf ears. In some sense the Iraqi Jews had the hardest time acclimating to the horrific conditions which awaited them — new poverty is more acutely felt.

Absorption camps, or *ma'abarot*, were set up haphazardly by a government that had not anticipated such an enormous population of refugees and immigrants. Conditions rapidly deteriorated into filth and misery. Immigrants were housed in tin shacks, tents, and tarpaulin or wooden huts, which were all penned in by barbed wire fences guarded by armed soldiers. Within the camps immigrants stood in long lines three times a day for food, and for hours awaiting medical assistance. There was not enough water or electricity. Sojourns within the *ma'abarot* were supposed to be temporary — the plan had been to process and then relocate immigrants to permanent housing — but there weren't any housing units into which the immigrants could be moved. Many remained in those camps for years. The grudges and the furies which account for much of the subsequent political history of the state were developed in those shantytowns.

The logistical nightmare was coupled with coerced cultural assimilation. Mizrahi students were sent to Ashkenazi schools and Ashkenazi yeshivas. The Ashkenazi elite expected these new immigrants to pick up the rakes and hoes that they had just put down, and take their turn engaging in the backbreaking labor which had a semi-mystical status in Israeli culture. Settling the land had been an honor for the *yishuv* pioneers, but such work had no analogous respect for Jews from Muslim countries, and they resented bitterly the expectation that they would work the fields for their European counterparts. It took until the end of the 1960s for the "development towns" into which the Mizrahim ultimately ended up to achieve economic stability. Even when social mobility and economic prosperity became possible, the association between dark-skinned Israelis and cultural "backwardness" had become nearly indelible. Eventually, in 1984, Rabbi Ovadia Yosef, the giant who presided over the Mizrahi community, founded a political party called Shas (an acronym for Shomrei Sephardim, or guardians of the Sephardim) in order to agitate politically on behalf of Mizrahim. Shas now sits in Netanyahu's government, as it did in previous governments.

The Labor elite expected the Mizrahim to Westernize and scorned the patriarchal, anti-egalitarian traditionalism that characterized Mizrahi society. The first generation of Mizrahim succumbed to the forced assimilation into Ashkenazi culture — *hitashkenazut*, or Ashkenazification — but their descendants hated the Ashkenazi paternalism masquerading as progressivism. They never forgave Labor and the Ashkenazim for perpetrating their humiliation. They stewed and yearned for vengeance. Their time came. As my friends and I were leaving the protests on that rainy Saturday night, we were taunted by a few pro-Netanyahu Mizrahim. "What do you want?" one of my friends angrily shot back, "Revenge?" The man looked coldly at him and said: "Yes."

In 1964 Ben-Gurion's stature, and the stature of the Labor party, was severely shaken. The political crisis that precipitated his downfall is distinctly pertinent to Israel's current tribulations. The crisis, which became known as "the Lavon affair," began with Operation Susannah, a failed Israeli operation in Egypt in the summer of 1954. Egyptian Jews were recruited by the Israeli military to plant bombs within Egyptian, American, and British theaters, libraries, and schools. They were set to detonate hours after closing times to avoid casualties. The Israelis hoped that the attacks would create enough upheaval to upset British plans to withdraw from Egypt. The plan was bungled. No civilians were killed, but two operatives committed suicide and two were tried, convicted, and executed by the Egyptians. Pinhas Lavon, the minister of defense, professed no knowledge of the operation and accused Shimon Peres, the Secretary General of the Defense Ministry and Ben-Gurion's protégé, of having organized it. Prime Minister Moshe Sharett commissioned a board of inquiry which found no conclusive evidence that Lavon had any ties to the mission, but Sharett publicly sided with Peres anyway. Lavon resigned. Sharett, who had not known about the operation before it was executed and had vociferously and embarrassingly denied Israel's involvement, resigned as well, and was succeeded by Ben-Gurion, thus returning him to the premiership.

Six years later evidence surfaced that seemed to support Lavon's protestations of innocence. Lavon demanded that he be exonerated on the basis of these new discoveries, but Ben-Gurion refused his request, arguing that it was not the prime minister's place to rule on questions of guilt or innocence. Infuriated, Lavon recklessly appeared before the Knesset and read aloud a list of grievances and accusations levied against the defense establishment. This oration was leaked to the press. An appointed ministerial committee ruled that Lavon had not given the order for operation. Ben-Gurion resigned. And here is the rub: Ben-Gurion protested that the scandal had injured the power of Israel's Supreme Court, which had been politically by-passed in the whole ordeal, and thus damaged the country's already thin separations of power. For the next five years he continued to speak out against the Lavon Affair, insisting that awarding ministers the power to indict or to exonerate anyone was a dangerous precedent that undermined the procedures of democratic governance and the integrity of the judiciary.

The public grew tired of his obsession with the Lavon affair, but history has proven him right. Ben-Gurion sacrificed his own reputation to defend an independent judiciary which he knew must be bolstered and defended in a democratic state. Netanyahu's outrageous attempt to subordinate the judiciary to the executive has been interpreted correctly by the Israeli public. They rightly see that his maneuver to concentrate political power within the executive branch is symptomatic of an autocratic lurch. "Judicial reform" is the emblem for, and only one facet of, that alarming turn, taken in defiance of Ben-Gurion's warning against what we would now call post-liberalism. Ben-Gurion's fall from grace cost the Labor Party a lot, but it was not enough to shake Labor from its throne. That took another twenty years, and the colossal failure of the Yom Kippur war.

The first time that protests of a size and intensity comparable to the current protests wracked the Jewish state was in the year after the Yom Kippur war. Israelis were terrified and infuriated by the unprecedented failure in intelligence which had almost led to military defeat and resulted in the deaths of thousands of Israeli soldiers. The proportions of that error were so enormous that it has since become known simply as the *mehdal*, or the failure. As Anita Shapira, the great historian of Israel, explains:

> The Yom Kippur War was the momentous event that brought about the demise of the labor movement. The public perceived the *mehdal* as an expression of the Labor Party's political ineptitude, and this led to a loss of faith that was the party's most valuable asset during its years of rule. People viewed it as the natural ruling party, which knew how to steer the ship of state to a safe haven.

What goes up must come down, and no force propels an Israeli politician or party downward like the failure to protect the country. In the early years of the state, neither Ben-Gurion nor anyone else really believed that his party, Mapai, or any Labor party, would ever be thrown out of office. He died in 1973, one month after the *mehdal,* and four years before that cataclysm resulted in the political "earthquake" which put an end to Mapai/Labor rule and installed his rival, Menachem Begin, in the premiership.

Begin was a right-wing Revisionist Zionist who, during the *yishuv* period, led the Irgun, a Jewish paramilitary organization that broke away from the mainstream Labor policy of restraint in the use of violence. After the establishment of the state he led the opposition in a series of political parties that culminated in the Likud. He could not have won the election in 1977 if the previous three-and-a-half years had not yielded repeated political disasters for the left. Labor's grip had to loosen to permit his ascension. But Begin relied on sturdier political stuff than post-war anger. His base was "the other Israel," the Jewish minorities who had for decades felt politically disenfranchised. Thus began the long tradition of right-wing Ashkenazi politicians capitalizing on Mizrahi resentment. Begin shared their innate suspicion and even hostility toward Arabs, and condemned what he considered the Labor's naïve passivity towards Arab aggression. (Never mind the hard and triumphant military history of Labor years.) And, in his steadfast commitment to "Greater Israel," or to a Jewish State encompassing all the land promised by God to the Jewish people, he appealed also to the religious right, then in the first stages of settling the West Bank.

Begin, like the current prime minister who was once one of the "young princes" of Begin's party, knew how to manipulate his base. He played on ethnic and cultural divisions and stoked Mizrahi rage. And the Mizrahim were natural political allies of the religious right, since both abhorred liberal secularism. Directly after his election, Begin appeared in a yarmulke and recited a traditional blessing, and soon he could be seen celebrating his victory with a Torah scroll in his arms. He did not have a religious bone in his body, but he revered tradition and he played politics. In the years of his rule, socialism and all its furnishings were despised as symbols of a coercive Western (and Marxist) culture. By this time, of course, Israeli socialism was disappearing. But along with it the founding ideal of Israel as an egalitarian and pluralistic bastion, Hebrew more than Jewish, pluralistic and tolerant, began to erode. Jewish ethnonationalism began to assert itself and grew increasingly virulent. A new narrative of the history of the state began to be written, in which Begin and the Irgun, and not Ben-Gurion and the Haganah, played the foundational role.

Yet Menachem Begin was a complicated man. It was he who gave back the Sinai to Egypt and brokered peace with Sadat.

Jordan later followed in Egypt's footsteps and the Arab-Israeli conflict morphed into the more local and more intractable Israeli-Palestinian conflict. Begin, the conservative right-wing Revisionist, was in no way a post-liberal. He despised the left, but he believed deeply in liberal democracy. He was eloquent throughout his career about individual rights and minority rights. Just a few months ago, there presciently appeared an important and revealing collection of Begin's speeches and writings on his political philosophy. It is skillfully edited by Dror Bar-Yosef and it is called (in Hebrew) *Begin's Way: An Anthology of the Liberal-Nationalist Thought of Menachem Begin*. Here, for example, are some of Begin's thoughts about the Israeli judiciary and the Supreme Court. From 1951: "Law and jurisprudence must be independent of the ruler, even if he was chosen by the people. The various executive authorities have no right to confer upon themselves any power relevant to the power of judging." From 1958: "Experience shows that in its essence [the Supreme Court] guarantees individual freedom against attacks upon it even by a majority in the legislature." From 1960: "One of the most magnificent visions of the state of Israel is our judicial framework. We have all contributed to the elevation of the judiciary in Israel, so that it will be independent, supreme, autonomous. This is what gives reason for our lives, sanctity to our efforts, greatness to our aspirations — its name is justice."

Decades later Begin's political successor, the present-day leader of the Likud, has lost all interest in securing minority rights or in checking executive tyranny. Netanyahu's constituencies — the Mizrahim, the settlers, the ultra-Orthodox — together preach a blood-and-soil nationalism and a supremacy of Jewish religious law unbridled by liberal scruples. They have counterparts in capitals around the globe — Washington among them — where tribalists have lost patience with the strictures of democratic governance and elementary tolerance.

It is no surprise that two of the most influential contemporary theorists of nationalism, liberal and illiberal, are Israeli. Yoram Hazony has emerged as the voice of illiberal nationalism. He was born in Israel but grew up in New Jersey, where his family moved when he was a year old. Hazony majored in East Asian Studies at Princeton before getting a doctorate in political philosophy at Rutgers. The supreme object of his nationalist devotion is the Jewish state, but his style and his tone are distinctly American. One of Donald Trump's aides remarked that Hazony's book *The Virtue of Nationalism* was foundational to Trump's foreign policy, and Hazony's Wikipedia page is part of a series entitled "Conservatism in the United States." He writes his Israeli ethnonationalist books in English. Much of his work rails against the Americanization of the world order, of which he is ironically an example. Hazony's Americanness is one of the greatest ironies of his work, though hypocrisy is in his case a rhetorical asset. Propagandists do not lose arguments by having a tenuous relationship with honesty — they win them that way.

It is important to note that Hazony is not a nationalist in the sense that he believes that every nation has a right to a state. Quite the contrary. He believes that certain nations do not deserve a state (he doesn't name names, but one can guess which stateless group tops his list). He is a nationalist in the sense that he believes that nation-states, or states comprised of homogeneous peoples bound by mutual natural loyalties, are the healthiest, the most tolerant, and the most peaceful sort. As he puts it, "the world [is] governed best when nations are able to chart their own independent course, cultivating their own traditions and pursuing their own interests without interference." Hazony's ideal is Herder's "extended family" state, one so small and homogenous that its identity is based on the primal bond that one shares with one's family. But of course this is a chimera: there are no states like this and there never have been. *There are always minorities.* Even when atrocities are committed to expunge them, no polity achieves perfect homogeneity. Such ethnic purity is a sick fantasy. Hazony's cult of likeness grants bigots license to despise, to disenfranchise, and to abuse the inevitable pollutants — the minorities and the immigrants and the asylum seekers — which corrupt his dark ideal.

Hazony's book *The Virtue of Nationalism* reads as, among other things, a hackish justification of the Mizrahi resentment of the West, which is the bedrock of Netanyahu's political base. Among its many bizarre tenets is that liberalism is itself imperialistic because of its universal aspirations — it is nothing short of imperialism, in his view, when liberals attempt to persuade non-liberals to adopt their principles, as if an idea that is true in North America devolves into falsehood while migrating eastward. Why does his imperialistic view of persuasion not hold also for post-liberals who seek to influence liberals? What about the sustained American neoconservative attempt to re-shape Israeli politics — is that different, or higher? When officials of the Netanyahu government consulted Polish and Hungarian politicians about judicial reform and protest management, were they the victims of Eastern European imperialism?

Hazony's theory is revolting nonsense, but arguing against

it is a vain exercise. You cannot persuade someone who is post-argument, who is unbothered by truth or history. Those who seek to convert Hazony's followers by poking holes in his reasoning have brought a philosophy book to a gunfight. His followers do not admire him because they believe he has properly understood history, or human nature, or political science; they admire him for his rigidity, for the licenses that he grants and the moral relaxation that he dispenses, for his prescription of precisely the tribalism which liberalism labors to constrain.

Consider only a few of Hazony's sophistries. He professes horror at the dearth of intellectual diversity in liberal empires:

> Under a universal political order in which a single standard of right is held to be in force everywhere, tolerance for diverse political and religious standpoints must necessarily decline. Western elites, whose views are now being aggressively homogenized in conformity with the new liberal construction, are finding it increasingly difficult to recognize a need for the kind of toleration of divergent standpoints that the principle of national self-determination had once rendered axiomatic. Tolerance, like nationalism, is becoming a relic of a bygone age.

What he is gesturing towards is the phenomenon of wokeness, the ideological intolerance of the progressive left. But the cultural power that the left wields in America, or in other Western countries, is not remotely as threatening to freedom of expression as the political power of the autocrats who govern the nation-states that Hazony reveres. (Anyway, wokeness is not a fulfillment of liberalism but a perversion of it.) Hazony weirdly posits that homogenous nation-states are the only sort capable of fostering an intellectually diverse and tolerant citizenry, but how exactly does likeness generate difference, or tolerate it? Ethnically homogeneous states solve the problem of diversity by denying it. The variety of nationalism that Hazony supports never fostered a "toleration of divergent standpoints." Group self-love does not breed tolerance. It is among the most powerful mechanisms for conformity.

Another of Hazony's favorite theories is that American aid is corrupting the globe and forcing submission to the American empire:

> This peculiar fact – that Americans continue to provide the financial and military resources needed to keep peace in Europe at relatively little cost to Germany and France – has been an underlying reason that Europeans are so smitten with the love of liberal empire. Afterall, why should anyone stand up for principles of national independence and self-determination if it is Americans that give these countries their safety without their having to work to attain it, much as the oil gushing from the ground brings the Saudis wealth without their having to work for it?

Hazony is not offended by Putin and so does not worry about what will happen to Europe without America's backing. But he appears not to understand the first thing about moral and strategic alliances. And what about his beloved tribe? What about Israel? Where would Hazony's favorite nation-state be without the beneficence and the muscle, and the billions upon billions of dollars annually doled out to it, by the imperialistic USA? Does Hazony really want to usher in an age in which that aid ceases? Of course not — Israel could not survive in such a world.

The other significant Israeli theorist of nationalism is Yael Tamir, an academic and politician who was a founder of Peace Now in the late 1970s and served as a member of the Labor party from 2003 to 2010 and as a minister in the government of Ehud Barak. Tamir wrote her dissertation on liberal nationalism with Isaiah Berlin at Oxford. Her understanding of nationalism, as impeccably laid out in her book *Liberal Nationalism*, is rigorous and sophisticated where Hazony's is coarse and simplistic. Tamir's theory is predicated on a view of the person —not human nature, which she considers too finicky and didactic a term — that is informed at once by liberalism and nationalism, and which asserts that people have a right to communal belonging, to cultural expression, *and* to personal autonomy. She is neither an individualist nor a communitarian. She believes in the nation but not in the *Gemeinschaft*; her nation must answer to standards not of its own devising. Since liberalism seeks to secure human rights, liberalism must be enlisted in the struggle for nationalism despite the obvious tensions in such an alliance.

As Tamir shows, the view of liberalism — promulgated not only by post-liberal reactionaries like Hazony, but also by certain communitarian liberals — which holds that liberalism actively disrupts communal ties in service to an atomistic, deracinated cosmopolitanism misrepresents the tradition of liberalism itself. John Rawls, the villain of the communitarian liberals, himself recognized that "we need one another as partners in ways of life that are engaged in for their own sake, and the successes and enjoyment of others are necessary for and complementary to our own good." Communities, in other words, must flourish within a liberal society in order for that society to be healthy. But liberalism does not legislate the quality and the content of those shared commitments. Rather, it protects the citizen's right to determine them for herself. Unlike Hazony, Tamir insists that every individual has a right to choose her own community and tradition. Hazony does condone conversion or naturalization, but he believes that those processes must include a complete assimilation into the dominant culture; deviation from the majority tradition, or personal interpretation of it, is eschewed. But Tamir recognizes that "the era of the illusion that homogenous and viable nation-states are possible is over since such states never existed."

Tamir's theory might suggest that liberal nationalism is best applied to multicultural and multiethnic countries, since those are the societies in which the citizen has the most options from which to choose. Yet there are certain communities, she contends, that cannot fully achieve cultural expression, and realize their "right to culture," without a state. (Yes, the criteria for the state-worthiness of various groups need to be clarified. When is the distinctiveness of a culture sufficient to qualify for sovereignty or to justify separatism? This is not a simple problem.) For such communities — namely, nations — the only way to protect their right to cultural expression is to facilitate the establishment of a nation-state. Identity politics is the tool that minorities use in multi-ethnic states to preserve their culture. A liberal identity-politics, like liberal nationalism, is concerned with the preservation of a community's (and of course an individual's) rights. An illiberal identity-politics, like illiberal nationalism, demands total loyalty and conformity, the self-immolation of minority identities in exchange for membership.

If the legitimacy of a nation-state is based on the individual's right to cultural expression, then the government of a nation-state is responsible for creating conditions in which citizens are at liberty to choose how to fulfill and develop their various traditions as they wish. Religion must be free and not prescribed. This is the opposite of Hazony's primitive idea that a nation-state derives its legitimacy from "natural bonds"; in Tamir's liberal nationalism, the strength and the limits of restrictions upon religious (and other culturally specific) practices would be determined by the individual and her community rather than the government. The government would be interested only in securing the liberties required for individuals and groups to participate in their own culture.

In contrast, in an illiberal nation state, the government will itch and swell to coerce the citizenry to express its preferred version of the national culture. Multiethnicity is regarded by illiberal nationalists as a plague. Their ethnic and autocratic overreach is abundantly evident not only in the Israeli government's disdain for Israel's Arab citizens, but also in the hunger of Netanyahu's right-wing coalition to legislate religious behavior. Never mind that the largest plurality of Israeli Jews are secular, and the second largest is "conservative"; and that the Haredim are the smallest of the denominations. In a few decades, however, owing to its infamous birthrates, the size of the Haredi community, in combination with its *de facto* secession from Israeli society and its duties, will pose a significant challenge to the coherence of the Israeli polity. This coming demographic change is one of the reasons that the Israeli right has allied itself strategically with the Haredi community, which is non-Zionist or anti-Zionist and theocratic about civil life, but abhors the secular left and can deliver a meaningful number of parliamentary seats to a coalition that will meet its legal and financial demands. Now its opportunism has joined with Netanyahu's to produce the most morally dubious government in Israel's history. Netanyahu, who has for decades projected the image of Israel's protector, has allied with people who insist the study of Torah provides Israel with as much security as the army does, and therefore shirk mandatory conscription. His cynicism is bottomless.

This time Netanyahu's unbridled self-interest may have raised the left from the dead. But this left is unlike the left that began its slouch towards impotence in 1977. It is a new, liberal left. The liberal nationalism currently on display in Israel's streets has risen to the standard of liberalism enshrined in the country's Declaration. And there is reason to hope that it will gain political muscle: it accounted for nearly half the votes cast in the last election. Time will tell.

There is an idea that grounds much of what is said in defense of Israel's new government, in Israel and abroad. The idea is "Jewish exceptionalism," which is a kind of metaphysical expansion of the right's political concept of Jewish supremacy. Hazony is a Jewish exceptionalist: his nationalism is informed by an abiding faith that the Jews deserve a state because the Jews are special, because they really are the Chosen Ones. Jewish exceptionalists have co-opted the religious doctrine of chosenness to agitate for a Jewish exemption from universal moral principles and to justify the corruption of democracy.

Simcha Rotman, a member of Knesset from the Religious Zionism party and a prime mover of the government's "judicial reform," once remarked that "in my view, democracy is doing what God tells you to do. That is why anybody who goes around without a *kipah* damages democracy." Now that is exceptional! And consider this:

> Unless you believe in Israeli exceptionalism, in the biblical covenant of divine election, and in the sacred bond between the Jewish people, its creator, and its promised land, there's no reason, under any condition, to tolerate much deviance from the broadest and most inclusionary contours of every other liberal Western democracy. Why should Israel be an exception?... [But] if you believe that it [Zionism] is a Jewish liberation movement whose work begins, not ends, with the establishment of a Jewish state and whose energies come from the redemptive vision of the prophets of Israel, then Zionism ought to be recharged and tasked with nothing less than the re-founding of the State of Israel — this time as a Jewish state, rather than simply a state for Jews.

Those words were written recently by Liel Leibovitz in *Tablet*, which has become the shameful organ of post-liberalism and proto-Trumpism in the American Jewish community. Liebovitz's arrogance is breathtaking. The "state for Jews," of which Herzl dreamed and for which thousands of Jews gave their lives, and which is certainly a miracle by the standards of Jewish history, does not satisfy him. The actually existing Israel, with all its struggles and its accomplishments? He is not impressed. "The broadest and most inclusionary contours of liberal democracy," perhaps the greatest achievement in the history of human politics, is too paltry for the Jews, who are an "exception." It is remarkably irresponsible for a Jew to disparage the rights secured for them by liberal democracy — to be nostalgic for a time before liberalism or hopeful about a time after liberalism. And it is similarly irresponsible for a Zionist to insist that Israel's right to exist is based on divine election. If Israel's existence is predicated on its special relationship with the Jewish God, why should any non-Jew, or any godless Jew, honor it? Why insist on such a vulnerable justification for statehood?

Liebovitz's variety of Jewish exceptionalism is designed to raise Jews above the standards of decency to which every other people and country must conform. His belief in his own tribe's specialness is, ironically, not all that special. It is a common conception of non-liberal states and their apologists. Many peoples think of themselves as chosen. Putin believes that Mother Russia need not answer to "Western" values. Germany believed in its *Sonderweg*, its special path. China insists upon "Asian values." And post-liberal apologists for autocratic Muslim states demand that we respect "Islamic exceptionalism" even to the point of being patient with Islamism. This is the company Leibovitz keeps, and the milieu into which he would banish the Jewish state.

It is worth emphasizing here that liberal Zionism is hardly hostile to the distinctiveness of the Jews, which is historically incontrovertible. Why is distinctiveness not enough? Why must Israel be an exception? Liberal Zionism does not dishonor the unique trajectory and civilization of the Jews; it merely honors also the difference, the distinctiveness, of others as well — of its own minorities, and of those who live beyond its borders. Liberal nationalists are secure enough in their own cultural and religious identity not to deny the same dignity to others. Jews are acquainted with the brutality of such a denial. Liebovitz is a poor scholar of the tradition that he labors to defend. He should have another look at those prophets whom he reveres. Their writings are riddled with universal values, especially about justice. Isaiah was not a tribalist.

The normalization of the Jewish people and the establishment of a liberal Israel will not yield a state hostile to Jewish distinctiveness nor will it deny the importance of religion in Israeli identity. It was not intended to do so before 1948, and it is not intended to do so today. The Jewish state was meant foremost to end forever the powerlessness of Jewish life in exile and its attendant sufferings and indignities. That was Zionism's most urgent mission. But Israel was not conceived only as a haven. The Zionist inspiration was to establish a Jewish State that is defensible also morally, respectful and protective of minority cultures, and sensitive to religious and spiritual sensibilities and ways of life. That is the future for which the protestors surge into the streets on Saturday nights. It is the only worthy one.

LEON WIESELTIER

Same But Different

I

The heaviest stone that melancholy can throw at a man is to tell him he is at the end of his nature.

W.G. SEBALD

All my life I have pondered my failure to live up to the romance of transformation. I have been born only once. I studied mystics but saw no visions. I read about voices but heard none. When I made changes, they turned out to be only revisions and modifications. I have been engulfed by certain experiences, but their effects were left on the old substance. There was the night, many decades ago in a dark room in a sixteenth-century manor house in Oxford, when I heard, for the first time, on a rickety gramophone next to my bed, Beethoven's fifteenth string quartet Op.132, and the third movement, the celestial one "in the Lydian mode," lifted me up, and terrified me with its demands — but when the music was over I was low again, the elevation was ephemeral. I felt that I had disappointed the music, and to this day I stay away from it unless I have made some spiritual preparation for it. In my religious life I envied converts: choosing is a greater achievement than inheriting; but since I myself have never found a reason to convert — or looked for one, since I am once and for all honored by my grand and taxing inheritance — the best I could do in this regard was to make myself into an advocate of welcome, so that those who acted on their dissatisfaction with their own *données* would know that there is safety on the other side. There is nothing I comprehend less about Christianity than its concept of grace, which is of a kind of coup from on high, or a monotheist's karma, and I regard miracles merely as the name we give to improbable events for which we are stupendously grateful. I mostly respect other people's new beginnings, though some transitions arouse my suspicions, but I have no talent for new beginnings, no matter how weary I become of myself.

Who has not performed the old exercise of clarifying one's principles by imagining what party he would have chosen in moments of truth gone by? One of those moments of truth that my mind visits often is America in the 1850s, and I long ago grasped that I would not have been a radical abolitionist but a moderate one. (On the other hand, there are villains in history whom I would have unhesitatingly shot dead, or so I would like to think.) In my writing, especially about history and politics, I have been the one who grimly endeavors to be sober about metamorphosis, who wishes to spoil the giddy celebrations of discontinuity and direct the attention of the celebrants to the continuities that are hidden in the revolutions, who is afraid of the millennium, every millennium, and wary of the disruptiveness of progress that I myself support, who refuses to toy and tamper with institutions and ideas that will not easily come again after they are destroyed. (The next Jewish millennium will arrive in 2240 and I am glad that I will miss it.) I am a hawkish dove, a conservative progressive, a late adoptor. Of course there are sufferings in the world that explode this rueful patience, and sometimes I have violated the rule of my temperament to go slow and demanded instead that power be used immediately against evil. There are historical actions that cannot wait. We are all selective about the consequences that trouble us.

I have always been a little embarrassed about my willingness to watch justice come slowly — why would you defer the dawn? Yet I do not trust speed, because it is so heedless of what is to its right and to its left, and I do not trust efficiency, because it flattens reality and deludes us about our powers, and I do not trust unprecedentedness, because it is almost always an exaggeration and usually inculcates a thoughtless antinomianism, and I do not trust wholeness, because it represents the end of possibility. In the realm of historical action, in sum, I do not trust transformation. And in the realm of the self, when I hear the ubiquitous praises of transformation (or, in the American vernacular, of redemption and closure), my back goes up, because this almost recreational Proteanism promises an end of meaning, or more precisely, an end of the meaning for which I have been searching, or even more precisely, an end of the search. I do not wish to be told to shut down and start over. The questions were the right ones. The arena was the appropriate one. I was getting somewhere. Transformation looks to me like quitting.

Many years ago I published a book about my mourning for my father, in equal parts scholarship and reflection, a spiritual diary of a year of sorrow in which I investigated the mourner's customs that I was practicing with insufficient understanding. A review of the book by Harold Bloom appeared in the *New York Times Book Review*, enthusiastic and sloppy in Bloom's way, and amid its flattering remarks it made an objection that rankled me. Bloom complained that in the course of my narrative the narrator did not change. An epic, he said, requires a hero's transformation. Whether or not I was a hero, he was correct. I did not conform to the canonical plot. I was not transformed by my year of spiritual intensification. Enriched, but not transformed. This was a matter of fact: I was reporting on events in my mind and my heart, and relying less on my imagination. Perhaps it was evidence of my limitations that I was never bathed in light. But the important point is that I did not hunger for transformation, or for a new philosophical framework, or for a new mode of perception. Transformation is a sort of obliteration, however salvific. But my beliefs about the world seemed defensible to me, and on the right track. I sought only to understand a certain human predicament that previously I had not understood. If I was wiser when it was over, it was still I who was wiser — I came out of sorrow as I went into sorrow, only less poor; and the continuity, after a period of sharp pain and diligent study, was exceedingly precious to me. Anyway, anybody who has prayed regularly in a crowded religious institution knows that they are not the best settings for transfiguration. If I had come away from my spiritual exercises with a pretense to a new identity, I would have felt like a fraud. Bloom was imposing upon my experience a literary requirement, as if my life were literature. The truth is that I find growth without transformation, or change without the dissolution, far more interesting.

I discovered a motto for my continuist disposition, my preferred conception of identity-in-change, in an unlikely place. In Basel, on a wall in the medieval church known as Basel Munster, a red sandstone Romanesque structure that was completed in 1500, hangs a plaque that marks the tomb of Jacob Bernoulli, *mathematicus incomparabilis,* a distinguished mathematician in a family of distinguished mathematicians, who taught at the University of Basel for fifteen years and died in 1705. (Erasmus is also buried in the church.) Bernoulli made many mathematical discoveries that bear his name and participated in the almost unimaginably rich philosophical and mathematical culture of the seventeenth century, corresponding with many of its luminaries. Set into an elaborately carved oval wooden frame with a globe at the top, a stony black surface gives the personal and professional details of the deceased, and at the bottom of the plaque, parallel to the globe, is a small black circle on which was carved, at Bernoulli's request, his credo.

Eadem mutata resurgo, is the credo. The most accurate translation is, "Having changed, I rise again the same." There were some who suggested that in its churchly context the phrase must be a reference to the resurrection of Christ, but grammar and doctrine rebut such an interpretation. Bernoulli's statement was personal, and its suggestion of individual resurrection was more exercised by the condition of the individual who will have survived the crucible. The definition of the change is sublimely mixed. Bernoulli's credo was based on a mathematical emblem of individual life and individual development — specifically, on a geometrical emblem taken from the geometry of shapes. The Latin adage, carved in gold letters, wraps around a circular representation of a spiral seen from above, also outlined in gold. It was supposed to have been a logarithmic spiral, whose defining characteristic is that it does not alter its shape as it grows larger — we most commonly encounter it in the exquisite patterning of snails and mollusks; but these are arcane matters, and the craftsman mistakenly depicted not a logarithmic spiral but an Archimedean spiral. Bernoulli had requested a representation of a logarithmic spiral because (as he wrote in a treatise about it called *Spira Mirabilis,* or *Wondrous Spiral)* this spiral "may be used as a symbol, either of fortitude and constancy in adversity, or of the human body which, after all its changes, even after death, will be restored to its exact and perfect self." Bernoulli coined the motto *eadem mutata resurgo* to describe the logarithmic spiral and its complicated model of development; and when he chose it also for his memorial plaque, he transposed it from the realm of mathematical significance to the realm of human significance. He wanted the words to describe himself.

The mathematical study of spirals, the classification of the different properties of different spirals, is an ancient pursuit; Archimedes composed a treatise on the subject. A spiral is a curved line that originates in a point and moves farther away from it as it revolves around it. A logarithmic spiral, which exercised Bernoulli (and before him Durer — perhaps the greatest geometrician among the painters — and also Leonardo) is the type most commonly found in nature. Its distinction is that it retains its shape as it grows in size. Which is to say, it changes and it stays the same. The name given to this property by mathematicians is self-similarity. A self-similar object repeats its form through changes in scale. The study of fractals revealed that self-similarity does not have to be perfect; it obtains also when an object changes but remains mostly like itself.

Self-similarity, moreover, is emphatically not the same as identity. Leibniz famously posited in his metaphysics that two numerically distinct objects cannot be the same in all of their properties, or else they would be indiscernible from each other. The aim of this axiom about "the identity of indiscernibles" was to secure the integrity of discrete individuals, to prevent similarity from climaxing in sameness and thereby erasing the distinction between existentially separate entities. Things can have many properties in common, but they cannot have all their properties in common and still be themselves. Leibniz's law was developed out of a medieval debate about the nature of angels, and it had a religious implication: "therefore," he wrote, "every substance is like an entire world and like a mirror of God, or indeed of the whole world which it portrays, each one in its fashion." We might call this the metaphysics of diversity.

Bernoulli understood that these geometrical truths can serve also as symbols of ethical values. He affectingly interprets the consistency-through-change of the logarithmic spiral as "fortitude and constancy in adversity" — the steadfastness of the self in the storm of circumstances. Here it is worth noting that Bernoulli's family had fled to Basel, where he was born, to escape the "Spanish fury," the reign of terror that the Spanish army inflicted upon the Netherlands in the 1570s. Immigrants and refugees are people for whom the retention of identity is a matter of honor. They seek only partial transformation. They are like the curve that travels far but always as itself. They exhibit both the swervingness and the unswervingness of these whorled patterns.

When I first read Bernoulli's motto, my heart quickened. Here was a formula for spiritual development that rendered moot an entire field of concepts with which the reflective and adventurous soul has traditionally been burdened: infidelity, inauthenticity, defection, betrayal, treason, heterodoxy, heresy, deviationism, apostasy. (A wise psychoanalyst once described my own psychic situation as "defection-in-place," which was my first hint of *eadem mutata resurgo*.) What if the dream of transformation is only a necessary fiction for bestirring a person or a people, for getting started? What if continuity is the very condition of right and lasting change? Personal growth must never be an apocalypse. The inalienability of one's origins and one's idioms is an obvious psychological and biographical fact about even the most restless individuals, but usually it is regarded as lamentable, an embarrassment to our freedom or our will, a weakness before the greater power of tradition or society. Perhaps it is better to consider the goal of transformation as a trap that will lead to crushing disappointment. The breathless eschatologies of self-invention and self-fashioning are the antithesis of wisdom about existence in the world. Nietzsche set us up. And as regards the history of transformation as a political objective, we have known at least since Tocqueville's analysis of the French revolution that total revolution is a myth and a murderous one.

When Bernoulli was elaborating his mottled ideal of change, a similar model of metamorphosis began to appear in the work of scholars with whom he corresponded — biologists who were vexed by the problem of generation, or what the historian Elizabeth Gasking described as "how differentiated parts could ever form from unorganized matter." How does the worm become a moth? How does metamorphosis work? There were many theories, and they all look absurd now that we possess a knowledge of genetics. Some argued for spontaneous generation; no less an authority than

William Harvey wrote that "whereas some animals are spoken of as spontaneously reproduced, others are engendered by parents." Sometimes spontaneous generation was attributed to an invisible force, but nobody could provide much information about that force. There was a school of thought, for a long time dominant, that generation was the result of "preformation": every feature of a mature animal existed from the start in its earliest and tiniest form, and organisms grew in a mechanical way, all its parts steadily enlarging. The invention of the microscope made it possible for researchers to see features of plants and insects that were not visible to the naked eye, and one scientist claimed that could detect the form of a chick in an unincubated egg. There were religious versions of this notion, according to which generation over time never happened, because these creatures had been formed by God at the beginning of time and then gradually appeared.

The preformationist view concentrated attention on the stages of growth, and begged the question of how the stages are related to one another. Gasking noted that "it must be remembered that whereas modern biologists speak of the grub, the pupa, and the adult as stages in the life cycle of one individual butterfly, Harvey and his contemporaries always regarded the grub as one individual and the butterfly as another." Transformation after transformation after transformation; new organism after new organism after new organism. The scientist who put paid to this theory of serial metamorphoses — of change as an abundance of transformations, of zoological identity as a sequence of complete and disconnected Humean moments — was a correspondent of Bernoulli's named Jan Swammerdam, a Dutch biologist and master entomologist. He was a scientist caught up in the pietist movements of his time: "Behold I offer you the Omnipotent

Finger of God in the anatomy of a louse!" He opposed the idea of spontaneous generation because it excluded certain creatures from God's labor of creation and thereby offended God's majesty. Swammerdam's monumental researches on insects decisively invalidated the theory of metamorphosis: "In reality the caterpillar or worm is not changed into a nymph, nor to go a step further, the nymph into a winged animal; but the same worm or caterpillar, which on casting its skin assumes the form of a nymph becomes afterwards a winged animal." (A nymph – no Ovidian excitements here — is an early phase of the butterfly's development, approximately like the larva or the pupa; the modern science of butterflies no longer recognizes a nymphal phase.) I wonder whether Bernoulli and Swammerdam acknowledged that they shared the same anti-cataclysmic model of growth, the same poised and steady paradigm for individual development. Having changed, says the butterfly, I rise the same.

Bernoulli's motto appears to have receded into obscurity, but centuries later it enjoyed a delightful resurgence. *Eadem mutat resurgo* became the motto of Pataphysics — excuse me, 'Pataphysics. This doctrine, a mad and enchanting parody of science, was one of the most lasting and subversive jokes in modern culture. The term was apparently coined by a bunch of schoolboys in Rennes in the 1880s, one of whom was the young Alfred Jarry, poet, painter, playwright, showman, cyclist, and hallucinator *extraordinaire*. He first used the term in one of his early plays, when he was twenty, in 1893, and then elaborated the pataphysical gospel. What was, or is, pataphysics? There is a plenitude of definitions, and there is even an academy devoted to the conundrum — the College de 'Pataphysique, an institutionalization of the hoax which was founded in 1948 and has included many illustrious writers and artists among its members, and may be found today on the Boulevard Diderot in Paris, not far from the Gare de Lyon.

In the 1890s Jarry wrote a novel called *Gestes et Opinions de Docteur Faustroll, Pataphysicien, Roman Neo-Scientifique suivi de Speculations* — or *The Exploits and Opinions of Doctor Faustroll, Pataphysician, a Neo-Scientific Novel followed by Speculations* — which was not published until 1911, four years after he died wretchedly of tuberculosis and drugs. (Doctor Faustroll is the permanent dean, or Immovable Curator, of the College, and for some years the vice-dean was a crocodile.) In his novel Jarry included a few pages from a theoretical exposition of his philosophy: "It is the science of that which is superimposed on metaphysics, extending as far beyond metaphysics as the latter extends beyond physics. Pataphysics will be, above all, the science of the particular, despite the common opinion that the only science is that of the general. Pataphysics will examine the laws that govern exceptions. It is the science of imaginary solutions." The governing intellectual impulse in pataphysics seems to be a recoil from generalization. The French writer Rene Daumal, a spiritualist and an early surrealist and a prominent pataphysician, pronounced in 1920 that pataphysics is "the knowledge of the specific and the irreducible." All this strains towards a radical notion of particularity, toward a property of uniqueness that is common to all things. (Now there is a generalization!) Insofar as they are themselves, all things are exceptions. It brings to mind Duns Scotus' notion of *haecceitas*, or "thisness" — the attribute of individuation, of the perdurability of the singular. For all its convoluted concepts, there is something anti-intellectual about pataphysics, in the way that there is something anti-intellectual about existentialism: its abstractions are a campaign against abstraction, a crusade for thisness. But in the age of the masses — in the early years of the massification of politics and culture and consumption — there was also something deeply stirring about these warnings against the dilution of the one into the many and the subsumption of the human into categories and classifications, about these howling protests on behalf of the individual.

Nothing Jarry did was more howling than *Ubu Roi*, or *King Ubu*, his play that set a new standard for artistic transgression. It premiered in Paris in December 1896, and as soon as its first word was uttered — "*merdre,*" says Pére Ubu as he steps out of the wings — pandemonium broke loose. Yeats was in the audience that night, and the event provoked his famous dark premonition: "After Stéphane Mallarmé, after Paul Verlaine, after Gustave Moreau, after Puvis de Chavannes, after our own verse, after all our subtle color and nervous rhythm, after the faint mixed tints of Conder, what more is possible? After us the Savage God." Ubu is the sinister Count of Sandomir and King of Poland and Aragon, a grotesque monster, a sadistic tyrant, whose speech is as revolting as his appearance. (In the 1970s we used to compare Idi Amin to King Ubu.) He is a hugely bloated creature, wearing a high pointy hat and carrying a toilet brush for a scepter. He looks a lot like one of Phillip Guston's klansmen. And on the front of his sheet, covering his hideous paunch, is his symbol: *un grande gidouille* — a large logarithmic spiral! This design was the work of Jarry himself, in a woodcut called *Veritable Portrait de Monsieur Ubu*, or *True Portrait of Mister Ubu*, in 1896. (At the same time that Jarry was devising this infernal physiognomy he was also composing a commentary on an etching by Durer and hatching a plan, never fulfilled, to publish a journal that would reproduce the entirety of Durer's graphic work — Durer, who called the logarithmic spiral "the eternal line.") The spiral later became the official emblem of the College de 'Pataphysique, which issued it in different colors to signify its differentiations of rank.

Why the spiral? As with all things pataphysical, it is impossible to know. Commentators have pointed to the spiral's prodigious energy, its suggestion of infinity, its insinuation of madness (recall James Stewart's dream in *Vertigo*), its duality of presence and absence; there has even been an attempt to link it to one of Mallarme's most hermetic speculations. I myself see nothing pataphysical about Ubu, except for his emblem. And I keep coming back to the idea of the persistence of the individual, the hallowing of actual existents. Leibniz, again: "It is not true that two substances may be exactly alike and differ only numerically." The pataphysicians, too, were at war with indiscernibility — with the melting away of distinctiveness, which they hilariously construed as eccentricity. Strictly speaking, however, they were right: eccentricity is another term for individuation.

Like Bernoulli, the pataphysicians adopted *eadem mutata resurgo* as their slogan and the logarithmic spiral as their symbol. They must have relished the apparent contradiction in the Latin words — but I suspect that, like Bernoulli, they saw in them a novel and sagacious way of regarding human trajectories. The rigorous genius of seventeenth-century rationalism and the wild explorers of the twentieth-century imagination endorse the same complication. For there is no contradiction in *eadem mutata resurgo* unless you believe that change is linear and complete, that development is orderly directionally clear, that a human life must perfectly cohere. But which life does, really? Who ever beheld in human affairs a pure discontinuity, except death? The tracks of the old do not compromise the new; they launch it, and serve as its conscience. Except for desperate people, there is no shame in the persisting substrate. Jarry's crazy reverence for the specific and the small, his defiant and scatological love of the exception, was a plea for the unassimilability of the human, which is a kind of plea for freedom. His last words were "*je cherche, je cherche, je cherche,*" I seek, I seek, I seek. Then he asked for a toothpick and died.

II

The question of whether excellent old art is preferable to inferior contemporary art is pretty complicated and painful. I am sure, at least, that excellent old art is not enough.

DONALD JUDD

Historical change can be even more inebriating than personal change. For a start, it is less lonely, and can seek vindication in numbers. It promises a thrill of participation and even absorption, though the latter may nullify the agency required for the former. Many of the notions that we use to describe personal change — including the very notion that personal change should be viewed historically — are owed to old theories of historical change, to historiosophies of various kinds, such as the American grail of "redemption." We are a teleological nation. The other American contribution to the popular understanding of change is the bias toward it, the feeling that change is itself, intrinsically, in its own right, a good; and closely related to this assumption is an interest in its acceleration. We preen ourselves on how often and how fast we move. We have a horror of stillness and of stasis; if we are not gaining ground, then we are losing ground. We detest time and we devour it. This addiction to dynamism is owed to many things — to the competitive frenzy of capitalism, to the epic of the frontier and the song of the open road, to the appetites of immigrant populations, to the unfettered tempo of scientific discovery and technological invention. Our anti-philosophical inclinations have also contributed to it, so that we turned practicality itself into a philosophy.

In America it was Henry Adams who first realized that the speed of change may be the primary characteristic of modernity. He was stupefied by the amount of scientific, technological, and material progress that he witnessed in his own lifetime. (He was born a decade before the Mexican War and died a few months before the end of the First World War.) He proposed that modern history has "a law of acceleration" which "cannot be supposed to relax its energy to suit the convenience of man." It was now and henceforth will always be the case, he wrote about the year 1900, that "the next great influx of new forces seemed near at hand, and its style of education promised to be violently coercive." This is how things looked to Adams a little more than a century ago: "Power leaped from every atom. Man could no longer hold it off. Forces grasped his wrists and flung him about as though he had hold of a live wire or a runaway automobile, which was very nearly the exact truth." And he concluded: "Prolonged one generation longer, it would require a new social mind."

The prophet seems a little quaint now. The pace that horrified him was superseded long ago. We have gone beyond speed to simultaneity. Does the law of the acceleration of historical change imply that every generation will look nostalgically upon the challenges of the previous one? Yet we must not condescend to earlier fears: Adams' apprehension was more than just a cranky anti-modernism, he lived in the dynamo about which he warned, and for us he should be exemplary for attempting to offer some resistance to it, for refusing to lose his head over all the transformations that he witnessed. The problem that he posed is still with us; it has never been with us more. It may be that nothing in the history of technological progress has more strenuously tested our capacity for equilibrium in flux, for selecting the wisest spiritual and social course in confronting extreme change, than what was done to us, and by us, just this year. I am referring, of course, to generative artificial intelligence. Its sudden availability had the aspect of a magical, or black magical, intervention; all of a sudden it was here and it was everywhere. Now everything, we are assured, is going to be different. Prepare to be swept away, or enjoy the sweeping.

The velocity terrifies me. I have nothing to add to all the dystopian alarm about what has been unleashed. In this instance I even welcome a measure of hysteria, except of course from Elon Musk, who is merely looking for a way into the action. The harmful potentialities of this great imposture machine, this weapon of the mass destruction of the sense of reality, seem limitless. The history of technology demonstrates that all technologies are deployed before they are adequately understood, but how helpless must we render ourselves? The precipitousness with which the technology corporations release their transformational devices is enough to make you despise capitalism. They are much too vain, out there in California: after all, they know enough to build these contraptions but not enough to understand their effects. How much knowledge is that, really? *They are just engineers.* They like to think in terms of scale, but the scale of an innovation tells you nothing about its merit. A change in the lives of billions may be a blessing or a curse, or a blessing and a curse. But the expertise of the people who produce these technologies does not extend to the intellectual equipment that is required for evaluating blessings and curses. Ethical responsibility cannot be assessed algorithmically. The values that we must clarify and uphold in an AI world cannot be culled from data sets.

At the beginning of the digital era we heard a great deal about Prometheus. At the beginning of the AI era we are hearing a great deal about Pandora. I suggest that it is time to dwell on the other member of the family of Titans, on Prometheus' brother and Pandora's husband — on Epimetheus, whose name translates as "afterthought" or "he who thinks too late." Prometheus championed the human race against the gods by stealing fire for us; in Aeschylus' version, he gave us also arithmetic, agriculture, architecture, "every art of mankind." As a consequence of Prometheus' defiance, Zeus angrily arranged for the creation out of clay of the first woman, and for the Olympians to provide her with many gifts. Her name was Pandora, which means "all gift." To deliver her presents Pandora was dispatched not to Prometheus, who shrewdly suspected Zeus of plotting against humanity, but to the hapless Epimetheus, who is the Fredo Corleone of Greek mythology. Ever zealous for the welfare of humankind, Prometheus, whose name means "forethought," warned his brother not to accept any gifts from Zeus, but Epimetheus gave the warning no heed. Among Pandora's gifts was a large storage jar — a jar, not a box — which contained all the evils that afflict us. Epimetheus received her warmly, Pandora opened the jar, the miseries became ours. We are not Pandora, we are Epimetheus. Or rather, we are Prometheus, Pandora, *and* Epimetheus. Technologically we are living in an

Epimethean age. Again and again we prefer enthusiasm over reflection, credulity over prudence. All that remains for us are afterthoughts. We swing vertiginously between being on the cutting edge and being too late.

And yet, while everybody is praising or denouncing the imminent tectonic shifts, I see some continuities, and their power to console and to fortify is immense. Much to my surprise, I found some consolation and some fortification in an encounter with AI art. I was not predisposed to welcome this lavishly hyped development: brushes and chisels and cameras have been my idea of art's best instruments. But my friend Bennett Miller, the film director who recently devoted years to an as-yet-unreleased colossal documentary project about the interpretation of the digital age — I have seen enough of it to testify that it holds treasures — threw himself into a long period of experimentation with the images produced by an early version of the AI generator DALL-E, which is designed to translate written prompts into high-fidelity imagery. The software is an inventory of hundreds of millions of images. Miller gave the commands, or prompts, and the program responded with its "understanding" of his pictorial intentions. The prompts were both general and specific. The results invariably surprised him, and there began, for each image, a lengthy process of revision, of interaction between the man and the machine. Thousands of prints were produced. Every one of these compositions reflected the strange dialectic of surprise and design that was characteristic of these many exchanges. Eventually nineteen prints in various sizes were selected for a show at the Gagosian Gallery in New York.

When confronted by art that is unfamiliar, the most common response is to associate it with art that is familiar — to see old art in new art. This assimilation of the unknown to the known has a basis in the essentially iconographic nature of pictures: images do refer to one another, not only in the minds of their creators but also in the minds of their beholders, so that we can create filiations that help with the reading of things seen for the first time. In the windswept hair of an unforgettable portrait of a girl that Miller calls "Lucy," I saw Julia Margaret Cameron — a continuity! In his rocky landscapes and dusty wastes I detected Timothy O'Sullivan and Carleton Watkins — another continuity! (The danger of repairing immediately to earlier and familiar images is that we imprison ourselves in a cage of references and never escape the encrustations of culture, which are often an impediment to perception.) Miller's pictures were printed in sepia and had the unmistakable look of early nineteenth-century photography. He had asked DALL-E for that effect. The pictures show people and places, abstract studies of fogs and mists, strange juxtapositions of figures and objects, mock-historical events, chilling incidents of individuals falling from obscure crags. All of them have a touch of the uncanny, an oneiric quality, a mood of reverie and realistically represented unreality. Can artificial intelligence have seances? The tells about the medium are in the details of the pictures, in the implausible proportions of heads to bodies, and especially in the eyes of the figures, which are eerie, even creepy. Poor DALL-E, those were the best eyes it could do.

The jarring thing about my visit to the gallery was that these images were aesthetically undeniable. Some of them are very beautiful. They please the eye, they provoke the mind. The more I looked at them, the less I worried about their validity. I mean, their validity as art. There are many reasons to distinguish AI art from other kinds of art, but a reactionary panic is foolish, and not only because we must learn to live with these new powers. Miller and DALL-E were engaged in acts of creation that are formally and historically recognizable. This may be helpful: "The mind of artists is full of images which they might be able to produce; therefore, if a man properly using this art and naturally disposed to it were allowed to live many hundreds of years he would be capable — thanks to the power given to man by God — of pouring forth and producing everyday new shapes of men and other creatures the like of which was never seen before nor thought of by any other man." That was written by Durer in 1523. Another continuity! In an earlier statement of his aesthetic theory, in 1512, Durer similarly described the artist as "full of figures," which is a fine description, when raised to a mind-numbing magnitude, of Miller's machine.

Of course, it was not DALL-E that produced these pictures; it was Bennett Miller. This was a collaboration — but artists have always "partnered" with mechanical innovations. The evidence of human intention is everywhere in these AI works. Many people get hung up about the question of intentionality, because they expect it in a work of art and they cannot attribute it to a computer program, but really the question of intentionality is moot, because DALL-E did not produce these images on its own, and even in a more directly artisanal practice the work of art always exceeds the intentions of its maker. It is important not to mistake human intention for human control. What these AI works lacked was not human intention but human control. Or rather, complete human control. But then we must think carefully about human control in art, and about its limits. Some varieties of art have allowed for more control than others, and other varieties of art have welcomed the incompleteness of the artist's control or renounced the aspiration to control altogether. Some media are more resistant to the artist's will than others. Titian put his brush exactly where he wanted to put it, but Pollock's hurling brush made a friend of randomness. Patterns emerged in Pollock's greatest paintings, but not because he mastered every drop of his paint. (This was the case, in fact, with more traditional painters, from Rembrandt to Soutine, and the late Titian too, who trusted local chaos.) Duchamp introduced a higher degree of serendipity, so that found objects could be exhibited in art museums. The bizarre juxtapositions of the Surrealists surrendered any allegiance to conventional notions of coherence and instead looked for coherence after the fact. Film directors, their most elaborate set-ups notwithstanding, are always wishing for luck, and when they get certain shots they marvel at their good fortune. My own favorite example of the aesthetics of limited control is the art of ceramics. The artist prepares the clay, shapes it into the form of the vessel, creates the glaze according to a chromatic or iconographical plan, applies the glaze to the surface of the clay — and consigns the whole thing to the fire. For a determined time and at a determined temperature, the fire is sovereign. The finished pot is the result of the action of an uncontrollable force upon a highly articulated object. (I am the grateful owner of a luscious ceramic bust of a woman named Flora by Vally Wieselthier, who was the head of textiles and ceramics at the Wiener Werkstätte, and my legendary cousin; the top of the head is flattened and scorched, but Vally appears to have accepted the fire's damage as a contribution to the work.)

So Miller's dependence on DALL-E was not a violation of the artistic calling, not at all. It may not suit certain tastes, but it cannot be excommunicated. Even in the maelstrom of artificial intelligence, *eadem mututa resurgo*. In this connection Miller's experiments represent the latest challenge to Walter Benjamin's constricted vision of art in "The Work of Art in the Age of Mechanical Reproduction," an essay that for too long has provided an alibi for philistinism about certain artistic media. "The uniqueness of the work of art is identical to its embeddedness in the context of tradition," Benjamin wrote, "but the technology of reproduction detaches the reproduced object from the sphere of tradition." This technology, moreover, plays into the hands of the vulgar masses, with their "desire to 'get closer' to things and their equally passionate concern for overcoming each thing's uniqueness." All this destroys "the artwork's auratic mode of existence."

That paintings and sculptures possess an aura which cannot be captured by reproductions of them is undeniable. But Benjamin was not railing against posters and tote bags. He was excluding from the realm of art everything that is not made by human hands and is therefore not one of a kind. (He did not discuss the auratic status of non-mechanical reproduction, which was how many Renaissance and early modern painters and their workshops earned their livelihoods.) When he declares that "to an ever-increasing degree, the work reproduced becomes the reproduction of a work designed for reproducibility," he is referring to photography and film, and denying them aesthetic legitimacy. It is true that there is no unique original of a photograph or a film, even though there are better and worse prints, and the production of photographic and filmic images is certainly mediated by machines. But what is the use of a criterion for visual art that excludes photography and film? I am reminded of Lukacs' theory of the novel, which was dazzlingly brilliant except for its denial that Dostoevsky wrote novels.

Anybody who never has an auratic experience before a photograph or a film has eyes but does not see. And anybody who has an auratic experience before every Old Master painting or carving is a fool or a snob. Some of Miller's images have auras. They cast a spell, they posit a mystery. As with photographs, the image is unique even if its iteration is not. (This is true, by the way, of every line ever written by Shakespeare or any other great writer, which is why bad productions of good plays are tolerable: there remains the auratic language.) Where a genuine artistic sensibility is at work, the mechanical mediation will be no obstacle to art. The machine will be another medium, which like every medium is capable of kitsch or beauty, of objects with presence or without. And meanwhile, as the culture is engorging itself with futurist fevers, men and women with brushes and chisels and cameras will go on with their work, stubbornly adhering to the old methods, which no time and no technology can ruin. The aesthetic honor of a culture anyway depends on the small company of the truly serious, however they choose to create. Having changed, we will return the same. I wish I could be so confident about the impact of artificial intelligence in other spheres of private and public life.

III

Come, and releive
And tame, and keep downe with thy light
Dust that would rise, and dimme my sight.

HENRY VAUGHAN

But how prosaic, how timid, how glumly realistic, how tempered in the hope for transfiguration, must we be? Did the poet err in inferring from his experience of an ancient marble torso that he must change his life? Is incrementalism, spiritual as well as political, an expression of cowardice? These are the questions that haunt the anti-apocalyptic mentality, and also the liberal one. It would be infinitely sad to settle for too little, for less than might be within our grasp. Whereas there have been no societies that achieved justice by means of revolution, there are reports of souls who went very far towards a state of transcendence, and I cannot work up the impertinence to declare that they are all lies. One of those reports was about a friend of mine.

Michael Gerson died last November in Washington DC. He was fifty-eight years old. He was a Christian conservative who gave both Christianity and conservatism a good name. He served in the administration of George W. Bush, first as a speechwriter and then as an assistant to the president on matters of policy. In his former capacity, he wrote the most unforgettable sentence I have ever heard in an inaugural address: "no insignificant person," Bush said in 2001, "was ever born." The humanism of those words was thunderous, and cut across all distinctions of right and left, religious and secular. In his latter capacity, Mike was responsible in large measure for the United States President's Emergency Plan for AIDS Relief, or PEPFAR. It must be the greatest act of mercy that any modern government ever performed: it has so far saved the lives of more than twenty million people. Now that is American imperialism! After his service at the White House, Mike became a columnist for *The Washington Post*, where his writing unfailingly displayed a natural eloquence. Later, in the gloom of the Trump years, he was, of all the conservative columnists, the most steadfast in his criticism of the president. (President Ubu.) There is perhaps nothing as withering as the contempt of a good man. Even more admirably, Mike, along with his friend Pete Wehner, regularly castigated the Christian evangelical community, his own community, for falling into line behind the leadership of such a sordid figure, such an advertisement for sin. The surest sign of a man's intellectual honesty is his willingness to criticize his own congregation.

What fascinated me most about Mike was the obvious depth of his religious belief. I have always been susceptible to the charisma of genuine faith, however rarely I find it. I had a thousand philosophical quarrels with the substance of Mike's faith, of course, but they were beside the point. Mike exemplified in his person the belief in belief — in thoughtful belief, which is not one of the most salient attributes of religion in America; and he inflected his Christianity with a universal compassion that showed in everything he wrote. May a liberal Jew say that he brought honor to Jesus? He did.

Mike was afflicted with depression, and cancer, and Parkinson's. He was cruelly tested. A few months after he died a memorial service was held in the National Cathedral, where in 2019 Mike had delivered a renowned sermon about depression. Among the remembrances was one by his old friend Scott Baker, which included this:

> On my first visit to the hospital, about a week or so before he died, I was alone in the room with him for a few minutes. He'd been sleeping and suddenly came to. After gathering my presence, he said quietly but with bright eyes, "I've been given a special privilege." I leaned closer. He said, "A woman came to me and said I no longer needed to be a being oriented to the world of physical objects." This was not the conversation I was

> expecting. And I understood, to a degree, the role of medication and the stage of things. Some of you may have a scientific explanation for this. But I don't need to hear it and I won't believe it. I said, using a Celtic phrase for those rare moments when heaven and earth seem to touch — "Michael, do you feel like you're in one of those thin places?" And he said — "Oh, yes! Exactly!" When I saw him a week later he couldn't say much. But his eyes still had those moments of brightness.

This nearly knocked me over. "A woman came to me and said I no longer needed to be a being oriented to the world of physical objects." Who was this woman who found these words for this man? Was she a nurse or a sibyl? I am with Baker in his reluctance to attribute the entirety of the experience to chemistry. After all, Mike in his dying was sufficiently in his powers to describe the new dispensation as "a special privilege." He recognized that the life that was left to him would be an altered life, that he was now another sort of being, that he had been unburdened of his cognitive duties and delivered to a new plane of awareness, in which the material world would no longer be the field of cognition. (And Mike was a journalist, remember, a perspicacious one, for whom the duties of cognition are also a professional responsibility.) He would see less, but his eyes would be happy. Or "bright," as Baker recalled. Mike's happiness at his own reduction was the mark of a strong inwardness. He embraced the subtraction as an addition.

The lines from Henry Vaughan that I have cited above in my friend's memory come from a poem called "Distraction," published in 1650.

O knit me, that am crumbled dust! the heape
Is all dispers'd, and cheape;
Give for a handfull, but a thought
And it is bought;
Hadst thou
Made me a starre, a pearle, or a rain-bow,
The beames I then had shot
My light had lessend not,
But now
I find my selfe the lesse, the more I grow....
But now since thou didst blesse
So much,
I grieve, my God! that thou hast made me such.
I grieve?
O, yes! thou know'st I doe; Come, and releive
And tame, and keepe downe with thy light
Dust that would rise, and dimme my sight,
Lest left alone too long
Amidst the noise, and throng,
Oppressed I
Striving to save the whole, by parcells dye.

I venerate this poem because I have spent a lifetime worried about the price of my worldliness. A rich life in this rich world is a life dispersed, and the soul, once dispersed, is hard to gather together, and to keep long gathered. My distractions, if distractions they were, have been wonderful. They have dripped with meanings. Sometimes I wish I could pray with the poet to be relieved of the material world — but then I remember that there is another side to the whole question. There is the powerful view that the material and visible world is our only avenue of access to what is immaterial and invisible, that it is futile for a corporeal and sensual being to ignore the conditions of its knowledge and its significance, that the beauty of abstract forms begins with the beauty of concrete forms. Poet against poet: "The thing seen becomes the thing unseen," Wallace Stevens wrote. "The opposite is, or seems to be, impossible."

The best that I can conclude is that a compound being's work is never done. But there was Mike in his hospital bed, emancipated from objects and "parcells," his sight "dimmed" but acute. What did he see in the "thin place" that brightened his eyes? Thinness of perception was the poet's dream. I am at a loss to describe Mike's gain. I do not know how to think or to imagine in the absence of differentiation. But in my ignorance I bow my head before Mike's affirmation of an undifferentiated reality — "Oh yes! Exactly!" It is more than Bernoulli thought possible, even if the human truth may have been on Bernoulli's side.

CONTRIBUTORS

KATHERINE C. EPSTEIN is a professor of history at Rutgers University.

CASS R. SUNSTEIN is the Robert Walmsley University Professor at Harvard Law School and is the author, among other books, of *This is Not Normal*.

MARIO VARGAS LLOSA won the Nobel Prize in Literature in 2010. This essay was translated by Adrian Nathan West.

MARK EDMUNDSON is a professor of English at the University of Virginia. His most recent book is *The Unwelcome Guest: The Super-Ego in the Age of the Internet*.

MOSHE HALBERTAL is the author, among other books, of *The Birth of Doubt: Confronting Uncertainty in Early Rabbinic Literature*. This essay was translated by Daniel Tabak.

LESLIE WILLIAMS is the author of *Even the Dark*.

ELLIOT ACKERMAN is the author most recently of *Halcyon*.

JAMES WOLCOTT is the author of *Critical Mass: Four Decades of Essays, Reviews, Hand Grenades and Hurrahs*.

NOGA ARIKHA teaches philosophy and the history of ideas in Florence. Her book *The Ceiling Outside: The Science and Experience of the Disrupted Mind* appeared last year.

CARLOS FRAENKEL is the James McGill Professor of Philosophy and Religion at McGill University.

DAPHNE MERKIN is an American critic and novelist.

JAMES R. RUSSELL is Mashtots Professor of Armenian Studies, Emeritus, at Harvard University. **MISAK MEDZARENTS** was a modern Armenian poet who was born in 1886 and died, young of tuberculosis, in 1908. His *Complete Lyric Poems*, edited, annotated, and translated by James R. Russell, was published a few years ago.

ROBERT ALTER is professor emeritus of Hebrew and Comparative Literature at University of California at Berkeley, and the author of a forthcoming study of Amos Oz.

HELEN VENDLER now writes from Laguna Niguel, California, where she is inventing a new life near her son and his family in Laguna Beach.

RACHEL CONNOLLY is the author of *Lazy City*.

CELESTE MARCUS is the managing editor of *Liberties*.

LEON WIESELTIER is the editor of *Liberties*.

Liberties — A Journal of Culture and Politics is available by annual subscription and by individual purchase from bookstores and online booksellers.

Annual subscriptions provide a discount from the individual cover price and include complete digital access to current and previous issues along with the printed version. Subscriptions can be ordered from libertiesjournal.com. Professional discounts for active military; faculty, students, and education administrators; government employees; those working in the not-for-profit sector. Gift subscriptions are also available at libertiesjournal.com.

As a matter of principle, *Liberties Journal* does not accept advertising or other funding sources that might influence our independence.

We look to our readers and those individuals and institutions that believe in our mission for contributions — large and small — to support this not-for-profit publication.

If you are interested in making a donation to *Liberties*, please contact Bill Reichblum, publisher, by email at bill@libertiesjournal.com or by phone: 202-891-7159.

Liberties — A Journal of Culture and Politics is distributed to booksellers in the United States by Publishers Group West; in Canada by Publishers Group Canada; and, internationally by Ingram Publisher Services International.

LIBERTIES, LIBERTIES: A JOURNAL OF CULTURE AND POLITICS, is published quarterly in Fall, Winter, Spring, and Summer by Liberties Journal Foundation.

ISBN ISBN 979-8-9854302-1-9
ISSN 2692-3904

Printed in Canada.

The insignia that appears throughout *Liberties* is derived from details in Botticelli's drawings for Dante's *Divine Comedy*, which were executed between 1480 and 1495.